ALPHA BRAVO DELTA
GUIDE TO
WARPLANES

D0063739

ALPHA BRAVO DELTA
GUIDE TO
WARPLANES

LT. COL. GEORGE A. LARSON, USAF (RET.)
AND MICHAEL BENSON

ALPHA

A member of Penguin Group (USA) Inc.

International Standard Book Number: 1-59257-232-4
Library of Congress Catalog Card Number: 2004105322

06 05 04   8 7 6 5 4 3 2 1

Interpretation of the printing code: The rightmost number of the first series of numbers is the year of the book's printing; the rightmost number of the second series of numbers is the number of the book's printing. For example, a printing code of 04-1 shows that the first printing occurred in 2004.

Printed in the United States of America

Note: This publication contains the opinions and ideas of its authors. It is intended to provide helpful and informative material on the subject matter covered. It is sold with the understanding that the authors and publisher are not engaged in rendering professional services in the book. If the reader requires personal assistance or advice, a competent professional should be consulted.

The authors and publisher specifically disclaim any responsibility for any liability, loss, or risk, personal or otherwise, which is incurred as a consequence, directly or indirectly, of the use and application of any of the contents of this book.

Most Alpha books are available at special quantity discounts for bulk purchases for sales promotions, premiums, fund-raising, or educational use. Special books, or book excerpts, can also be created to fit specific needs.

For details, write: Special Markets; Alpha Books, 375 Hudson Street, New York, New York 10014.

DEDICATION

For 100 years aviators have climbed into an aircraft's cockpit and left the ground to engage in aerial combat—or to maintain the peace. This was just as true during both world wars as it was during the Cold War when the Strategic Air Command aircrews stood nuclear alert. It is just as true today.

This book is dedicated to those aviators who set today's airpower standards, and, more specifically, to my father, George W. Larson.

In my office I have a photograph of my father beside a Boeing B-29 Superfortress, marking his part in the history of warplanes. He is on Tinian Island, during World War II, as a member of the United States Navy Construction Battalion (Seabees). There he assisted in the building of the four runways on North Field. From these runways 20th Air Force B-29s bombed targets in Japan, first with conventional high-explosives, then with incendiaries for large fire-bombing raids, and finally, on August 6 and 9, 1945, with the two atomic bombs that ended World War II.

During January 1981, I had the opportunity to walk in the steps of my father when he visited Tinian Island and North Field. I also had the opportunity to show him, at that time, a modern warplane. It was the Boeing B-52D Stratofortress, which—as part of the 43rd Strategic Wing on Andersen Air Force Base, Guam—stood nuclear alert. I joined the Air Force because of my father, and now as a military historian I strive to tell the stories of military warriors and the aircraft they flew or supported.

CONTENTS

FOREWORD

Aircraft win wars.

The aircraft—plane, helicopter, dirigible, drone—has a 100-year history of deciding the outcome of battles and of campaigns.

Whether fighting at the edge of the stratosphere or slugging it out down in the weeds, the combat aircraft has become the dominant weapon in the profession of arms.

This book tells how we got there.

Alpha Bravo Delta Guide to Warplanes is about today, but only because it's also about the past hundred years, when air warriors made the leap from cocked revolvers to satellite-guided precision munitions, and warplanes went from fabric-and-wood construction to microchips, electrons, and high-tech composites.

Never before has one volume put together the three key ingredients of the story of aerial warfare—the historical backdrop, the people, and the planes—to tell us how military aviation was conceived, evolved, and matured.

George Larson and Michael Benson take us through a world that changed when great advances in technology collided with history's most difficult moments.

Pilots have traded their jodhpurs, goggles, and leather jackets for G-suits, helmet-mounted aiming systems … and leather jackets. One thing you learn on the pages that follow is that no matter how much air warfare changes, it never changes completely.

World War I German air ace Baron Manfred von Richthofen captured the spirit of the air warrior in a brief quote: "The fighter pilots have to rove in the area allotted to them in any way they like, and when they spot an enemy they attack and shoot him down. Anything else is rubbish."

Richthofen was talking about fighter pilots and his words could still be found in early 2004 in the ready room of the 494th Fighter Squadron at Lakenheath, England, where F-15E Strike Eagle pilots and weapons officers had just returned from Operation Iraqi Freedom.

He might, as easily, have been talking about B-17 Flying Fortress and B-24 Liberator crews who braved flak, fighters, and frigid air high over Hitler's Fortress Europe, or combat transport pilots who nudged their C-46 Commando transports over ice-encrusted Himalayan peaks in 1944, or F-86 Sabre jocks who shot down nine MiGs for every plane they lost in Korea.

The men—and, in recent wars, women—retain more today than just the attire of a Richthofen, a Chennault, or a Tibbets. They still have the fighting spirit. It has never slackened.

But this book is a story of change, from the wheezing, sputtering Spad fighter of World War I to the white flying triangle called the XB-70 Valkyrie in the 1970s; from shooting through the propeller (or not) in 1917 to firing heat-seeking missiles in Operation Desert Storm; from leather-padded bucket seats to rocket-propelled ejection seats.

On the pages that follow, you'll fight in a Messerschmitt, go on patrol in a Catalina, and strike at Afghanistan in the B-2 stealth bomber. *Alpha Bravo Delta Guide to Warplanes* tells us not only how things work but why. It's a saga of adventure and achievement, never seen between two covers before. Prepare to be unable to put this book down.

Robert F. Dorr

Robert F. Dorr is the author of *Alpha Bravo Delta Guide to the U.S Army* and 60 other books of military history. He is an Air Force veteran and contributes the weekly column "Duty, Honor, Country" to the *Army Times* newspaper.

INTRODUCTION

From the moment the first dogfight took place over Europe in 1914, warplanes became a fascination for aviators and non-aviators alike. Today, 90 years later, warplanes remain the favorite subject of modeling hobbyists. In addition to bringing a new level of romance and adventure to warfare, warplanes also took over the lead role. It has become a rule of thumb for military strategists that "he who controls the air, controls the war." With the development of aircraft carriers and the policies of power projection, the oceans became ruled by airpower as well.

For the last 60 years the United States has dominated the air, one of the key reasons it is the world's last remaining military superpower. American-designed and -built military aircraft surpass those of any other country.

This book presents a look at the development of airpower, using significant historical aviation events, and when possible, focusing on those who were there.

The aircraft selected present a broad perspective of combat aircraft. The current generation of warplanes have earned their spurs in the modern, high-tech battlefield, allowing aircraft to go "where no one has gone before."

Acknowledgments
The authors wish to thank the following: Lt. Col. Dean E. Abbott, USAF (Ret.); Lt. Gen. William E. Brown, USAF (ret.); and John Cugini, Paul Dinas, Robert F. Dorr, Jake Elwell, Gary Goldstein, Dr. Michael H. Gorn, Mitch Highfill, Charles Hinton, K. V. Horstmanshoff, David Jacobs, Dianne Knippel, Lockheed Martin Aeronautics Company, Timothy J. Kutta, and Philip Semrau.

CHAPTER 1

NOT LONG AFTER THE WRIGHT BROTHERS ...

The first men to defy gravity with the help of a man-made device were chemistry professor Jean-François Pilâtre de Rozier and French army major the Marquis François d'Arlandes. The device was a hot-air balloon and the men took that brave first flight six minutes before two in the afternoon on November 21, 1783.

Their balloon, which had been built by two French brothers, Joseph-Michel and Jacques Etienne Montgolfier, was 50 feet wide and 72 feet high. It had been tested once before, safely carrying a chicken, goose, and sheep aloft and returning them to Earth. Hot air was later replaced by hydrogen, so that keeping a fire lit was no longer a necessity.

While balloons became an increasingly standard way to fly over the next 100 years, they remained a poor weapon. They could be used to spy at night under certain conditions, but, being balloons, they were simple to shoot down. Balloons were used by the military as far back as the Napoleonic Wars.

WILBUR AND ORVILLE

The invention that truly gave birth to military airpower made its debut on the morning of December 17, 1903, at Kitty Hawk, North Carolina. That was when Wilbur and Orville Wright successfully flew their plane, named *Flyer I*, for the first powered flight in history.

Orville was the pilot and he was stretched out on his belly, his face toward the ground. The first flight was not a spectacular one. It only lasted 12 seconds, and for most of that time the plane was only a few feet off the ground.

Although we recognize this first flight as a key moment in history, it was not recognized as such at the time. After all, every flight before the one at Kitty Hawk had resulted in failure. Crashes remained the norm for experimental aviators in the first years after *Flyer I*'s ascent. Who in their right mind would ever get into a so-called "aeroplane"?

Then there was the considerable portion of the population who simply refused to believe that the airplane was possible. The Wright brothers did not get an immediate patent on their invention because the patent department ruled that the airplane defied the laws of science.

The Wright brothers built a second aeroplane that flew in 1907. Most of the flying action was in Europe, where, that same year, a Frenchman by the name of Henri Farman flew in a plane for longer than a minute before safely landing.

Germany's first plane was called the *Ellehammer IV* and it flew in 1908. The following summer the British joined the "heavier-than-air" era with a plane with three wings called *Triplane I*.

HEAVIER-THAN-AIR AIRCRAFT AS WEAPONS

The U.S. Army had been looking into the possibility of using heavier-than-air aircraft as weapons as far back as 1898 when it commissioned inventor Samuel Langley to build an aircraft. Langley's machine—christened the *Aerodrome*—was a failure.

Since public money had been spent, some congressmen and segments of the press set up a howl. Once burned, the army had become twice shy about backing other flying machines.

In 1907, the army established an Aeronautical Division within the Signal Corps. By 1908, military brass had seen the light—with the help of prodding by President Theodore Roosevelt—and commissioned a biplane from the Wrights.

Major Douhet Has an Idea

Credit for the idea of using heavier-than-air aircraft during a time of war officially goes to Italian major Giulio Douhet. In 1909 Douhet wrote: "At present we are fully conscious of the importance of the sea (in war). In the near future, it will be no less vital to achieve supremacy in the air."

By 1910, there was experimentation with aviation all around the world. In the United States, aviation pioneer Glenn H. Curtiss was already experimenting with flying planes off of ships, so that military air and sea power could be combined. (We'll discuss Curtiss and the start of naval aviation later in this chapter.)

Maj. Douhet's theory was quickly proven to have a practical application as, in 1911, Italy found itself at war to conquer Libya and used the airplane in a military capacity. On October 23, 1911, Capt. Carlo Piazza flew the first reconnaissance flight. A week later, on November 1, 2d Lt. Giulio Guidotti flew the first bombing raid.

GLENN CURTISS

American aviation pioneer Glenn Curtiss was born on May 21, 1878, in Hammondsport, New York. He raced motorcycles as a teenager. Before he turned 30 he became known as the fastest man on the planet after he rode a V-8-powered motorcycle at a record 136.3 miles per hour (mph).

That same year, he got together with balloonist Thomas Baldwin and created a gasoline-burning engine that would power one of Baldwin's balloons, thus creating the first American dirigible. The first U.S. Army aircraft was the dirigible SC-1, with an engine built by Curtiss.

Also in 1907, Curtiss got together with the man who invented the telephone, Alexander Graham Bell, and formed the Aerial Experiment Association (AEA). One of the AEA's first aircraft had ailerons—the moving part of a wing that provides lateral control. It was called the *White Wing*. The AEA also built the first seaplane, a plane designed to take off from and land on water.

Although five years had passed since the Wright brothers' first flight, there had never been a public demonstration of mechanized flight. In 1908, Curtiss invited the public and flew a plane called *June Bug* more than ½ mile before landing safely.

In 1909, Curtiss took his latest plane, the *Golden Flyer,* to France where he competed in and won the grand prize at the Rheims Air Meet. His plane flew two laps around a 6.2-mile triangular route at an average speed of 47 mph.

In 1910, one of Curtiss's planes was used by pilot Eugene B. Ely to take off from an aircraft carrier for the first time. (More about that in our sea-based planes section, a little later in this chapter.)

The NC-4, a Curtiss plane, was the first to fly across the Atlantic Ocean in 1919. During World War I, the Curtiss Aeroplane and Motor Company was the largest aircraft manufacturer in the world.

1911: WAR IN THEIR FUTURE

In 1911, French captain Ferdinand Ferber was asked by a reporter, "How could a fight take place between two airplanes?" Captain Ferber replied, "In the same way as all fights between two birds have ever taken place."

By 1911, many of the countries of Europe knew that war was in their future. Italy's successful use of the airplane as a weapon was the catalyst for several brand-new research and development plans.

Great Britain and France

In Great Britain, the first military aviation unit was formed in 1911 and was called the Air Battalion of the Royal Engineers—although the name was changed to the Royal Air Corps the following year. Pilots were trained to observe the land below, mark enemy positions on a map that they carried, and take intelligence photographs.

These planes flew their missions at approximately 3,000 feet. That altitude kept the risk of being hit by antiaircraft fire from the ground reasonable, yet allowed clear photographs of the ground to be taken.

Since surveillance was all the planes were intended to do, the speed of the plane was not of much importance. The engines used in the first warplanes built by France and England had power plants that produced in the 70 to 80 horsepower range.

Also in 1911, France formed a unit of aviators who were trained in more than how to spy. They were trained to shoot rifles and handguns from their cockpits as well.

Germany

Germany as well began to build military airplanes in 1911. However, aviation experts in that country were still concentrating on airships— a mechanized balloon like dirigibles and today's blimps.

In Germany, Count Ferdinand von Zeppelin had been so impressed by the performance of tethered observation balloons as reconnaissance platforms and artillery spotters during the American Civil War that he was inspired to create the airship that bore his name.

But when World War I began in August 1914, the German High Command and the military planners of most of the belligerent nations expected more than observation from lighter-than-air ships. They envisioned zeppelin fleets conducting massive bombing raids. But zeppelins proved to be ineffective during the war. As many were lost to bad weather as were brought down by enemy gunfire.

It was the heavier-than-air, motor-powered aircraft which proved to be the decisive weapon—not just in World War I, but in every war since.

The first German planes were much more powerful than those being produced at the same time in England and France. The Germans put Mercedes engines in their planes, which produced upwards of 200 horsepower.

HOSTILITIES COMMENCE

The world went to war in August 1914. The German army invaded Belgium to get to France, where they planned to encircle the French army. A French counteroffensive at the Marne halted the German advance.

By November of that year, the mobile war bogged down and trench warfare began, setting the stage for the greatest mass slaughter in the history of the world. General staffs on both sides believed that a large enough offensive would break the stalemate, but failed to reckon with the death-dealing capabilities of the Machine Age: machine guns, barbed wire, heavy artillery, and poison gas. As a result, battles were fought in which hundreds of thousands of troops were slaughtered to gain a few dozen yards of territory—territory that was lost when the enemy counter-attacked.

Pushers and Tractors

The first warplanes fell into two categories: pushers and tractors (pullers). The pushers had the engine in the rear while the tractors had the engine in the front. The pushers were slower and less maneuverable than the tractors.

But there were still old-fashioned military leaders who failed to see the significance of the airplane in all future wars. For them, seeing would be believing, and planes and their pilots would have to prove themselves in battle before the elder military planners would take note.

Next to the airplane itself, the most significant invention leading to the creation of the fighter plane was the machine gun. The gun was invented at the end of 1914, by which time World War I was already in progress. Before that, planes were still used mostly in a reconnaissance role. Planes would be used to fly over and spot the locations of the enemy. Troop movements and artillery locations could be monitored during these recon flights. The pilots were given whatever weapons were handy—sometimes a rifle and sometimes a handgun—so they could fire back if fired upon.

Reconnaissance Only

Though the earliest World War I planes were designed for reconnaissance only, planes on opposing sides did encounter one another—and they were not friendly.

The first dogfights of the war were between British reconnaissance planes overflying German-captured land in France (where they hoped to gather information about and photograph enemy positions and troop movements) and the German aircraft sent aloft to make the British fight for their information.

Originally, reconnaissance planes flew alone, and then in pairs, so that one plane could keep an eye on the other's tail. Eventually teams of planes went aloft simultaneously and team fighting was developed.

FIRST BOMBING RUNS

The first bombing runs of World War I were flown by warplanes before the first year of the war was over. The newer airplanes had stronger engines and could therefore carry heavier loads aloft. This allowed for the planes to carry a small bomb load, bombs that could be dropped directly onto enemy personnel.

Compared to the bombing missions that would be run in the next war 30 years later, these early bombs were terribly inaccurate and relatively harmless—but they proved that dropping bombs on the enemy from airplanes could be done.

One primitive but useful new weapon was used during the first dogfights along the war's Eastern front. It was the invention of one of Russia's top aces, Capt. Alexander Alexandrovich Kazakov. The weapon was a heavy hook at the end of a cable. Kazakov dangled the hook off of his plane and used it to tear at opposing planes. Many early World War I planes were covered with canvass, which could easily be ripped.

FIRST FIGHTER PLANES

The first fighter planes—planes designed specifically for pilots to combat enemy pilots in their aircraft—were being built. The dogfight had been born, and the new flying aces were accommodated by designers with ever more powerful, agile, and deadly aircraft.

The one thing that separated the fighter plane from other kinds of warplanes was its machine gun. Without the invention of the machine gun, the fighter plane may never have evolved. The machine gun, once installed in a plane, was clearly more than just a defensive weapon used during a reconnaissance flight. With a machine gun a pilot could *attack*.

Once machine guns were used extensively by the fighter pilots of the First World War, even Kazakov stopped dangling his hook. This was progress. Using the machine gun, the pilot could attack both targets on the ground and enemy planes in flight.

Attack from the Front

The winners of dogfights soon recognized the advantage of attacking a foe while making a pass in front of him. The opposing pilot could not fire his machine gun straight ahead without shooting off his own propeller. (At the same time they learned never to fly directly at their foe, or they couldn't shoot without harming their own propeller.)

Several systems were used to try to avoid the machine gun/propeller problem. Some planes—such as the Nieuport 11—mounted the machine gun on a wing so that it would shoot around the propeller, but this made it more difficult for the pilot to aim the gun.

The other attempt to fix the problem involved redesigning the plane. Planes with propellers in the middle or in the back appeared. With the propeller moved, the machine gun could be mounted right in the nose of the plane.

The Deflector System

The first solution to the firing-through-the-propeller problem was invented by Roland Garros of France in 1915. Garros had been France's greatest pre-war stunt pilot. He invented the deflector system, which fixed deflector blades to the propeller blades along the line of fire so that any bullets that would have hit the propeller were deflected.

The system was installed in the Morane-Saulnier L, a monoplane (a plane with one wing) that has been called the first "real fighter." Since steel deflected the shots, pilots at the time learned to shoot at the man, not at the machine.

Aerial combat came of age during three hectic weeks in the winter of 1915. During that time, a French single-seater, flown by Garros himself, shot down six German planes. This put the German air force into a panic. By then, many planes had been outfitted with machine guns, usually mounted on the tail and fired by the observer—but they had been largely ineffective in shooting down enemy planes.

The nose-mounted machine gun of the Morane-Saulnier N caused a frightening improvement in accuracy that greatly upset the German air force. But the Germans learned the secret of the N model when a French pilot was forced to glide his N model to a landing behind German lines and was captured before he had an opportunity to burn his plane.

Fokker's Synchronization System

By 1915 a machine gun/propeller synchronization system was established by airplane designer Anthony Fokker for the German air force. After that, a machine gun could be fired without striking its own plane's propeller.

At first, the German High Command was skeptical of Fokker's invention. "There is one way to test this gun," Fokker was told. "Take it to the front, teach a pilot how to use it and then let him go up and shoot down an enemy plane. This will prove that the gun works in combat."

They wanted Fokker to test the gun himself, but he declined the "honor." On August 1, 1915, Max Immelmann, piloting a Fokker E-1 with synchronized machine gun, shot down an enemy bomber. For a time the synchronized machine gun gave the Germans air superiority, clearing the skies of Allied aircraft.

This superiority lasted for four months when a German plane equipped with the gun was forced to land behind enemy lines. The secret of the synchronized gun was learned and copied, and the day of the combat pilot officially arrived.

FLYING BOATS AND SEAPLANES

Many of the air forces participating in the First World War featured flying boats or seaplanes. These were ship-based planes that could land in the water. They would be placed in and retrieved from the water by cranes aboard the ships. These planes were used over the North and Adriatic seas, as well as over the Mediterranean.

Austria

Austria had two of these types of craft during the first years of the war. One, the Lohner E, was a reconnaissance craft. About 40 of these were built. The other, the Hansa-Brandenburg CC, was a fighter.

The recon plane was built by Jacob Lohner Werke & Co. in Vienna. It was first flown in 1914, was powered by an 85 horsepower six-cylinder liquid-cooled in-line Hiero, and became the prototype for all of the flying boats flown during the war. It had a wingspan of 53 feet and 2 inches and had a top speed of 65 mph. Holding a crew of two, it could fly to a ceiling (the highest altitude at which it could function) of 13,120 feet with a four-hour endurance between landings.

The fighter was manufactured by Phönix Flugzeug-Werke AG and used to defend Atlantic ports. First flown in 1916, this flying boat was powered by a 150-horsepower six-cylinder liquid-cooled in-line Benz Bz III. It had a wingspan of 30 feet and 6 inches, and had a maximum speed of 109 mph. The one-man crew was armed with a single machine gun. Both Austrian planes had the engine mounted to the upper wing, well above the boat-hull fuselage (the main body of an airplane designed to carry the crew and cargo).

Italy

Italy's flying boat was the Macchi L.1, manufactured by SA Nieuport-Macchi, which built 140 of them. The boat first flew in 1915 and its missions were of reconnaissance only. It held a two-man crew and was powered by an Isotta-Fraschini V4a six-cylinder liquid-cooled in-line engine producing 150 horsepower, which was attached to the upper wing. The wingspan was 53 feet, 10 inches. It was armed with one machine gun and could fly at a maximum speed of 68 mph. It flew to a ceiling of 14,760 feet and had a four-hour endurance.

France

France's flying boat was known as the FBA Type C. It was flown by the Russian and Italian navies as well as by the French. This recon plane, which first flew in 1915, was built by Franco-British Aviation. Its power plant was the Clerget nine-cylinder air-cooled rotary engine, later to be associated with the great Sopwith planes. With a wingspan of almost 45 feet and a length of 28 feet, 10 inches, the plane held a crew of two and was armed with a single machine gun. The plane had a maximum speed of 68 mph, could fly to a ceiling of 11,480 feet, and had a range of 186 miles.

Germany

Germany built seaplanes that didn't use their fuselages as the hull of their boat, like the flying boats listed previously. The German planes landed on a pair of skis, allowing the engine to be mounted on or in the fuselage. The Germans built two types of seaplanes, both fighters.

The first was the Rumpler 6B 1, which was developed from a land plane by E. Rumpler Flugzeug-Werke GmbH, and first flew in 1916. Thirty-eight of them were built. It was powered by a Mercedes D III six-cylinder liquid-cooled in-line engine producing 160 horsepower. The wingspan was a fraction of an inch longer than 40 feet. It could fly 95 mph and could reach a ceiling of 16,405 feet. It had a four-hour endurance and was armed with a single machine gun.

The other German ski-plane was the Hansa-Brandenberg KDW, which was considered superior to the Rumpler. It was designed to defend German flying-boat bases along the Adriatic and North seas. About 60 of them were built. It was powered by a 150-horsepower six-cylinder liquid-cooled in-line Benz Bz III, the same engine used in the Austrian air force's Hansa-Brandenburg CC. It had a wingspan of 30 feet, 4¼ inches, and could fly to a maximum speed of 106 mph. It had a ceiling of 13,123 feet, and endurance of three hours. The one-man crew was armed with one machine gun in the early editions, and with two machine guns in later models.

THE CONCEPT OF SEA-BASED AIRCRAFT

The first naval officer to suggest combining sea and airpower was Britain's Rear Adm. Henry Knowles who, in 1803, had a frigate customized so that it could operate a hot-air balloon. Fifteen years later, Charles Rogier, also from England, did Knowles one better. He had a ship outfitted to operate a fleet of pilotless hot-air balloons, each of which carried bombs that could be dropped on enemy ships. These flying weapons were never used, however.

On July 12, 1849, the first act of war that originated from a ship-launched aircraft took place. The attack was by the Austrians, who were besieging Venice, Italy. Diminutive pilotless balloons, rigged to drop explosives, were launched from the Austrian steamer *Volcano* in the general direction of the enemy. The Austrians had no clue when the balloons were and weren't over the enemy. For the most part the balloons dropped their bombs harmlessly. It was clear that any balloon attack launched from a ship would require pilots.

On August 3, 1861, during the American Civil War, the first piloted balloon was launched from a ship. Pilot John La Mountain, who was fighting for the North, launched from a tugboat that had been converted into a transport called *Fanny*. There were enough balloons being used by the Union Army, mostly for reconnaissance, that a Union Balloon Corps was formed. A larger ship would be needed to operate the sea-based balloon operations, so in August 1861, a coal barge was converted into the first ship configured exclusively for aerial operations. The ship, which came from the Washington Navy Yard, was known as the *George Washington Parke Custis*.

Later in the war, in 1863, reconnaissance balloons were also launched from an army gunboat named *Mayflower*. The *George Washington Parke Custis* remained the state of the art in what would develop into aircraft carriers until the end of the nineteenth century.

Birth of Naval Airpower

So far, all of the aerial warfare experiments from ships had involved balloons, or the occasional kite. After the Wright brothers successfully flew the first airplane at Kitty Hawk, the usage of motorized aircraft from oceangoing vessels began almost immediately.

In 1908, a German steam liner company announced that it was making plans to fly planes off of its ships. The announced reason was to speed up cross-Atlantic mail, but the United States feared that the real reason was military. In response to this announcement, the U.S. Navy began making plans to launch an airplane from one of its own ships. The German plans did not come to fruition, but the plans the United States made in response did.

Plane vs. Battleship

On May 31, 1910, American airplane builder Glenn Curtiss—whom we discussed earlier in this chapter—addressed a banquet of army officers, political leaders, and bigwigs in the manufacturing community and made a bold claim. He said that one airplane could sink a battleship.

There was some laughter. It seemed preposterous. To prove his point, Curtiss began a few experiments. In late June 1910, he dropped several dummy bombs—they were actually lead weights with streamers attached—from a plane at Hammondsport, New York, from heights of 500 and 800 feet.

His target was not a battleship but rather a raft anchored in the center of Lake Keuka. A reporter who had been invited to watch the experiment wrote that the bombs had been quite accurate. Curtiss's comment was that the accuracy was nothing compared to what could be accomplished by a plane with a two-man crew. He'd had to both pilot the plane and aim the bombs. If he'd had a copilot to aim the bombs while he flew the plane, he'd have been more accurate.

Vision of the Future

Also in 1910, navy captain Washington Irving Chambers had a vision of the future and it included naval aviation. In order to convince the admirals that his vision was more than poppycock, he knew that he would have to demonstrate the feasibility of operating airplanes off of ships.

He first asked the Wright brothers if they would fly a plane off the deck of a ship. They refused. But Glenn Curtiss, the man who "bombed" Lake Keuka earlier in the year, agreed to help—as long as he didn't have to be the pilot.

Officials of the Hamburg-American Steamship Company offered Curtiss the use of their steamship SS *Pennsylvania*. A large platform was built on the stern of the ship. The *Pennsylvania* was to load a Curtiss plane aboard the platform and then travel 50 miles out to sea.

A pilot named McCurdy had volunteered to fly the experimental flight. The plane never got off the ship, however, because an oil can placed carelessly on the wing of the plane fell off and broke the propeller. The experiment was cancelled. But they tried, tried again, and the next time history was made.

Ely's Historic Flight

On November 14, 1910, a pilot took off in an airplane from a ship for the first time. This time the pilot was 24-year-old Eugene B. Ely. He took off in a 50-horsepower Curtiss plane from an 83-foot-by-24-foot wooden platform built atop the bow of the USS *Birmingham* (CL-2), a light cruiser.

Finding Ely had not been easy. Many established pilots wanted no part of taking off from a ship. Ely was a stunt pilot who worked in a daredevil show, and looked forward to the opportunity to add to his death-defying resumé.

At the time of Ely's historic first takeoff from a ship, the *Birmingham* was at anchor in Hampton Roads, Virginia. The experiment was delayed all morning because winds were too strong. In the afternoon a heavy mist came up and limited visibility.

Finally, with the weather getting no better, the pilot decided to take a chance. The flight barely made it. The plane descended after leaving the platform and actually touched the water. A spray came up as the propeller struck the water and the whole plane vibrated just before it began to rise.

Ely flew blind for the next several moments, as the spray from the propeller striking the sea had covered his goggles with saltwater. After a frightening few seconds, he managed to clear his goggles enough so that he could once again see the sky above and the water below.

The short flight ended moments later when Ely—who was a friend of Curtiss—landed on a strip in Willoughby Spit about 2½ miles away.

First Landing on a Ship

The first man to take off from a ship became the first man to land on a ship when Eugene Ely landed his Curtiss pusher on a platform built atop the USS *Pennsylvania*, an armored cruiser, during the late morning of January 18, 1911. The ship was at anchor at the time in San Francisco Bay.

Ely took off from Camp Selfridge and flew up the coast, over San Francisco, and across the harbor to the Navy Yard. He circled the ship once before making his approach for the landing. Ely landed with the help of 22 transverse hemp ropes stretched across the platform and held in place with sandbags. Ely's plane was fitted with hooks that hung down from the fuselage.

For this experiment the weather cooperated. It was a calm and clear day. Ely went from touching down to coming to a complete stop in

33 feet. Forty-five minutes after landing, Ely took off again. Though the wheels of his plane almost touched the water before he began to rise, the takeoff was successful and he returned to Selfridge Field in San Francisco.

First Catapult

One problem with launching planes from ships is getting them up to speed for takeoff before they fall off the edge of the ship. To give the planes a boost, a catapult was developed.

The first catapult designed to launch an airplane was built by the Wright brothers in 1912. It consisted of a heavy weight suspended in a framework tower. A system of pulleys led a rope from the weight to the aircraft. When the weight was released, the plane was thrown forward. Capt. Washington I. Chambers brought high technology to the catapult, also in 1912, when he designed one that functioned with compressed air.

It wasn't until the outbreak of World War I that the admirals of the world first began to take Curtiss's idea of using ships as floating airfields seriously. In Japan, Adm. Isoruku Yamamoto announced that the most effective warships of the future would be those that carried airplanes. His countrymen didn't exactly laugh at him, but it was another decade before anyone agreed with him.

FIRST AIRCRAFT CARRIER

During the summer of 1919, less than a year after the end of World War I, the Naval Appropriations Act for Fiscal Year 1920 contained a provision that was to change the U.S. Navy forever. The act provided for the conversion of the *Jupiter*, a collier (a ship that transports coal), into the first aircraft carrier. Plans were modified that autumn.

The *Jupiter* had a flat platform built on top, extending its entire length. Catapults were put on both ends of what was called the "flying-off deck." Later this portion of an aircraft carrier would be known as the flight deck. Because the flying-off deck had been placed atop the ship without any consideration for aesthetics, the nickname given to the new carrier was "Covered Wagon."

The ship was renamed the USS *Langley*. Even before it was converted into a carrier, this was a precedent-setting ship. The *Jupiter*, which launched on August 24, 1912, at the Mare Island Navy Yard in Vallejo, California, was the U.S. Navy's first electronically propelled ship. The *Jupiter* traveled east into the Atlantic for its conversion.

The navy was pleased with the *Langley* and immediately sought more ships with naval aviation capabilities. Congress authorized the conversion of the unfinished battle cruisers *Lexington* and *Saratoga* as aircraft carriers on July 1, 1922. When the conversion of those ships was completed, all pilots assigned to them had been trained by taking off and landing on the *Langley*.

After six months of flight operations and tests in the Caribbean, in June 1923, the *Langley* sailed to Washington, D.C., where it demonstrated takeoff and landing for a gathering of dignitaries. From there it went to Norfolk for more tests and alterations, and then made the long trip to San Diego late in 1924, to join the navy's Pacific fleet.

CHANCE MILTON VOUGHT

Although the very first planes to take off from ships were Curtiss planes, the man most responsible for adapting aircraft to the needs of naval aviation was Chance Milton Vought.

Vought was born on February 26, 1890, in New York City. He studied engineering at the Pratt Institute, New York University, and the University of Pennsylvania. After school, at age 20, he went to work for Harold F. McCormick, an aircraft backer. Vought got his flying lessons from the inventors themselves, the Wright brothers. He was the 156th to receive his pilot's license. In addition to being a pioneer pilot, he also edited a magazine called *Aero & Hydro*.

Vought designed his first plane in 1914, the Mayo-Vought-Simplex. It was used as a training plane by the Royal Air Force. Two years later he joined the Wright Co. of Ohio as its chief engineer. Although he only worked there for a brief period, he did develop the Model V Wright flyer. With partner Birdseye Lewis, Vought formed his own company in 1917, and their aircraft, the VE-7, was considered the state of the art at the time. When the USS *Langley* was ready for launching and receiving aircraft in 1922, it was a Vought VE-7 that accomplished the feat.

Naval airpower was effective because it accomplished a projection of power. Using ship-based planes, aircraft could attack areas that would be impossible to reach from friendly airstrips on land. The airpower could now go anywhere the ship could go. This would be a key factor in World War II, especially in the Pacific Theater.

But we're getting ahead of ourselves. Let's return now to World War I, the land-based planes of that war, and the progressive nature of dogfighting in the skies over Europe.

CHAPTER 2

EARLY LAND-BASED PLANES OF WORLD WAR I

World War I (WWI) broke out on August 1, 1914. At that time, Germany possessed long-range bombing capabilities, using its rigid airships or zeppelins, as well as fixed-wing, multi-engine biplane aircraft.

When people discuss the "Battle of Britain," they are usually referring to the aerial combat between the Germans and the British that took place over England during the early years of World War II. But that was the second Battle of Britain.

FIRST BATTLE OF BRITAIN

When World War I began, German kaiser William II prohibited the military from bombing England; he had an English mother and was the eldest grandson of Queen Victoria. He did not want to conduct aerial bombing of his English cousins. He viewed the dropping of bombs as not the act of a gentleman. As the death toll and fighting rose on the Western Front in horrible trench warfare, his concept of appropriate behavior during wartime changed. The first attacks over English soil were made by zeppelin. This is the story of the first Battle of Britain, which was started in 1914 by fixed-wing German aircraft flying across the North Sea, picking up from or supplementing the zeppelin bombing raids against England.

In preparation for fixed-wing bombing of England, the Imperial German Air Service created the High Command Bomber Group (Kampfgeschwader de Obsertein Heeresleitung) to create a long-range, fixed-wing bombing force. The German High Command Bomber Group collected a small aircraft force of three dozen two-seat Aviatker AG reconnaissance aircraft, modified to carry bombs under their wings. The Aviatker AG only had a maximum speed of 62 mph, a service ceiling of 9,000 feet and a range of 225 miles. It could barely reach London and would be at great risk from attacking fighters.

FIRST STRATEGIC BOMBING RAID

It was the British who changed Kaiser William's view on the prohibition on aerial bombing of England. On November 21, 1914, three Royal Flying Corps (RFC) aircraft took off from a forward airfield at Belfort, France (close to the German lines along the Rhine River), to bomb the large wooden zeppelin hangars (sheds) on Lake Constance (a round trip air distance of 120 miles).

This limited, strategic bombing raid only damaged one zeppelin inside the wooden shed. The German military command officers wanted to immediately retaliate against targets in England, and convinced Kaiser William to authorize the bombing of England. Kaiser William relented.

Retaliation

The first German fixed-wing bombing raid against England was flown on the night of December 21, 1914, by a German navy seaplane. The seaplane's mission was to bomb the Admiralty Pier located at Dover, England, but the two bombs missed, exploding harmlessly in the water.

The first bombs to hit English soil from a German fixed-wing aircraft fell on December 24, 1914. A German navy seaplane dropped two small bombs on the town of Dover. A second German navy seaplane attempted to repeat the attack against Dover on Christmas Day 1914, but this time, English antiaircraft artillery (AAA) guns and one airborne fighter drove the attacking German aircraft from the city. The German seaplane dropped its bombs into the North Sea before landing back at its base. These were classified as nuisance raids, preliminaries of larger raids to follow.

The German army prepared a forward airfield at Ghistelles, Belgium, located on the North Sea coastline, within flying distance of Dover. The German High Command Bomber Group stationed single-engine fighters, modified with bomb racks that carried 5- to 10-pound bombs, one or two at a time.

The bomb-carrying fighters conducted 20 single aircraft bombing raids against Dover, across the North Sea. Kaiser William, even though he had authorized zeppelin bombing of London and its surrounding area on February 12, 1915, placed limits on what could be attacked. Bombs could only be aimed at ...

- military bases and supply dumps
- military barracks
- oil and petrol (gasoline) stocks and storage facilities
- the London docks

The zeppelin raids over London began in May 1915 but, in reality, given the primitive bombing equipment and dead reckoning navigation, it was difficult to identify and bomb the correct targets.

Germany's ability to bomb England improved by the autumn of 1916, as did England's ability to defend itself. The outcome of the first Battle of Britain will be discussed in Chapter 3.

BIRTH OF THE DOGFIGHT

In the early days of the war, planes were unarmed, although sometimes the observer carried a rifle, and the pilot was usually armed with a pistol (to defend himself in case he was shot down behind enemy lines). The observer was the second member of a reconnaissance plane's crew, who often sketched geographical landmarks and enemy positions.

Shots were sometimes exchanged between passing enemy planes, usually to no result. Grenades, too, were sometimes carried. France had a not particularly effective antipersonnel weapon, a small bomb packed with fléchettes (small darts).

Although they started the war flying mostly British planes, France was quickest to appreciate the possibilities of air war apart from simple bombing. Its planes were the first to be armed with machine guns. It pioneered the concept of the three-plane hunting squad, whose mission was not scouting, but shooting down enemy planes. Its aircraft also bombed such German cities as Cologne and Freidrichshafen, site of the zeppelin factories.

During the first year of the war, English pilots would joke that Europe's prevailing westerly winds were a larger threat than was German antiaircraft fire (which they called "Archie"). Missions were always flown with the wind and the return trip was into the wind's teeth. The early reconnaissance flights often frustrated British pilots and observers, because they would see targets that should have been attacked right then and there, and yet with no armament they could only return to their base where an attack from the ground would be ordered. So the crews were given bombs, which had to be dropped over the side by hand.

Firebombs were also used. These consisted of an aerodynamic container filled with gasoline. Dropped over the side they would burst into flame upon impact with the ground.

GREAT BRITAIN'S EARLIEST LAND-BASED WARPLANES

The Royal Aircraft Factory R.E.5 was a two-seater that worked both as a reconnaissance plane and as a light bomber in 1914. It received its power from a Beardmore six-cylinder liquid-cooled in-line engine that produced 120 horsepower. It had a 44-foot, 6-inch wingspan, and flew at a maximum speed of 78 mph.

The B.E.2a model was used both for reconnaissance and as a light bomber. Its engine was a Renault eight-cylinder air-cooled in-line V that produced 70 horsepower. It held a crew of two. Its wingtips were 35 feet, ½ inch apart. When flying in anger, it carried 100-pound bombs. With a top speed of 60 mph, the B.E.2a model was a favorite of pilots because of its stability and because it offered the observer an excellent view of the ground.

The British also flew the Sopwith Tabloid, granddaddy of the Camel. The one-seater's power plant was a nine-cylinder air-cooled rotary that produced 100 horsepower. With a wingspan of 25 feet, 6 inches, it could fly at a maximum speed of 92 mph and up to a ceiling of 15,000 feet. It had an endurance of 3½ hours and was armed with a machine gun. (Much more about Sopwith planes later in this chapter and in Chapter 3.)

Martynsyde Ltd. produced the Martinsyde S.1, a biplane one-seater that was designed as a fighter plane. The engine was a Gnome rotary producing 80 horsepower. The wingspan was 27 feet, 8 inches, and it flew at a maximum speed of 84 mph.

England also flew the Avro 504 beginning in 1914. The reconnaissance/light bomber held a crew of two and was armed with both a machine gun and 80-pound bombs. It was powered by a Gnome seven-cylinder air-cooled rotary engine producing 80 horsepower. It had a wingspan of 36 feet, flew at a maximum speed of 82 mph up to a ceiling of 12,000 feet, and had an endurance of 4½ hours.

FRENCH SITTING DUCK: B.E.2

When the war started, and newborn heavier-than-air aviation transformed so rapidly into military airpower, some nations were left disastrously behind the curve. Though they quickly caught up, this was true in France, where the French air force had to use British planes that were not designed for warfare, until warplanes could be designed and built.

One example of this was the Blériot Experimental 2, built by Great Britain's Royal Aircraft factory, which was a state-of-the-art plane in 1912. But when forced into a military role, it became a sitting duck in the skies over Europe. In a 1912 competition in Britain, the two-seater B.E.2 broke the British altitude record by climbing to 10,590 feet.

The B.E.2 was upgraded in 1913 with a more powerful engine and became known as the B.E.2a. The following year this became the first plane used in warfare by the French. B.E.2b and B.E.2c models quickly followed.

The planes, nicknamed "Quirk," were designed for reconnaissance and the modifications that led to the new designations involved wing and tail configurations designed to provide a smooth ride. The smoother the ride, the better the reconnaissance photography.

But nothing was done to provide the B.E.2 with extra maneuverability, although the C model was given a pair of 7.7mm machine guns. German aircraft quickly cleared the skies of the smooth-riding Quirks. In total, 3,535 B.E.2s were built.

OTHER FRENCH AIRCRAFT OF 1914

Let's look at the French aircraft at the start of the Great War.

The Morane-Saulnier H, built by Société Anonyme des Aéroplanes Morane-Saulnier, was a reconnaissance plane that first flew in 1913. It had a Gnome rotary engine that produced 80 horsepower. Its wingspan was an inch shy of 30 feet. It flew at a maximum speed of 85 mph. The one-seater could fly up to a ceiling of 3,280 feet and had an endurance of three hours.

Louis Breguet and the Breguet Bomber

Almost twice as heavy was another French plane, this one a customary biplane, the Breguet AG4, first built by Louis Breguet in 1914. The two-seater had a Gnome rotary engine producing 160 horsepower. Its wing-span was 50 feet, 4 inches, and it had a maximum speed of 62 mph. It could fly up to a ceiling of 4,290 feet.

> ### FIRST U.S. ACE
> The first American pilot to shoot down an enemy airplane was Lt. Stephen W. Thompson of Dayton, Ohio. He accomplished this feat on February 5, 1918, while riding as observer in a Breguet bomber.

This first Breguet effort of the war was a reconnaissance plane, but soon he was designing bombers. The Breguet Bomber would turn out to be France's premiere bomber of the war. The first of these bombers was the Breguet Br. M.5, which first flew in 1915. It was powered by a Renault liquid-cooled in-line V that produced 220 horsepower. It could carry 661 pounds of bombs and was further armed with a pair of machine guns.

BREGUET BR. M.5 SPECIFICATIONS

Wingspan: 57 feet, 9 inches
Length: 32 feet, 6 inches
Height: 12 feet, 9 inches
Weight empty: 4,235 pounds
Maximum speed: 88 mph
Ceiling: 14,110 feet
Range: 435 miles or five hours

Among the first French warplanes were four other monoplanes. The French monoplanes, all used for reconnaissance in the First World War, included the Deperdussin TT, a two-seater manufactured by S.P.A.D.; the Nieuport 6M, a one-seater produced by Société Anonyme des Établissements Nieuport; and the Blériot XI, a two-seater nicknamed "The Bird Cage" and built by Louis Blériot.

Morane-Saulnier N

An early French plane, which roared across European skies as early as 1915, was the Morane-Saulnier N model. It was a monoplane as opposed to the double-winged plane we most often associate with the dogfighting of WWI, or the triple wing of the Red Baron's Fokker. The N model was designed in 1914 by French flying ace Roland Garros and veteran airplane designer Raymond Salnier.

The resulting plane was introduced to the front during March 1915. Plane experts looked at the plane with skepticism at first. The fixed Hotchkiss machine gun fired through the propeller blades without synchronization, and so the propeller was covered with steel bullet deflectors.

The skepticism quieted in April 1915, when Garros strapped himself into the cockpit and shot down an enemy plane. The Morane-Saulnier N went on to serve both the British Royal Flying Corps and the Russian 19th Air Squadron until 1916.

EIGHT WINNER'S TIPS FOR DOGFIGHTING

Here, according to German aviation instructor Capt. Oswald Boelcke, are eight concise rules for fighter pilots:

1. Try to secure advantages before attacking. If possible, keep the sun behind you.
2. Always carry through an attack once you have started it.
3. Fire only at close range and only when your opponent is properly in your sights.
4. Always keep your eye on your opponent, and never let yourself be deceived by ruses.
5. In any form of attack it is essential to assail your opponent from behind.
6. If your opponent dives on you, do not attempt to evade his onslaught, but fly to meet it.
7. When over the enemy's lines, never forget your own line of retreat.
8. Attack on principle in groups of four or six. When the fight breaks up into a series of single combats, take care that several do not go for one opponent.

The Red Baron himself, Lt. Manfred von Richthofen, wrote during the war that "Everything Boelcke told us was Gospel." Boelcke died in a midair collision in October 1916.

GERMAN AIRCRAFT, 1914

The top German plane of the early years of the war was the Fokker E (for Eindecker), which we discussed in Chapter 1. The addition of the synchronized machine gun to Fokker planes led to the "Fokker Scourge," or air superiority. But there were other effective German aircraft being flown during 1914.

The Deutsche Flugzeug-Werke GmbH company produced the D.F.W. BI, a two-seated reconnaissance biplane with a Mercedes six-cylinder power plant producing 100 horsepower. It was unarmed and had a 46-foot wingspan. It could stay in the air for up to four hours on a single tank of gas. It flew at a maximum speed of 75 mph to a ceiling of 9,840 feet.

The Albatros BII was built by the Albatros Werke GmbH. Its power plant was a Mercedes six-cylinder liquid-cooled in-line producing 100 horsepower. The two-seater had an endurance of four hours and flew at a maximum speed of 66 mph up to a ceiling of 9,840 feet.

The Germans also flew the Aviatik BI, a reconnaissance plane with a Mercedes six-cylinder liquid-cooled in-line engine producing 100 horsepower. It held a crew of two and could stay in the air for four hours at a time. (The similarly named Aviatik BII was built by the *Österreichische-Ungarische Flugzeugfabrik Aviatik* and first flew for the Austrian Air Force in 1915. It had a crew of two and carried 44-pound bombs.)

One of Germany's top fighters during the first years of the Great War was the LFG Roland C-II Fighter Biplane. It held a two-man crew and ran on one water-cooled Mercedes D six-cylinder in-line engine that generated 160 horsepower. Used from 1915 to 1917, the plane had a wingspan of 33 feet, 8 inches, and weighed 2,822 pounds when fully loaded.

BRITISH AIRCRAFT, 1915

In 1915, in order to catch up with planes being produced in Germany by Fokker, Geoffrey de Havilland designed the D.H.2 biplane for the British Aircraft Manufacturing Company. It was a pusher, which as you'll recall, means that the engine was behind the cockpit. The machine gun, therefore, could be mounted right on the nose of the plane without worry of shooting the propeller off. By the beginning of 1916, the D.H.2 had taken away the air superiority claimed by Fokker and the Germans.

Twelve Royal Aircraft Factory FE 2b Fighter Biplanes were ordered by the Royal Flying Corps at the outbreak of WWI and all 12 saw frontline service from early 1916, until the autumn of 1917. In all, 2,190 of the two-seaters were built. The craft proved in combat that it was superior to the German Fokker monoplanes.

The Royal Air Force FE 2b had a top speed of 91 mph, much faster than the Fokker. The plane had a 47-foot, 9-inch wingspan. The power plant was a water-cooled Beardmore in-line engine that produced 160 horsepower.

DEVELOPMENT OF THE NIEUPORT

During WWI, some of the top French planes were built by the Nieuport company and designed by Gustave Delage. They were among the first real fighters to be used by the Allies, and continued to develop and improve until the end of the war.

The Nieuport XI, which first flew early in 1915, was nicknamed the Bébé because it was developed from the French Bébé racing aircraft of 1914. The plane was highly maneuverable and led to many victories when in the hands of a good pilot. It was powered by an 80-horsepower rotary piston engine—some made by Gnome and some by Le Rhône. They were fast and could climb well. The plane's weak point was in its wings, which proved to be fragile.

GEORGES GUYNEMER

France's beloved ace of aces was Georges Guynemer. Rejected five times by flying corps as physically unfit, he managed to break three aircraft in 12 days after finally being accepted. He was flying a Morane-Saulnier monoplane when he made his first kill. On one morning, he shot down three German planes.

He flew a Nieuport XI Bébé biplane single-seat fighter over the fiercest battles of Verdun and the Somme, scoring 53 victories. Guynemer flew with a French squadron known as the "Storks."

In one two-month stretch he waged 388 combats, downed 36 German planes and three balloons, and forced 36 other planes to land. On September 11, 1917, he took off on a mission, flew into a cloud, and was never seen again. A generation of French schoolchildren believed that he had flown so high he could not come down.

The Nieuport XI's lone machine gun was mounted on the top wing so that it shot over the nose-mounted propeller. This plane was originally built only in France, but eventually also was manufactured in the Netherlands, Spain, and Russia.

In January 1916, the new-and-improved Nieuport, the XVII, hit the skies. The wings were now larger and stronger, and the power plant produced 110 horsepower. The XVII turned out to be one of WWI's most effective aircraft. The Germans eventually copied it, producing the Siemens-Schuckert DI, which we'll be discussing in Chapter 3. Among the WWI aces who flew the XVII were Billy Bishop, Albert Ball, Charles Nungesser, and Georges Guynemer. In both of the earlier Nieuport models, the top wing was much larger than the lower one.

NIEUPORT XVII SPECIFICATIONS

Wingspan: 26 feet, 10¾ inches
Length: 19 feet, 7 inches
Height: 8 feet
Power plant: Le Rhône rotary piston engine, producing 120 horsepower
Weight empty: 825 pounds
Maximum takeoff weight: 1,235 pounds
Maximum speed: 106 mph
Ceiling: 17,550 feet
Range: 155 miles
Armament: Two 7.7mm machine guns, one mounted on the top wing, one synchronized to shoot through the propeller.

In June 1917, the Nieuport 28 made its debut. This was the first plane flown by pilots of the American Expeditionary Forces (AEF). In this version, the lower wing was almost as large as the top. The Spad (to be discussed in Chapter 3) knocked the Nieuport off its throne as the top Allied fighter, but the 28 was still a successful plane with an excellent kill ratio.

The power plant now produced 160 horsepower, and top speed was 121 mph. This was the plane of the top U.S. ace, Eddie Rickenbacker (also to be discussed in Chapter 3), before he switched to a Spad.

BRISTOL FIGHTER

The Bristol F2A Fighter was a British Fighting Scout type plane that held a crew of two. It was manufactured by the Bristol Aeroplane Company and contained a 190-horsepower Rolls Royce Falcon I power plant. The wings had a span of 39 feet, 4 inches, and its overall length was 25 feet, 10 inches. The plane, which was nicknamed "Biff," could fly 125 mph at sea level but only 108 mph at 13,000 feet. It was armed with one Vickers and either one or two Lewis guns. It could also hold 112-pound bombs below its wings.

The F2A made her maiden voyage in September 1916, and was used in action on the Western Front for the first time on April 5, 1917. The first F2As made up Number 48 Squadron, Royal Flying Corps of the Army, commanded by Capt. William Leefe-Robinson VC. The "VC" at the end of his name means he received the prestigious Victoria Cross medal. (The Royal Air Force did not become an independent air branch until 1918.) This squadron suffered heavy losses over the Western Front in April 1917. While it was true that the fuselage was mounted high between the wings and the pilot had an excellent view, the plane had poor defensive tactics which German pilots quickly learned to exploit. The F2A was vulnerable, it turned out, both from below and from directly astern.

In the fall of 1917, Bristol manufactured the first F2B Fighters, which were F2As with a stronger engine. The new models had a 275-horsepower Rolls Royce Falcon III engine, giving the plane greater offensive capabilities. Despite the weight of the craft, the F2B could fly as fast and maneuver with just as much agility as any German one-seater. In fact, the F2B was the best diver on the Western Front. Though it held a crew of two, pilots soon learned to fly it like a one-seater, using the forward-firing Vickers gun. The second man fired rearward, using a pair of Lewis guns. When the war ended, 3,100 of the F2B had been manufactured, supplying 14 squadrons.

SOPWITH PUP AND TRIPLANE

The first important plane to be manufactured by Sopwith was the Admiralty Type 9901. But, because of its small wings, it became known then and forever more as the Sopwith Pup.

The Pup was used both from the land and off of British aircraft carriers beginning in 1916. It set a new mark for maneuverability at high altitudes. It flew to a ceiling of 17,500 feet and could do all of its aerobatic tricks as high as 15,000 feet.

The plane was powered by a Le Rhône 80-horsepower rotary engine. Pilots shot down the enemy with one forward-firing synchronized Vickers 7.7mm machine gun. There was also room for four bombs to be carried beneath the fuselage.

The Pup had a wingspan of 26 feet, 6 inches. It flew at a maximum speed of 112 mph. It could fly to its maximum altitude in 35 minutes and was able to fly for three hours without refueling.

INSIGNIA SOUVENIRS

Just as WWI planes were known for their colorful insignia—logos painted on their sides to identify them—WWI flying aces were known for being souvenir-takers.

When an ace shot down an enemy plane, he often visited the crash site and took the insignia from the crashed plane as a souvenir. The insignia was usually painted onto the fabric that covered the fuselage, so it could be easily removed.

The follow-up to the Pup was the Sopwith Triplane, which first flew on May 28, 1916. It was basically a Pup with a third wing added. Although the third wing did not make the plane more maneuverable, it increased the rate of climb, enabling it to climb at 1,200 feet per minute up to a ceiling of 20,500 feet. It was powered by a Clerget 130-horsepower rotary piston engine, and was armed with the same forward-firing Vickers machine gun as the Pup. The Triplane had a wingspan of 26 feet, 6 inches. It could fly at a maximum speed of 117 mph and had an endurance of two hours and 45 minutes.

The triplanes had their biggest effect on the war between February and July 1917. Only 140 triplanes were built but they were credited with shooting down 87 enemy planes during that six-month period.

THE CIRCUS IN THE SKY

The glory and romance of WWI's land warfare died during the first three weeks of the war in 1914. Trench warfare had turned into a meat grinder into which the politicians and generals flung an entire generation of young men.

Aerial combat, on the other hand, became more romantic and glorious as the war progressed. The aerial duels of the aces echoed earlier days, when individual champions gave battle in single combat. The pilots were called Knights of the Sky and the war in the air was seen as the last bastion of chivalry.

By autumn 1916, aircraft quality was improved on all sides. In Germany, Max Immelmann was put in charge of his own Jagdstaffel, a 12-plane hunting pack consisting of two swarms of six planes, further divided into "chains" of three planes. Basically, it was an elaboration on the French three-plane units, and continues even today in the three-man team of a leader and two wingmen. Immelmann scored 16 victories before his luck ran out. Fokker's synchronized machine gun didn't have all of the bugs worked out of it and Immelmann accidentally shot off his own propeller. The plane broke in two and crashed. The body was identified by the "Blue Max" (named for Emperor Maximillian Friedrich) worn around his neck, a decoration coveted by every German ace.

Oswald Boelcke, the man whose "Eight Tips For Dogfighting" we learned earlier in the chapter, took up where Immelmann left off. His Jagdstaffel 2 scored many victories. He was not only a great flyer, but he had an eye for talent as well. He discovered the man who became known as the Red Baron.

THE RED BARON

The most famous ace of WWI, German or otherwise, was Manfred Freiherr von Richthofen, known as the Red Baron.

Born in Breslau, Prussia, on May 2, 1892, the eldest of three brothers, Richthofen was a true baron, the right to that title having been granted to his family by Frederick the Great. Well-to-do, Richthofen spent his childhood hunting, riding, and swimming at various family estates before entering officer training school. He emerged, at age 19, as a lieutenant best known for his horseback-riding skills. So, when the war began, he was assigned to the cavalry.

On horseback, Richthofen once rode so deep into Poland, behind enemy lines, that he was nearly captured by the Russians. It was not until May 1915, that he was transferred to the Air Service.

For the first five months, Richthofen served in an observer's capacity, riding along on flights over the Russian front and over Belgium with a long-range bombing unit. He decided to attend flying school in October 1915, after a chance meeting with the German flying ace Oswald Boelcke in a railroad dining car.

At pilot school, Richthofen seemed the least likely to become a flying ace. He failed his first two pilot's tests. On his first solo flight, he crash-landed.

He passed his pilot's test on Christmas Day 1915, on his third and final attempt. It wasn't until Richthofen entered the world of air combat that his superior skills began to show: By October 1916, he had shot down six enemy planes in his sleek Albatros D.II. His first combat plane was made of plywood, light yet strong. It had a 160-horsepower in-line Mercedes engine and was armed with twin Spandau machine guns.

Manfred Freiherr von Richthofen, the Red Baron.

Military Technical Journal

Loss of His Mentor

On October 28, 1916, Richthofen lost his mentor when Oswald Boelcke died in combat while attempting to support an infantry attack. The Baron was determined to be as good as Boelcke. He began to build his own legend on November 9, 1916, when he shot down and killed the British air hero Maj. Lanoe Hawker.

In January 1917, Richthofen and his fellow German pilots received upgraded planes. Their new Albatros D.IIIs climbed faster and performed better at high altitudes than had the old models.

The Red Baron, whose squadron was known as the "Flying Circus," scored the final 21 of his 80 victories in a red Fokker Dr.I Triplane, which he first flew late in 1917. The new plane not only had three wings but also had a supplementary airfoil on the undercarriage which enabled it to outclimb and outrun contemporary Allied craft. It was small—18 feet, 11 inches long with a wingspan of 23 feet, 7 inches—and had a small Oberursel engine that produced only 110 horsepower, but its maneuverability almost always gave the Baron an edge over his adversary.

Death of Richthofen

It was said at the time that the only way to shoot down a triplane was to attack it from above. And so it was that, 11 days before Richthofen's twenty-sixth birthday, on April 21, 1918, he was finally vanquished in battle by 24-year-old Capt. A. Roy Brown of Canada, flying a Sopwith Camel, attacking from above.

The Red Baron was flying air cover during Germany's big spring offensive. He led part of a squadron on an attack on two Allied scout planes.

During the confusion of the dogfight, Brown fired into a red triplane, and then lost sight of it. It glided to a landing near a position manned by Australian troops, who also fired at it. Richthofen lay in the cockpit, shot dead by one bullet.

In an Allied ceremony, the Red Baron was buried in France. Seven years after the end of the war, his body was disinterred and paraded through Germany on a ceremonial train to a hero's burial in Berlin.

CHAPTER 3

LATER PLANES OF WORLD WAR I

The increasing intensity of British air defenses against zeppelins forced the German military to switch almost exclusively to fixed-wing aircraft to conduct bombing raids against England, beginning on October 8, 1916.

There had been fixed-wing bombing raids on Dover and elsewhere in England, as we discussed in Chapter 2—and unsuccessful bombing raids of London by zeppelin beginning in May 1915—but on that night, October 8, a German Navy seaplane conducted the first fixed-wing bombing attack on London, dropping six small bombs.

GERMAN BOMBERS

By the beginning of 1917, the German military had developed three long-range, fixed-wing bombers with sufficient range to attack London with a significant bomb-carrying capacity. The first was the Siemens-Schuckert RI (a 1915 German aircraft design), powered by three engines.

Unfortunately, it was a poor design. The aircraft carried a crew of seven, had a maximum range of 320 miles and a service ceiling of 12,500 feet, and was able to carry a 230-pound bomb load. However, it was easy prey to existing French and British fighters, once the German bombers were located on their way to or from London. By this time, of course, pilots were no longer tossing the bombs over the side by hand. As early as late 1914, bombs were stored in a bomb bay at the base of the fuselage and released through bomb bay doors that opened when the plane was over its target.

The Gotha G-4

The Gotha Ursinus GI bomber first flew in the late months of 1915. The following variant, G-4, was used to attack London and other parts of England, beginning in May 1917. The bomber was powered by two 260-horsepower engines, fitted in a separate nacelle under the lower wings.

The blunt nose configuration allowed the two engines to be positioned closer together by mounting the tail fins in the engine's slipstream, which provided improved one-engine flying characteristics. However, if one engine stopped functioning, it was still difficult for the pilot to fly. The bomber had a maximum speed of 88 mph, maximum range of 522 miles, a service ceiling of 21,320 feet, and a 1,100-pound bomb load.

The bomber was defended by two machine guns, one mounted in the nose ahead of the pilot and the second behind. The positioning of the second machine gun made it difficult for the aircraft to be shot down by British or French fighters approaching either from above or below the rear of the bomber.

The aircraft had a plywood-lined tunnel in the rear fuselage compartment, with a V-shaped opening on the top decking for the rear gunner so he could fire down through the fuselage. Interestingly, this unique dual firing choice by the rear gunner, which made it appear there were two guns at the rear of the aircraft and not one, made it hard for attacking fighters to get close enough to fire their guns.

Landing Problems

During WWI Germany built 230 Gotha G-4s, a remarkable aeronautical accomplishment for a country at war. The bomber's design, unfortunately, possessed a major design flaw or structural weakness in the undercarriage system (landing wheels and supporting struts).

TYPE R

The Zeppelin Company also built a long-range, fixed-wing, multi-engine bomber, officially designated as the Staaken R, but commonly referred to as the Type R. This was a limited bomber production run, with only 32 Type Rs produced. Only 18 Type Rs actually flew bombing raids against London before the war ended.

During the bombing campaign against England, 36 Gotha G-4s crashed while landing, after a bombing mission. The landing wheels could not support the impact of repeated landings. Because the bomber had a nasty tendency to nose over when landing, two pairs of wheels became the standard undercarriage, one set under each engine, with a tail wheel for ground control.

German High Command Group

In the summer of 1917, the German High Command Group was created as a semi-independent bomber force to carry the air war to England.

The German High Command Group collected 50 Gotha G-4s, assigned to three separate bomb squadrons, operating from three different airfields located around Ghent, Belgium, approximately 170 miles from London. The scattering of the three bomb squadrons was to prevent the Allies from conducting reprisal raids against the bomber bases, catching all on the ground at the same time and at one airfield.

BOMBS OVER LONDON—NOT

On May 25, 1917, 33 Gotha G-4s took off in the first concentrated fixed-wing aircraft bombing raid of WWI against London. Because of the distance to London, after leaving the airfields around Ghent, they landed at Nieuwmunster to top off their fuel tanks, reducing the flying distance to London to 130 miles. This would enable the Gotha G-4s to reach London carrying a maximum bomb load, release their bombs, and return to the launch bases around Ghent.

The refueling stop provided a slim margin of airborne flight safety if the bombers consumed more fuel than expected. This extra consumption might be caused by...

- higher than expected head winds (weather predictions were hard to determine over England and the North Sea).
- bad weather (requiring the pilots to fly around thunderstorms, which could bring down the fabric-covered aircraft).
- the need to outclimb attacking British fighters once the weight of the bombs had been released, or because of reduced aeronautics caused from battle damage.

Later, because of increased fuel consumption, an additional reserve fuel tank was installed on the aircraft, but at the expense of bombs that could be carried.

Where Did London Go?

After refueling in Nieuwmunster, the German bombers encountered higher than predicted head winds and thunderstorms, which forced all the aircraft, except two, to abort and return to their airfields in Belgium.

The remaining two Gotha G-4s became lost, unable to determine ground location and reach London. One of the Gothas dropped its bombs on Folkstone, England, rather than jettisoning the bombs into the North Sea. The remaining Gotha released its bombs on the Canadian military camp located at Shorncliffe, killing 16 and wounding 100 troops.

British Retaliation

Even though only two Gothas released bombs on England, in retaliation the British launched 77 fighters in an attempt to intercept and shoot down the raiders. The two Gothas were highly visible during the daylight raid. Thousands of Britishers on the ground heard the sound of the British fighters passing above, trying to reach the retreating German bombers.

By the time the British fighters climbed to 14,000 feet, the two Gothas safely pulled away as the fighters, short on fuel, were forced to land. Some glided to landing areas without the engines running.

Second Try

On June 5, 1917, the Germans mounted a raid by 20 Gotha G-4s. The Gothas took off from their bases around Ghent, with a total bomb load of 12,000 pounds.

Four Royal Navy Air Service (RNAS) fighters took off from Dunkirk, attempting to break up the German bomber formation, but the Gothas were too far out to sea, heading toward land, for the British fighters to catch up. The fighters returned to base at Dunkirk, reporting by wireless that the Gothas were headed inland. The small fighters carried no wireless equipment, since it was too heavy and took away from their already limited engine power-to-weight ratio.

The wireless warning alerted British ground defenses, starting with AAA on Sheerness, Isle of Sheppy (located south of the entrance to the Thames River, the expected route for the bombers to take to inland or farther, to London). Those batteries shot down one Gotha G-4.

The British launched 66 fighters, but only two were able to climb to the altitude at which the bombers flew, making an uncoordinated attack. The Gotha bomber formation's combined machine guns fended off the two attacking British fighters. The Gotha G-4s maintained a precise formation, releasing part of their bomb loads on the docks and naval facilities at Sheerness. Then they turned toward Shoeburyness, across the Thames opening on the North Sea, north of the Isle of Sheppey, releasing remaining bombs on the Shoeburyness munitions factory.

The Gotha G-4s slowly turned to the east, out over the North Sea, heading back to Ghent. Wireless operators at Sheerness alerted the airfield at Dunkirk that the Gothas were headed their way and to get into the air.

Ten RNAS Sopwith Camel fighters took off to position themselves ahead of and above the approaching German bombers. Even with their combined machine guns, the Germans had a difficult time fending off the British fighters. The German bomber formation was saved from many losses by the arrival of a squadron of German fighters launched from a base in Flanders. The German fighters attacked from above and surprised the Sopwith Camel pilots, driving them away from the Gotha G-4s. Almost at the same time, the Gotha pilots started to descend to land in

Belgium. Two Gothas crashed while landing when their landing gear collapsed.

TEN THOUSAND FEET OVER LONDON

On June 30, 1917, 20 Gothas took off from Belgium, arriving over London at an altitude of 10,000 feet. Heavy clouds hampered navigation, forcing six to drop out of formation and turn away from London. These six Gotha G-4s released their bombs on targets of opportunity along the English coast before crossing the North Sea, and headed for home. It was too dangerous to land with bombs attached under the aircraft's lower wings.

Fourteen Gotha G-4s continued on to their intended target. Arriving over central London at 11:35 A.M., the German aircraft released part of their bomb loads onto the Royal Albert Docks and the Borough of East Ham. The Gotha G-4s then released their remaining bombs around Liverpool Station in downtown London.

German Gotha bombers appeared over London again on July 7, 1917, with their pilots displaying exceptional flying skill. Twenty-one Gotha GIVs, flying in a precise diamond formation (one in the lead, eight slanted in position to either side of the lead aircraft, with four filling in the rear of the bomber flight), dropped all their bombs on London.

TOP TEN GERMAN WORLD WAR I ACES

Pilot	Victories
1) Manfred von Richthofen	80
2) Ernst Udet	62
3) Erich Loewenhardt	53
4) Werner Voss	48
5) Fritz Rumey	45
6) Rudolf Berthold	44
7) Paul Bäumer	43
8) Bruno Lörzer	41
9) (tie) Josef Jacobs	41
10) Lothar von Richthofen	40
(tie) Oswald Boelcke	40
(tie) Franz Büchner	40

As the Gothas turned for the North Sea, one RNAS Sopwith Camel fighter shot one Gotha GIV down near Margate. Four Gotha GIVs, while landing at their bases around Ghent, crashed when the landing gears collapsed.

After this massed daylight Gotha raid, British prime minister David Lloyd George ordered British Imperial Army field marshall Jan Christian Smuts to improve and strengthen London's air defenses against the German Gotha GIVs. The "Smuts Committee" reached a series of suggestions on how to improve (short and long term) British home defenses, including the radical (for this time) creation of an independent Royal Air Force (RAF).

Nine fighter squadrons were assigned to home defense in 1918, including Sopwith Camels that were modified for night interception of German aircraft. The Sopwith Camel pilot was provided a wireless receiver, mounted inside the cockpit to allow him to receive report from ground stations, directing the aircraft to the airborne zeppelins or fixed-wing aircraft.

DOGFIGHTS OF AUGUST

Thirteen Gotha G-4s appeared over England on August 12, 1917. British fighters based at Felixstowe intercepted the Gotha G-4s as they crossed the coast, with additional fighters based at Hainault Farm as well as Sutton's Farm attacking the Gotha G-4s over Canvey Island before reaching Southend.

THE ROYAL AIRCRAFT FACTORY SE5A

The Royal Aircraft Factory SE5a was a one-seat British fighter plane manufactured in Farnborough, Hampshire. The plane, used in 1917 and 1918, was produced with a variety of engines (Hispano-Suiza, Wolseley W.4A Viper, Wolseley Adder, and Sunbeam Adder), all producing in the neighborhood of 200 horsepower, enabling the plane to fly at a maximum speed of 132 mph at 6,500 feet. It could climb at a rate of 765 feet per minute. The SE5a had a wingspan of 26 feet, 7½ inches. Its armament consisted of a fixed, synchronized, forward-firing Vickers machine gun and one Lewis machine gun on a Foster mounting above the top wing. The plane had the capability to carry four 25-pound Cooper bombs under its wings.

Attacked by British fighters over Southend, the Gotha G-4s were forced to bomb the naval base at Chatam. British fighters based at Rock Ford joined to attack the Gothas, after they released their bombs on the naval base, but none were shot down. A flight of additional fighters based at Walker finally succeeded in bringing down one of the Gotha G-4s, with the German aircraft crashing into the North Sea.

One final group of RNAS fighters took off from Dunkirk to attack the approaching Gothas coming back across the North Sea. Before the RNAS fighters could climb up to the Gothas, German fighters from Flanders intercepted the British aircraft, turning them back to Dunkirk.

Four Gothas crashed upon landing, again due to landing-gear collapse. Still, it was extremely frustrating for British pilots to have been in the air in force, and to have shot down only one German aircraft.

SWITCH TO NIGHT BOMBING

On September 2, 1917, in a daylight raid, Gotha G-4s bombed Dover's port facilities and surrounding military installations. However, as the number of British fighters and AAA increased, operating during the day became too dangerous. The German High Command Bomber Group decided to switch to night-bombing raids. Beginning on the night of September 28, 1917, three Type R-6s flew a bombing raid to England.

ALBATROS D-VA

Germany's Albatros D-Va Fighter Biplane was used from June 1917 until the end of the war. It had an advanced design but its lower wings had a tendency to snap during dive attacks. The one-seater ran on a water-cooled Mercedes D IIIa in-line engine that produced 180 horsepower. It had a wingspan of 29 feet, 8¼ inches, and weighed 2,072 pounds when fully loaded.

During WWI, these large bombers flew 28 bombing sorties against England. Although these aircraft could carry a large capacity of bombs, it was committed in too few numbers to make it an effective aerial weapon. Type R-6s ended their combat over England in May 1918.

Fire Bombs

The Germans began carrying incendiary bombs on the Gothas, in an attempt to ignite as many small fires as possible, which they hoped would join together into one large fire, overwhelming London's fire fighters. These incendiaries were small, however, approximately 10 pounds, and not large enough to start the fires the Germans wanted. The resulting fires were usually put out rapidly by the London fire brigade.

During one incendiary mission, the Gothas had to release their incendiaries short of London. As soon as the Gothas dropped the incendiaries, searchlights illuminated the bomber formation and bursts of AAA appeared around the aircraft. The incendiaries hit the ground, but failed to explode and ignite. None of the bombers was shot down, but five nosed over when landing in Belgium, with the aircraft bursting into flames, killing all aboard.

BLOCKBUSTER BOMB

On the night of January 6, 1918, three Type R-6s raided London. On February 16, 1918, one Type R-6 dropped one 2,200-pound blockbuster bomb, hitting the Royal Hospital located at Chelsea, and causing considerable damage to the building and loss of life.

Three Type R-6s bombed London again on the night of March 7, 1918, damaging or destroying 400 homes. Fortunately, considering the dense population of the area, only 12 civilians were killed. The people had taken notice of the air-raid sirens, and headed toward the nearest shelter.

During May 1918, the Germans launched a massed raid with 28 Gotha G-4s attacking London. The bombers successfully reached London, dropping their bombs on the city. British fighters shot down three Gotha G-4s, three were brought down by AAA, and three crash-landed at their home airfields. This was the highest number of Gothas lost on a single raid over England.

FINAL BOMBING STATS

By July 1918, the Germans made the decision to halt bombing raids over England. German fixed-wing aircraft had killed a total of 835 and wounded 1,971. In return, 60 Gotha bombers had been lost. Of those 60, eight had been shot down by British fighters, 12 had been shot down by British AAA, 36 crashed on returning to their bases located around Ghent, Belgium, and four never returned from bombing raids and were considered missing in action (downed in the North Sea).

The German bombing raids eventually were defeated by a layered British air defense system and the effects of weather on the fabric-covered aircraft. Still, the use of German fixed-wing bombers to attack England was a remarkable achievement. The bombers brought to British civilians the horrors of war for the first time—horrors that would be dramatically increased during WWII.

SQUADRON 124, THE LAFAYETTE ESCADRILLE

On April 6, 1917, the United States declared war on Germany, but one group of American airmen who couldn't wait to fight had been in it since the beginning. They were the men of Squadron 124, the Lafayette Escadrille.

They took advantage of legal technicalities by first enlisting in the French Foreign Legion (which, as its name implies, is the only branch of the French military open to foreigners), and then transferring to the flying corps.

Flying Nieuports, Voisins, and Maurice Farmans, they scored 199 confirmed victories over the Germans before finally being incorporated into the Air Service of the American Expeditionary Force in February 1918, as the 103rd Pursuit Squadron.

One of the pilots of the Lafayette Escadrille, Frank Luke, carved out a reputation for himself as a balloon buster. The Germans' sausage-shaped observation balloons were hard targets, being ringed with antiaircraft guns, high-angle machine guns, and a landing strip of fighter planes nearby. Making a successful run could be even more dangerous, since the fireball from the exploding gas bag could incinerate the attacker if he didn't peel off quickly enough.

Balloon-busting called for a cowboy approach, and Frank Luke was a cowboy from Phoenix, Arizona. He flew a Spad for the 27th Aero Squadron of the First Pursuit Group. After one month in action, he was dead, after having downed more than 20 balloons and planes. He was posthumously awarded the Congressional Medal of Honor.

Another outdoorsman, Canadian Billy Bishop, took bags of tin cans aloft over Europe, throwing them out and shooting them in the air to hone his accuracy with a machine gun. Flying a Nieuport, Bishop made 72 kills, including 25 planes in 12 days. Unlike the majority of his generation of pilots, he died in bed of old age.

EDDIE RICKENBACKER

The United States's premier flying ace during the Great War was Eddie Rickenbacker, who scored 26 victories over Europe, 20 of them during the last two months of the war.

Rickenbacker was born in Columbus, Ohio, in 1890, the son of immigrants. His father died when he was 13. So he grew up before his years helping to support himself with a series of factory jobs. When Eddie was 16, he learned that he was a natural at repairing race-car engines, a skill that earned him a job at a small automobile manufacturer.

By the end of his teen years, Rickenbacker was a race-car driver who was quickly earning fame. He raced in the Indianapolis 500. The newspapers referred to him as "The Wild Teuton." He was earning $35,000 a year and owned the land-speed record with a drive at 134 mph.

When the United States became involved in World War I, Rickenbacker lobbied the U.S. Army to form a squadron of fighter pilots composed exclusively of race-car drivers. The Army turned him down, saying that Rickenbacker's speed demons lacked the youth and education required in flight candidates.

So when Rickenbacker enlisted soon thereafter, his first job was as chauffeur for the American general staff in France. While doing that job, Rickenbacker found himself the driver for Col. Billy Mitchell. Eddie convinced Mitchell of his aptitude as a pilot, and so Mitchell sent him to the French flight school at Tours.

Rickenbacker was greatly different from his fellow students, who tended to be college-boy types. His salty language and roughhouse ways were not popular at the school. Nonetheless, he won his wings in a record 17 days.

By March of 1918, Rickenbacker was a member of the 94th Aero Squadron.

Eddie celebrated his first victory in his Spad Fighter Biplane (a plane we'll be discussing in detail later in this chapter) on April 29, 1918. He and fellow pilot James Norman Hall (later co-author of the classic *Mutiny on the Bounty*) were on patrol when their two planes encountered a German Pfalz fighter (another plane we'll be discussing later in the chapter). The Americans climbed above the German plane and attacked it out of the sun. (It's good dogfighting form to get directly between your opponent and the sun. That way, they can't look at you without also blinding themselves.) The German pilot successfully evaded Hall, only to fly directly into the path of Rickenbacker's guns.

Before becoming a Flying Ace, Eddie Rickenbacker was a successful race-car driver who drove in the Indy 500.

Rickenbacker's fifth victory brought him closest to death. Far behind enemy lines, Eddie shot down a German Albatros, but sustained damage to his plane in return. He flew his Spad with the top wing collapsed, all the way back to the 94th Aero Squadron's headquarters in Toul. The story goes that he grazed the roof of the 94th's hangar before pancaking onto the runway.

Military Technical Journal

Rickenbacker poses with his Spad.

RICKENBACKER'S PLANE: SPAD 13

Spad is actually an acronym for *Société Pour l'Aviation et ses Dérivés*. The first successful Spad military aircraft was the Spad S.7, which first flew in April 1916. It was built solidly and could fly very fast without any risk of breaking up in the air. That plane was built with two different Hispano-Suiza engines: the 8Ac, which produced 180 horsepower, and the 8Aa, which provided only 150 horsepower.

By September 1916, Spad S.7s were being flown by pilots of the French, British, Belgian, Italian, and Russian air forces. When American pilots joined the fight, they flew Spads as well. More than 6,000 S.7s were built.

SPAD S.13 SPECIFICATIONS

Wingspan: 26 feet, 6¾ inches
Length: 20 feet, 8 inches
Height: 7 feet, 8½ inches
Weight empty: 1,326 pounds
Maximum takeoff weight: 1,863 pounds
Maximum speed: 134 mph
Ceiling: 21,815 feet
Range: Two hours

The S.7 only had one machine gun. The upgraded model, which first flew in 1917, the S.13, had two 7.7mm Vickers machine guns. The Hispano-Suiza engine in the S.13 produced 220 horsepower.

In all, 8,500 S.13s were built. The Spad was as good or better than German fighters of the time until 1918, the final year of the war, when the Fokker D.7 surpassed it.

THE SOPWITH CAMEL

The Sopwith Biplane F.1, nicknamed the Camel, is the most famous plane to fight in WWI. Any chance of it slipping into obscurity vanished when Snoopy decided to fly one when fantasizing that he was the "World War I Flying Ace" in the comic strip *Peanuts*.

But the original reason it became the most famous plane of the Great War had nothing to do with fantasizing dogs. The Camel was simply the most dominant plane of the war. Sopwith Camels were credited with shooting down 3,000 German planes.

About 5,500 Camels were built—about 1,000 in 1917, the remainder the following year. The most notable variant of the Camel was the one built for aircraft carriers. This plane had a removable tail so more of them could be parked together on the flight deck and hangar deck of a navy flattop.

Built for Home Defense

Camels were used by the British for home defense. The variant used by these pilots had Lewis machine guns mounted on the wings rather than

Vickers guns on the nose. Along with pilots from Canada, the United States, and the United Kingdom, Camels were flown during WWI by pilots from Belgium, Greece, and the Slavo-British Aviation Group, who were fighting in Russia.

The Camel was much easier to handle than its Sopwith predecessors, the Pup and the Triplane. It had a forward center of gravity because its engine (usually a Clerget 130 horsepower nine-cylinder air-cooled rotary piston engine, although versions were also produced using the Le Rhône 9J, the Gnome Monosoupape, and the Bentley BR1), its armament (two 7.7mm synchronized Vickers machine guns), the pilot, and the fuel tank were clustered in the front 7 feet of the fuselage.

The plane had a wingspan of 28 feet. It could fly at a maximum speed of 117 mph, to a ceiling of 19,000 feet, and go for 2½ hours without refueling. It could climb to a height of 10,000 feet in 10 minutes and 35 seconds.

It was extremely responsive to a skilled pilot's wishes. The Sopwith Camel was a difficult plane to master, however. Many student pilots did not survive their training. But those who did turned the Camel pilot/plane combo into the toughest team of the war.

First Flight, First Victory

The prototype first flew on February 26, 1917. The first models were shipped to the front lines in June 1917. Only days later the Camel scored its first victory. Two days after that two more German planes were shot down by a single Camel. In addition to its double machine guns, the Camel was also armed with four 25-pound bombs which it carried below its fuselage.

The plane was also particularly deadly to German pilots because of its ability to make sharp starboard turns. Pilots could turn to the left more quickly by going three quarters of the way around a circle to the right, than by going the one quarter of a circle to the left. Though this dazzling and unexpected movement often proved to be the key to victory in dogfights, practicing the maneuver proved to be deadly to inexperienced Camel pilots as the extreme torque of the engine during the turn often forced the nose of the plane downward, causing a dive the pilot could not pull out of.

Nobody had a better day in the air during the war than Capt. J. L. Trollope of the RAF's No. 43 Squadron who, on March 24, 1918, during the Battle of Cambrai, shot down six German planes in his Camel.

On April 21, 1918, Roy Brown of the Royal Canadian Air Force used his Camel's machine guns to shoot down the Red Baron, Manfred von Richthofen. (This is the reason, of course, that Snoopy chose to fly one.)

On November 4, 1918, very near the end of the war, two squadrons of Camels attacked 40 Fokker D. VIIs. Twenty-two of the 40 Fokkers were destroyed or disabled.

In addition to German planes, Camels were also used along the Italian front against planes of the Austro-Hungarian air force.

THE DOLPHIN AND THE SNIPE

Making its debut only a few months after the Camel was the Sopwith 5F.1 Dolphin. The prototype first flew on May 22, 1917. The plane was powered by the Hispano-Suiza 200-horsepower piston engine. It was armed with two forward-firing synchronized 7.7mm machine guns mounted in front of the cockpit.

The Dolphin had a wingspan of 32 feet, 6 inches. It had a maximum speed of 112 mph. With a climbing capability of 855 feet per minute, it could fly up to a ceiling of 20,000 feet.

What was thought to be the plane's best design feature turned out to cause a lot of stress among pilots. There was a slot built in the center of the top wing, through which the pilot's head popped out. This gave the pilot a great view but tended to decapitate him when a poor landing led to the plane rolling over. This happened more than once, and a "crash pylon" was added. This was basically a roll bar, such as is found in today's race cars, and was mounted to the top wing above the pilot's head. The Dolphin also had a habit of stalling during turns, but as with the Camel, it could be deadly to the enemy if the pilot had a feel for the plane.

CHARLES NUNGESSER

Like Eddie Rickenbacker, Charles Nungesser was a race-car driver turned fighter pilot. He raced in South America and it was on that continent that he learned to fly.

He joined the French army in 1914 and was transferred to the French Flying Service the following year. He started out as a reconnaissance pilot, but an armed and aggressive one.

In November of 1915 he was transferred to a fighter squadron and by the war's end he had scored 45 victories, which put him third on the list of French pilots.

He flew Nieuport planes and struck terror in the hearts of his enemies by painting skull-and-crossbones designs on his aircraft. He was wounded many times during the war, both by gunfire and in crashes. One crash in 1916 broke both of his legs, but he was back in the cockpit two months later.

Also in 1916, a message was dropped on Nungesser's aerodrome challenging him to a duel, but when he flew to the assigned place at the assigned time he was ambushed by six German planes. Furious, he shot down two of the German planes, causing the other four to flee.

By August 1917 he was so banged up and exhausted that he sometimes had to be carried to his plane so he could fly his next mission.

Nungesser disappeared in 1927 attempting a flight from France to the United States.

The final Sopwith model to be introduced during WWI was the Sopwith Snipe. It first flew in September 1917. The Snipe was basically a larger Camel with a more powerful engine. It was powered by a Bentley 230-horsepower B.R.2 rotary piston engine. The armament was the same as in a Camel, and the plane's dimensions were all larger. The Snipe had a wingspan of 30 feet, 1 inch. It flew at a maximum speed of 121 mph. It had three hours of endurance and could fly to a ceiling of 19,500 feet at a climbing rate of 1,500 feet per minute.

SEAPLANES OF 1917 AND 1918

In Chapter 1, we reviewed the seaplanes used by Germany and the Allies during the first half of WWI. Here is a review of the seaplanes used by the participating air forces during the final two years of the war.

United States

In 1917, the United States produced three seaplanes, two of which landed on skis attached to the bottom of the fuselage. The other was a flying boat, the hull of which was the fuselage itself.

The first was the Curtiss N-9, which was powered by a Curtiss OX-6 eight-cylinder engine producing 100 horsepower. With a wingspan of 53 feet, 3¼ inches, it flew to a maximum speed of 80 mph and up to a ceiling of 9,850 feet, and could stay aloft for two hours at a time. Unarmed, it was flown as a trainer and held a crew of two: one pilot, one student.

The American-built Fairey Campania, also introduced to the war in 1917, was a reconnaissance flying boat powered by a Rolls-Royce Eagle VIII 12-cylinder liquid-cooled V producing 345 horsepower. Sixty-two of them were built. The plane was named after the HMS *Campania*, a British transatlantic liner that had been converted into an aircraft carrier, the very flattop upon which this plane served. Its wingspan was 61 feet, 7 inches; maximum speed, 80 mph; ceiling, 5,500 feet; and endurance, three hours. It was armed with one machine gun and carried a crew of two.

The other U.S. seaplane to make its debut in 1917 was the Felixstowe F 2A. It was a reconnaissance plane that was sometimes used as a bomber. The plane was derived from the Curtiss H-12 Large America. One hundred seventy of these planes were built. They were used extensively on patrol duty over the North Sea. The plane was powered by twin Rolls-Royce Eagle VIII 12-cylinder liquid-cooled V engines, which produced 345 horsepower each. Carrying a crew of four, it was huge compared to the other flying boats of the time, with a wingspan of 95 feet, 7 inches. It could fly 95 mph at 2,000 feet and had a ceiling of 9,600 feet and an endurance of six hours. Different models were armed with four to seven machine guns, and some carried 460-pound bombs. The Felixstowe F 2A was a menace to German submarines and was also extremely effective against zeppelins.

America's final flying boat of the war, introduced in 1918, was the Curtiss H16, manufactured by the Naval Aircraft Factory. It had two engines, a pair of Liberty 12-cylinder liquid-cooled in-line Vs producing 400 horsepower each. It had a crew of four, carried five or six machine guns, and was used for naval reconnaissance. It was a massive plane for the times, with a 95-foot wingspan. It had a maximum speed of 95 mph at sea level, flew to a ceiling of 9,950 feet, and had a range of 378 miles.

After WWI, further emphasis was placed on aircraft carriers. Planes that could be launched from a carrier were developed more frequently, with less development of new flying boats and seaplanes.

Great Britain

Great Britain's new ski plane of 1917 was the diminutive Sopwith Baby one-seater, which was used both for reconnaissance duties and as a light bomber. It saw extensive action over the English Channel and the North Sea, but also saw action in the Middle East, in Italy, and over the Mediterranean.

It had a Clerget 9-cylinder air-cooled rotary engine producing 130 horsepower. Here are its stats: wingspan: 25 feet, 8 inches; maximum speed: 100 mph; ceiling: 7,600 feet. It had an endurance of 2 hours, 15 minutes. It was armed with one machine gun and 130-pound bombs.

Austria

Austria's seaplane of 1917 was the Hansa-Brandenburg W12, built by Hansa and Brandenburgische Flugzeug-Werke GmbH. It was designed by Ernst Heinkel in response to a need for a naval fighter that wasn't an easy target for attackers from the rear.

The plane carried an armed observer at the rear so the plane could bite from both ends. In total, its two-man crew was armed with two or three machine guns.

Its engine was a Benz Bz III six-cylinder liquid-cooled in-line producing 150 horsepower. It had a wingspan of 36 feet, 9 inches, and flew at a top speed of 100 mph at sea level. It could fly to a ceiling of 16,405 feet, and had an endurance of 3 hours, 30 minutes.

The following year the same company made the similar but slightly faster Hansa-Brandenburg W29, which was a monoplane that could fly at 116 mph for up to four hours. Its lone wing was attached to the bottom of the fuselage with the twin skis attached to the bottom of the wing.

Italy

In 1918, Italy introduced two new flying boats: the Macchi M5 Mod and the Macchi M9. Both were manufactured by SA Nieuport-Macchi.

The Macchi M5 Mod was a reconnaissance/fighter one-seater armed with a pair of machine guns. It was powered by an Isotta-Fraschini V6B 6-cylinder liquid-cooled in-line engine that produced 250 horsepower. Its wingspan was 32 feet, 7¾ inches; maximum speed, 130 mph at sea level; ceiling, 16,405 feet; and endurance, 3 hours, 40 minutes.

The other Italian flying boat was the Macchi M9, which was a reconnaissance plane whose two-man crew was armed with a single machine gun. The engine was a Fiat 1-12 bis 6-cylinder liquid-cooled in-line worth 280 horsepower. It had a wingspan of 50 feet, 6 inches, and could fly as fast as 116 mph. Its ceiling was 18,500 feet and it had an endurance of four hours.

FRENCH PLANES CONTINUE TO DEVELOP: THE SALMSON

One of the top French reconnaissance planes of the final year of the war was the Salmson 2, a two-seater which had been designed the previous year by the *Société des Moteurs Salmson*. The strong point of the plane was a radial Canton-Unné engine. The nine-cylinder power plant produced 260 horsepower. The Salmson entered service during the first months of 1918.

SALMSON 2 SPECIFICATIONS

Wingspan: 38 feet, 8½ inches
Length: 27 feet, 10¾ inches
Height: 9 feet, 6¼ inches
Weight empty: 1,676 pounds
Maximum takeoff weight: 2,954 pounds
Maximum speed: 115 mph
Ceiling: 20,505 feet
Endurance: Three hours
Armament: Two or three machine guns

There were 3,200 Salmson 2s built, and they were flown extensively by both the French and the United States. Although designed as a reconnaissance plane, the Salmson 2 also proved to be effective on ground-attack and day-bombing missions.

THE GERMAN SIEMENS-SCHUCKERT (1918)

The German Siemens-Schuckert D.III was known for its engine, an 11-cylinder, 160-horsepower Siemens-Halske engine that gave the plane a phenomenal rate of climb (16,400 feet in 13 minutes), perhaps the best of the war. This engine, unlike others, had a crankshaft that rotated in one direction while the crankcase and cylinders rotated in the other. This doubled the engine speed, giving the plane its ability to climb. But there was a drawback. By this time in the war, only inferior oil was available to the Germans, and the Siemens-Halske engine had a tendency to overheat.

SIEMENS-SCHUCKERT D.III SPECIFICATIONS

Wingspan: 27 feet, 8 inches
Length: 18 feet, 8 inches
Maximum speed: 112 mph
Maximum takeoff weight: 1,598 pounds
Ceiling: 26,575 feet
Range: Two hours

The other drawback to the plane was that it could be deadly when operated by an inexperienced pilot. Landings demanded practice, and those who hadn't mastered the art often flipped the plane over after hitting the airstrip.

As mentioned in Chapter 1, the original Siemens-Schuckert plane, the D.I, was a copy of the Nieuport XI, which had been captured by the Germans. The D.I, however, was obsolete by the time it reached the front and was used mostly as a trainer.

There was also a D.IV, which had some of the D.III's problems ironed out, but it was not available for service until August 1918, only four months before the war ended.

PFALZ FIGHTERS

One of the top German fighter planes of 1917 was the Pfalz D.III fighter, a biplane built by the Bavarian company Pfalz, the same company that had built LFG-Roland fighters earlier in the war. Both strong and agile, the D.III was popular with pilots. One of the drawbacks of the D.III was the fact that the radiator was mounted to the top wing. When the radiator was shot up by enemy gunfire, boiling hot water would drip down onto the pilot. About 600 of them were built.

PFALZ D.III SPECIFICATIONS

Wingspan: 30 feet, 10 inches
Length: 22 feet, 9½ inches
Height: 8 feet, 9 inches
Weight empty: 1,532 pounds
Maximum takeoff weight: 2,061 pounds
Maximum speed: 103 mph
Ceiling: 17,000 feet
Range: 2 hours, 30 minutes
Armament: Two 7.92mm machine guns

In 1918, the Pfalz fighter received an upgrade and became known as the D.XII. The radiator had been moved. The Pfalz fighters were powered by a Mercedes in-line piston engine producing 180 horsepower.

FOKKER D-VII

The final Fokker model to see combat in WWI was the D-VII, which made its combat debut in May 1918 on the Western Front during Germany's unsuccessful spring offensive. It was notably maneuverable at high altitudes and had the advantage of being highly controllable even when flying at extremely low speeds.

The D-VII was considered by many to be the greatest fighter plane of the war. It was armed with two fixed 7.92mm Spandau machine guns and could fly anywhere up to a ceiling of 22,000 feet. At sea level the one-seater could fly as fast as 124 mph.

The wingspan measured 29 feet, ½ inch. The power plant—either a BMW IIIa or a Mercedes—was capable of developing 160 horsepower. It was designed by Reinhold Platz and, naturally, Dutchman Anthony Fokker. The craft was known for its lack of rigging wires in its wings, which had produced drag in earlier models. The rigging wires were rendered unnecessary by the new design's N-shaped interplane struts.

The Fokker D-VII could turn on a dime, a virtue of obvious value in a dogfight. The plane worked so well that, by the summer, the new Fokkers were featured in the attack of every squadron in the German Air Force.

After the Red Baron's death in the spring of 1918, Richthofen's squadron, his "Flying Circus," fought on without him in Fokker D-VIIs, fighting above the Second Battle of the Aisne during the early summer of 1918.

Among the German aces to fly the D-VII were Lt. Carl Degelow, who scored 20 of his 30 confirmed victories over a five-month period in a Fokker, and airman Rudolf Berthold, who scored 44 victories.

The D-VII arrived too late to save the war for Germany, but the plane made such an impression during its short time in battle (World War I ended in November 1918) that the Treaty of Versailles, the terms of Germany's surrender, specifically banned the plane.

CHAPTER 4

BETWEEN THE WARS

Only one generation got to enjoy the peace between the First and Second World Wars. An imperfect armistice left Germany anxious to conquer Europe, something it set out to do soon after Adolf Hitler and his Nazi party came into power in 1933. Between the wars, aircraft and theories of airpower changed, but at a more leisurely pace than during World War II, when air superiority determined who would live, who would die, and who would be in charge when the shooting was over.

GÖRING AND MITCHELL

Two very different individuals had absorbed the lessons of airpower learned in the Great War: Hermann Göring and Billy Mitchell.

As a pilot—first in Boelcke's staffel, then Richthofen's—Göring was a respected ace, with 22 kills to his credit. After the war he was an early member of the Nazi party. When Hitler took power in 1933, Göring was made air minister. The punitive terms of the Treaty of Versailles had come down hard on German militarism and sought to suppress any future manifestation of it. Germany was expressly forbidden to have an air force. But the armistice was barely signed before it began to be circumvented.

Generaloberst Hans von Seeckt was the hidden hand in charge of rebuilding Germany's air arm. He cut a deal with the Soviet Union to have German engineers build German planes in Russian factories. Presumably both countries would reap the rewards—and they did, although not as they had expected, when the Hitler-Stalin pact collapsed and their two countries went to war. Air cadet corps, universally popular among German youth, provided the organizational infrastructure for the coming air force: the Luftwaffe. Its chief was Hermann Göring.

As commander of the air force of the American Expeditionary Force in the Great War, Gen. Billy Mitchell scored a great victory during the Allied offensive of September 1918. A force of 1,500 planes under his command gave close support to ground troops at St. Mihiel, ceaselessly hammering the enemy, cutting off German troops from the main body.

After the war, Mitchell was a tireless campaigner for the cause of airpower. In a dramatic demonstration, he proved to the top brass that an airplane could sink a battleship. But he was a better prophet than he was a salesman, and his running feuds with high officials in the War and Navy Departments led to his court-martial in 1925.

Found guilty of insubordination, he was forced into retirement. His disciples, however, remained in the service, quietly working and waiting.

FIRST DIVE-BOMBERS

The biggest leap in air attack strategy between the wars came with the development of the dive-bomber, a plane that could attack a ground target while diving, leveling off and rising again just in time to keep from crashing.

The first successful dive-bomb attacks were made by Marine Corps flyers in Nicaragua in 1928. Going to the rescue of a besieged post ringed by attackers, the Curtiss OC-1 Falcons dove straight down at the enemy, dropping bombs with pinpoint accuracy.

Others were quick to seize on the possibilities. Ernst Udet, Germany's second greatest World War I ace with 62 confirmed kills, used the Curtiss Hawk dive-bomber to impress the Nazi brass in 1935. German designers incorporated features in what would become the Junkers 87. The Ju 87 was best known as the dive-bombing Stuka. Udet became a lieutenant general in the Luftwaffe's technical branch, but committed suicide in 1941 when confronted with irrefutable proof of the Nazi's extermination programs.

Military Technical Journal

One of the last planes debuted by the Luftwaffe was the Ju 87, an antitank plane equipped with two 37mm cannons.

VOUGHT AND THE PROBLEMS OF NAVAL AVIATION

It was during the 1920s that pioneer aircraft designer Chance Vought became involved with the particular problems presented by naval aviation. One problem of land-based aircraft was that they were too heavy and needed to develop momentum over a long runway in order to take off.

Vought sought to make every part of the plane lighter, including the engine. Pratt and Whitney designed a light engine for his purposes. Vought's first plane designed especially for naval aviation was the UO-1.

Along with having a lighter engine, it also was equipped to be launched from a catapult. During the 1920s, Vought's company was bought out by the United Aircraft and Transportation Corporation, but continued to function as a separate division.

Vought UO-1 made history when it became the first plane to be catapulted from a battleship at night. It happened on November 26, 1924, when Lt. Dixie Kiefer flew the plane off the USS *California* in San Diego harbor. The only light came from the ship's searchlights trained 1,000 yards ahead.

Vought's next plane designed specifically for carrier use was the O2U-1, the first Corsair, in 1928. More than 500 of them were built and they turned out to be amazingly versatile. They could take off and land on aircraft carriers. They could even be catapulted off battleships.

Vought died in 1930, unexpectedly, of blood poisoning, but quality naval aircraft continued to be made under his name. These included the F4U Corsair, the "Bentwing" which became famous during World War II, the F-8 Crusader, and the A-7 attack aircraft.

SOVIET WORKHORSE: POLIKARPOV I-16

Built in 1935, the Polikarpov I-16 fighter was one of the workhorses of the Soviet air force during World War II. This, despite the fact that, when it came time to return to Earth, the pilot had to *hand crank* the landing gear into place. It was a stubby (a little more than 20 feet long), single-seat monoplane.

The I-16 was combat tested even before World War II. During the Spanish Civil War (1936–1939), the plane flew on the side of the Loyalists, while the enemy, the fascist *Falange* (the movement of Gen. Francisco Franco), had on its side the Condor Legion of the German Luftwaffe. It was during the Spanish Civil War that American volunteer pilot Jackson Peck shot down a German plane, becoming the first American to do so since World War I.

The Condor Legion was established by the Luftwaffe's top man, Hermann Göring. The air unit that fought over Spain was commanded by Hugo Sperrie, with Chief of Staff Wolfram von Richthofen (cousin of Manfred von Richthofen, the "Red Baron").

During those dogfights, the I-16 was the fastest and deadliest aircraft over Spain. Technology passed the I-16 quickly, however, as World War II became the necessity that mothered many inventions. During most of the war against Germany, the Soviet fighter plane was obsolete.

German and Soviet air arms shared a common origin, in the chaotic aftermath of World War I. Historic adversaries, the two nations held a similar status, or lack of same, in the years between the world wars. According to military historian David H. Jacobs in the *Military Technical Journal*, "They were pariahs, outlaw states: Germany, because she had suffered defeat; and Russia, because she had gone Communist."

The German and Soviet Arms Race

The years between the wars saw an arms race between Germany and the Soviet Union. A mutually-agreed-upon race. Germany and the Soviet Union even formed an organization, called the GEFU, which included the German military elite and the ruling Bolshevik clique. The organization enabled both countries to industrialize their rearming processes.

As we mentioned, to circumvent the Versailles Treaty, the first German bases were set up inside Russia. Well into the later years of the decade, German pilots received their training at these bases. These airmen training inside Russia were the Luftwaffe, the German air force.

By 1928, after 10 years of civil war, Stalin had consolidated his hold on the Soviet Union. His next goal was Soviet industrialization, which he set about achieving with his customary ruthlessness and brutality. A succession of Five-Year Plans saw the Soviets make vast gains in industrial might.

The I-16 was a product of this phase, which also saw the inception of the Red air force. The Red army and navy each had its own arm of the Russian air force. Russia's strength lay traditionally in her army, and the development of the air force reflects the primacy of the army over the navy in that country's military history. Like the Red navy of the period, the Red navy's air force is only of secondary interest.

The Russian army's arm of the air force had the lion's share of the action in the air. In 1933, the year Hitler came to power in Germany, the Red Army Air Brigades became the Air Corps, mutating in 1936 to the First Air Army.

In 1934, designer Nikolai Polikarpov unveiled the I-15, a single-seat biplane with a Shvetsov engine. This was followed, a year later, by the single-wing I-16. In Germany, the Luftwaffe had not been idle either.

Spain would provide an arena for German and Russian pilots to test out their wings in actual air combat.

Proving Ground over Spain

By late 1936, Göring's Condor Legion in Spain had quite an operation going. The Condor Legion's men and materiel had been transported through Spain's Moroccan colony into Spain proper, working closely with Franco's "insurgent" ground troops. The first planes of the Condor Legion included Junkers 52 bombers and Heinkel 51 biplane fighters.

In the summer of 1937, the biplanes began to be replaced by Messerschmitt 109B-2 single-wing fighters. Other planes included He 111 bombers and the previously mentioned Ju 87 Stuka dive-bombers.

The Soviet air force was all set up inside Spain as well during the Spanish Civil War. The Red air unit stationed inside Spain flew the most recent version of the Polikarpov I-16: Type 10. They also flew the bomb-armed I-15 250. Both planes made their combat debut in 1937. Among bombers, the Tupolev SB-2 medium bomber was the mainstay.

DRESS REHEARSAL

The Spanish Civil War, for the air forces of Germany and the Soviet Union, served as a sort of dress rehearsal for the big one, soon to be known as the Eastern Front. There was even a preview of the hell airpower would cause to civilian populations during World War II. On April 26, 1937, Condor flyers bombed, burned, and strafed the village of Guernica, a historic first in airborne destruction.

The German Condors had reason to dread the I-16. The fighter was fast and tough, regularly besting not only the He 51 biplanes, but also the more advanced Messerschmitt Bf109 fighters. The Bf109E was a different story, faster and more agile than the I-16. (We'll be discussing that plane in greater detail in Chapter 5.) Its advent saw the end of the I-16's brief reign as the top-performance aircraft in the skies over Europe.

Once they achieved air supremacy, the Condors were able to escalate their bombing runs at will, paving the way for the ultimate victory of Franco's Nationalists in 1939.

The Luftwaffe had found Spain a valuable proving ground, where tours of duty were short, and pilots were quickly rotated to provide the greatest number of experienced pilots in the least amount of time. The lessons of Spain were put to use in the conquest of Poland and beyond.

The Soviets were less quick to change. Part of the reason was Josef Stalin's paranoid purges of 1937, which decimated the military high command of its best generals, sparing lesser lights whose mediocrity won the dictator's trust. One of the results was the unimaginative doctrine that aircraft should be used mainly as a tactical weapon in support of ground operations, rather than as the key strategic element to which the Spanish experience had served as a signpost.

Still, the tyrant was not unmindful of the importance of aircraft, and he wanted them. In the years running up to 1941, Russia manufactured about 3,500 aircraft a year. Most of these were I-15s, I-16s, and SB-2 medium bombers. In 1939, the reengineered I-16 Type 24 made its debut, as did the I-153 fighter-bomber.

I-16 SPECIFICATIONS

The I-16 Type 24, a single-seat fighter, was 20 feet long, with a 32-foot-long wingspan and weight (fully loaded) of 4,200 pounds. It was powered with an air-cooled nine-cylinder Shvetsov M62 radial engine with a two-stage compressor. The power plant produced 1,100 horsepower. Type 24 flew at a maximum speed of 326 mph. The plane had a range of 250 miles, and could fly up to a ceiling of 29,500 feet. Armament included two 20mm cannon with two 7.62mm machine guns.

Few Amenities

Soviet tanks were rugged and well built, but with few amenities for the crew. Russian aircraft were designed according to a similar philosophy. This was seen in the hand-crank crudity of the I-16's landing gear, which began in the initial design for the plane and never changed. The pilot had to make 44 hand-cranked turns to either raise or lower the landing gear. A distracting task during the best flying conditions, it could turn out disastrous in combat conditions. A pilot with a wounded arm, unable to crank down his landing gear, was doomed.

The I-153 single-seat fighter-bomber was the last of its line. It remained in production only until June 1941. Similarly equipped to the I-16 with a 1,100-horsepower Shvetsov engine, it had a top speed of 267 mph, a 293-mile range, and a ceiling of 35,000 feet. Armaments included pairs of 7.62mm machine guns, and a 220-pound bomb or six rockets.

In June 1941, the Red air force had a total of 18,000 aircraft, of which 59 percent were fighters. Personnel numbered some 200,000, including 20,000 pilots.

Operation *Barbarossa* was Germany's opening thrust in the war against Russia. It began on June 22, 1941. At the start of hostilities, at the front, the Luftwaffe launched 2,700 planes against the Soviet's 7,500. It was blitzkrieg, lightning warfare, from the air. The Russians were caught flat-footed. Despite abundant intelligence of Germany's aggressive intent, Stalin stubbornly refused to believe that war was imminent.

In the first 10 days of the war, the Luftwaffe destroyed 3,000 Red aircraft, including a claimed 2,200 I-15s in the first week. The I-16, making up 65 percent of Soviet fighter strength at the start of Barbarossa, also suffered greatly.

As a fighter, the I-16 was essentially obsolete in 1937, and subsequent improvements failed to bring it up to competitive levels. During the air war with Germany, it suffered terrific losses, but it remained in frontline service until the spring of 1943. During that time, and after, it achieved some success as a rocket-armed ground-attack plane.

DOUGLAS TBD DEVASTATOR

Douglas delivered the TBD Devastator to the U.S. Navy in 1937. At that time it was a state-of-the-art torpedo bomber. But, once World War II erupted, technology advanced in leaps and bounds. It replaced biplanes on the decks of navy carriers and was the first all-metal monoplane torpedo bomber.

It was also the first sea-based plane to have an enclosed cockpit. At the time, the wings of carrier-based planes had to be hand-cranked to fold down (necessary, as we've learned, so that more of them could be parked in the limited space of a carrier deck). The Devastator's wings, however, folded down automatically, with a hydraulic system.

There was a crew of three—the pilot, bombardier, and gunner—and there was room for one 500-pound torpedo, to be dropped into the water in the direction of an enemy ship.

DOUGLAS TBD-1 DEVASTATOR SPECIFICATIONS

Type: Torpedo bomber
Crew: Two, pilot and observer/rear gunner
Armament: One .30 cal machine gun firing forward, one .30 cal machine gun in rear cockpit, one torpedo, or one 1,000-pound bomb
Length: 35 feet
Height: 15 feet, 1 inch
Wingspan: 50 feet
Wing area: 422 square feet
Empty weight: 5,600 pounds
Gross weight: 10,194 pounds
Power plant: One Pratt & Whitney R-1830-64
Horsepower: 900 horsepower
Range: 716 miles
Cruise speed: 128 mph
Maximum speed: 206 mph
Rate of climb: 720 feet per minute
Ceiling: 19,500 feet

Soon after Pearl Harbor, the Devastator had some early successes versus Japanese ships. In the spring of 1942, Devastators sank an enemy aircraft carrier and heavily damaged another.

But there were problems. For one thing, the torpedoes launched by the aircraft often failed to explode when they struck their target. The plane was slow and lacked maneuverability.

The fact that the Devastator was obsolete was proven tragically during the Battle of Midway. Forty-one Devastators were sent to attack the enemy. None successfully hit its targets. Only six returned. By the summer of 1942, the Devastator had been withdrawn from service.

The Devastator was replaced by the Grumman TBF Avenger, which we'll be discussing in Chapter 6.

BOEING P-26 PEASHOOTER

After the end of World War I, the U.S. Army lived off equipment and supplies not consumed by the Great War, those still in the production pipeline when the fighting ended. By 1920, most of this equipment was worn out and surplus supplies consumed or deteriorated until useless.

Added to this shortage was the start of the Great Depression in the United States in 1929. The United States Army Air Corps (USAAC) fought to survive and replace obsolete aircraft and equipment. The USAAC needed an annual budget of $54 million to meet its minimum objectives in 1931, but it only received $36 million.

The 1930s was a terrible economic period because of the Depression and one of aviation transition from stick-and-wire aircraft construction to metal framework covered with fabric, to all-metal monoplane design for fighters, bombers, and transport aircraft.

During the limited between-the-wars aviation expansion, the USAAC acquired small numbers of new and improved aircraft. New aircraft had increased maximum speeds, improved rate-of-climb, higher service ceiling, better handling characteristics, and longer range.

First All-Metal Fighters

The USAAC's first all-metal fighter was the Consolidated Y1P-25, but only two prototypes were built. It was an all-metal, low-wing monoplane with retractable landing gear, enclosed cockpit for the pilot, and rear-facing gunner (rear portion of the gunner's compartment swung open), fitted with a three-blade propeller.

The Boeing Aircraft Company began design work on an all-metal, low-wing monoplane fighter, referred to as Model 248, in September 1931. Boeing built three prototypes with its own funds using USAAC-provided engines, instruments, and other equipment, designated as the XP-936. Boeing engineers wanted to incorporate a retracting landing gear and cantilever wing into the XP-936's design. Cantilever construction used an internal steel beam to support the aircraft's wings.

However, the USAAC specified that Boeing's design include an open cockpit, wire-braced fixed landing gear, and external wire-braced wings. The external wire bracing allowed for a lighter structure. The wires did produce less total drag than rigged struts.

Boeing started building the first XP-936 in January 1932, and completed it in February 1933, with its initial flight at the Seattle plant on March 10, 1932. Prototype one was delivered to the USAAC at Wright Field, Ohio, on April 25, 1932, for initial military air trials. Prototype two was also delivered to Wright Field for static, ground testing evaluation. Prototype three was delivered to the 1st Pursuit Group at Selfridge Field, Michigan, for operational testing with an active USAAC unit.

The production version was called the P-26A, nicknamed the "Peashooter," because of its small size. This aircraft became the USAAC's first mass-produced, all-metal monoplane fighter.

BOEING'S LAST FIGHTER

The P-26 was Boeing's last production fighter. After producing this plane, Boeing switched to building heavy bombers and large commercial aircraft.

On January 28, 1933, the USAAC ordered a buy of 111 aircraft, numbers 33-28 to 33-138.

The P-26A's construction used many advanced engineering techniques, although it was limited by USAAC design specifications, not taking advantage of all available aviation developments. The fuselage was semi-monocoque with brazier-riveted aluminum skin. *Monocoque* is a construction technique in which the fuselage skin carries the aircraft's stress loads. It is referred to as the fuselage's shell. The center section of the fuselage is load bearing, with fixed landing gear attached to the frame.

The fixed undercarriage added drag to the aircraft but at a reduced weight and structural complexity, while providing anchor points for the wing's flying wire bracing. The rear portion of each undercarriage leg consisted of an inverted tubular bipod fastened to the front and rear wing spars. The flying wires were attached to the apex and the wheel pivoted about the apex on an arm, with landing loads absorbed through the oleo shock-absorber strut connecting the wheel axle to the front spar.

The lower portion of the landing gear was enclosed by a streamlined wheel fairing, called a pant. A removable spreader bar kept the undercarriage rigid when the aircraft was serviced, usually with its wings removed. The production aircraft eliminated the fairing aft of the wheels, because it did nothing to increase dynamic characteristics.

The fuselage was fitted with aluminum bulkheads, longerons, and stiffeners. A longeron is a relatively heavy longitudinal structural member in the fuselage that runs continuously across a number of bulkheads.

The outer wing was constructed of riveted aluminum with round wingtips. Originally, the aircraft was not equipped with underwing flaps, retrofitted to existing aircraft to reduce landing speed from 83 to 73 mph. Because of the retrofit, the P-26's landing speed was too low for safe operations on the navy's aircraft carriers. Consequently, Boeing could not sell the aircraft to the navy, which was also looking to replace its biplane fighters then in service.

The U.S. Navy began designing an aircraft to replace its current generation of fabric biplanes, beginning with the Brewster F2A Buffalo, in 1936. It was an all-metal monoplane fitted with wing flaps, arresting gear, retractable landing gear, and an enclosed cockpit. The USS *Saratoga* was the first U.S. Navy carrier to be equipped with the Buffalo in June 1939.

Engineers referred to the P-26's rounded wingtips as elliptical with slightly diffused ailerons. The wings were supported or stiffened by the use of top and bottom external bracing wires.

The Peashooter Grows a Hump

Production models were altered to include handholds to assist the pilot's entry and exit of the aircraft. The headrest height was increased by 8 inches to protect the pilot during a crash or ground loop. Only one pilot was killed in such a crash. The alteration produced the P-26's distinctive humpbacked appearance. The fuselage was classified as a Boeing 109 aerofoil, thick at the center, ending in a taper. The USAAC also specified each aircraft was to be fitted with flotation gear for emergency ditching, manually activated by the pilot to keep the aircraft on the water's surface.

P-26A SPECIFICATIONS

Wingspan: 27 feet, 1¾ inches
Length: 23 feet, 7¼ inches
Height: 10 feet, ½ inch
Empty weight: 2,196 pounds
Maximum takeoff weight: 2,955 pounds
Power plant: One 52 horsepower Pratt & Whitney R-1340-27 air-cooled radial engine
Maximum speed: 234 mph at sea level; 227 mph at 10,000 feet; 210 mph at 20,000 feet; 174 mph at 28,900 feet
Cruising speed: 193 mph
Landing speed: 83 mph (Note: 73 mph with the installation of underwing, trailing edge flaps which were manually cranked down or up by the pilot)
Rate-of-climb: 2,260 feet per minute
Service ceiling: 27,400 feet
Absolute ceiling: 28,900 feet
Range: 635 miles
Armament: Two .30 caliber Browning M1 machine guns, mounted on left and right side of cockpit floor, each with 500 rounds of ammunition, firing through propeller, or one .30 caliber Browning M1 machine gun on left side of cockpit floor and one .50 caliber Browning M2 machine gun on right side of cockpit floor, each with 500 rounds of ammunition, firing through propeller
Bomb capacity: Two 100-pound high-explosive; or five 30-pound fragmentation; or two parachute flares

A C-3 gun sight was mounted ahead of the windshield. To record air-to-air combat, a C-4 gun camera was externally mounted on the right wing, close to the fuselage. The USAAC installed radios to complete the cockpit's communication equipment. The first production aircraft, serial number 33-28, was delivered to the USAAC on November 1933.

The first USAAC unit to receive the P-26A was the 20th Pursuit Group at Barksdale Field, Louisiana, in December 1933. The USAAC increased its initial production order to 136 aircraft, excluding the three prototypes. The last 23 production aircraft were delivered to the USAAC as P-26Cs, powered by a carburetor-equipped P-26A, 525-horsepower Pratt & Whitney R-1340-27 air-cooled radial engine. Three P-26Bs were fitted with a 600-horsepower Pratt & Whitney R-1340-33 air-cooled radial engine. Later, the P-26s were retrofitted with fuel-injected engines. These aircraft also included changes to the tail wheel, which used a taller, unfaired oleo-pneumatic shock-absorbing castoring tail wheel.

P-26 PAINT SCHEME

The standard paint scheme for the aircraft was olive drab or blue for the fuselage with wings and tail yellow. The USAAC star insignia was painted on the left and right side of the fuselage, as well as on the upper and lower wing surface. The rudder usually carried red and white horizontal stripes, with a blue vertical stripe at the hinge point. The lettering "U.S. Army" was painted in black on the bottom of both wings, U.S on the right and Army on the left. Individual squadron trim colors, numbers, and insignia decorated the fuselage, engine cowling, and vertical tail fin.

The USAAC equipped the 1st Pursuit Group at Selfridge Field, Michigan, and the 17th Pursuit Group at March Field, California, with the P-26A. The USAAC followed the procedure of equipping one pursuit group at a time with new aircraft as they came from the production plant. It chose not to mix aircraft during the transition. This slowed the introduction of new aircraft to operational units. Even with the arrival of the P-26 to operational units, the aircraft was barely able to catch the Martin B-12 at altitude, and then it could only make one attack pass. It was quickly outclassed by new fighters and bombers. In less than three years of active service, the P-26 was no longer considered to be a front-line fighter.

Secondary Flight Duties

By early 1937, the P-26 was relegated to secondary flight duties and training, and assigned outside the United States. In the spring of 1937, as part of the army's efforts to increase aircraft fighter strength in the Far East, the 4th Composite Group at Nichols Field, Philippines, received 21 P-26s. In 1940, the 37th Pursuit Group in the Panama Canal Zone received the P-26, based at Howard Field to protect the Panama Canal. The USAAC also shipped P-26s to the 15th and 18th Pursuit Groups at Wheeler Field, Hawaii.

Boeing applied for and was granted an export license for the P-26, but only built 12 Model 281s for overseas sales. China purchased 10, used by the Chinese air force's 17th squadron, based near Nanking. The squadron was commanded by Wong Pan-Yang, a U.S. citizen from Seattle, Washington, and staffed by Sino-American volunteers. The squadron's P-26s were in combat against the Japanese from late 1936 to 1937. Combat loses and primitive maintenance, aggravated by a lack of spare parts, ended their operational use.

One Model 281 crashed during a demonstration flight. The remaining aircraft was sold to Spain, used by the Republican air force, based at Getafe airfield. Spain's Model 281 began combat flying on July 18, 1936, and was shot down on October 21, 1936. It was piloted by Ramon Puparelli, who managed to safely bail out of the mortally damaged aircraft.

Peashooters in Battle

When the Japanese attacked Pearl Harbor on December 7, 1941, the air strike destroyed six P-26s and damaged one on the ground. By this time, the 21 P-26s shipped to the Philippines had been reduced in number to 16. These aircraft were now in the possession of the Philippine Army Air Corps (PAAC), based at Batangas Field, Luzon.

In the battle for the Philippines, the PAAC's P-26s fought a gallant battle against overwhelming Japanese air superiority. They had limited success in the air but did not change the battle's outcome. On December 12, 1941, PAAC Captain Jesus A. Villamor shot down a Japanese Mitsubishi G4M2 Betty twin-engine bomber. On December 23, PAAC Lt. Jose Kare shot down a Mitsubishi A6M2 Zeke fighter. But this was the last aerial combat victory for the P-26 against the Japanese. The remaining P-26s were destroyed on the ground by the PAAC on the evening of December 24 to keep them out of the hands of the advancing Japanese army.

Submarine Hunting

After Pearl Harbor, the P-26s in the Panama Canal Zone were used to patrol and hunt for German submarines. As more modern and longer-range aircraft became available, the remaining 11 P-26s were transferred to the Panama air force. The United States then transferred ownership of these aircraft to Guatemala in 1943.

The United States transferred seven P-26s to Guatemala, to meet an agreed-upon aircraft export commitment to that country. Guatemala also took possession of four nonoperational P-26 hulks to provide spare parts to keep the seven operational until more advanced fighters were acquired. The Guatemalan air force based its P-26s at Campo de la Aurora Field near Guatemala City. The Guatemalan air force flew the P-26s until 1950. In 1951, its P-26s were replaced with North American P-51 Mustang fighters.

MUSEUM DISPLAYS

Today, two original and one replica P-26 Peashooters remain, one on display at the Planes of Fame Museum at Chino, California, and the second at the National Air and Space Museum at Washington, D.C. The United States Air Force Museum at Wright Patterson Air Force Base in Dayton, Ohio, has a full scale replica of the P-26, fitted with an original engine.

The P-26 was an innovative design but one which was rapidly outclassed by following fighters. It was an important transitional fighter from the fabric covered biplane to that of the all-metal, low-wing monoplane fighter. The P-26 was the first mass-produced fighter, although fighters built during World War II numbered in the thousands, making the 151 Boeing production run for the Peashooter insignificant. The P-26 was the last open-cockpit U.S. fighter.

HAMILTON STANDARD'S HYDROMATIC PROPELLER

One of the major technological improvements in military aircraft between the wars was the invention of Hamilton Standard's hydromatic propeller. It saved thousands of aircrew members and hundreds of aircraft and engines. Here's how it happened:

The first great advancement in propeller design was the transition from wooden to metal blades. The new blades could be adjusted before a flight began to the best compromise pitch angle for both takeoff and cruise for a given aircraft/engine installation. A single pitch setting, however, for the entire flight regime was like driving a car with only one gear. It was impossible to get maximum performance from a plane's engine with a single pitch setting. When taking off, the plane's power plant could not reach full-rated horsepower without the blades being set at sufficiently low pitch. Conversely, the engine operated at higher than normal revolutions per minute in level flight without a higher blade pitch to fully absorb its power.

First Controllable-Pitch Propeller

Hamilton Standard of East Hartford, Connecticut, introduced the world's first controllable-pitch propeller in 1930. It was simple and effective. Military aviation historian John D. Cugini explained it this way: "To achieve maximum takeoff power, the pilot shifted a lever in the cockpit which sent oil, under pressure from the engine, to actuate a piston in the propeller hub. This mechanically twisted the blades into low pitch for higher revolutions per minute. When the aircraft reached cruising altitude, the lever was repositioned to automatically place the blades in high pitch via centrifugal force acting on two counterweights attached to the propeller hub. This was equivalent to the manual gearshift in an early automobile."

The controllable pitch propeller was heartily embraced by the airline industry and Hamilton Standard won the 1934 Collier Trophy from the National Aeronautics Association for that year's greatest achievement in aviation.

But Hamilton Standard was not through. In 1935, the company, in collaboration with the Woodward Governor Company, added the constant-speed governor to the propeller. The device was called the "automatic gearshift of the air." It allowed pilots to select and hold optimum propeller speed no matter what the flight conditions were.

More Advancements Needed

Still, more advancements would be needed. Stronger plane engines required larger, stronger propellers with greater, faster pitch-change capability. Faster aircraft demanded a wider range of pitch change, while more maneuverable aircraft needed quicker rates of pitch change to hold their revolutions per minute steady.

Introduced during this decade were multi-engined planes. This seemed like a no-brainer advancement in technology. If one engine failed, the plane could still survive. But it wasn't as simple as that. At first the multi-engine concept didn't work nearly as well as designers had thought it would. It turned out that, if an engine failed, the propeller would continue to rotate, causing excessive drag and vibration. This would sometimes become so severe that the engine would fall off the wing, destabilize the plane, and cause the very crash the extra engines were designed to prevent.

Hamilton Standard's solution to this problem was simple: To satisfy the need for higher actuation forces, engineers developed a system employing a larger piston in the propeller hub that could be actuated in both directions by hydraulic pressure.

This provided more precise controllability. To adequately house the piston, a large domelike hub was designed. Also, larger oil pumps and longer cams were used to facilitate this more positive action. With the longer cam, the travel path of the pitch change cam slot could be increased, permitting a wider range of pitch change. Larger cams also allowed for higher slope cam slots, which afforded a faster rate of pitch change.

Probably the most important design feature was the addition of a flat portion to the cam's slot and an independent oil supply, which provided the feathering feature. This allowed the propeller to an inoperative engine to be stopped by twisting the blade pitch past the high points so that the blade angle knifes into the airstream, offering no wind resistance. This eliminated windmilling and its consequent drag and vibration. This also stopped the engine itself from turning and, if its oil supply was depleted from battle damage, it prevented the engine from seizing or being badly damaged from the lack of lubrication.

The hydromatic propeller went on sale in 1937 and was eventually installed on the bombers the United States would use during World War II, such as the B-17, B-24, and B-29—many of which returned from their missions safely despite having one or more of their engines shot out.

DOUBLE WASP ENGINE

Three of the most successful American warplanes during World War II would be the P-47 Thunderbolt, the F6F Hellcat, and the C-47 Skytrain. These planes all had something in common: They were all powered by the R-2800 Double Wasp engine, made by Pratt & Whitney. There were different versions of the Wasp engine; they ranged from 400 to 3,000 horsepower and from 9 to 28 cylinders. There was the Twin Wasp, the Double Wasp, and the huge Wasp Major. Each model proved to be a testament to Pratt & Whitney's style of engineering: innovative and no nonsense.

Rentschler's Baby

The Wasp was the brainchild of Pratt & Whitney head honcho Frederick B. Rentschler, who had been a captain in the Army Signal Corps during World War I. His job during that war was to supervise the production of Wright-Martin Company aircraft engines. When World War I ended, Wright-Martin offered him an eventual presidency of a new aeronautical corporation.

And so the new Wright Aeronautical Corporation was born. It quickly became known as one of the world's great producers of aircraft engines and thrived. Rentschler only stayed with the company until 1924, however, leaving when he discovered he was the only executive there who believed the corporation's profits should be reinvested in experimental aircraft.

While most aircraft builders of the 1920s thought that airplanes would remain small, Rentschler believed that airplanes would grow bigger and thus need larger and more powerful engines. Therefore, he recognized that there was a huge vacuum in the military market for an air-cooled engine in the 400–500 horsepower range. Air-cooling would be the key, he reasoned.

Sure, liquid-cooled engines were more popular and slightly more efficient, but air-cooling would save great amounts of weight and reduce system complexity by eliminating the coolant, radiator, pumps, and plumbing. Rentschler was confident that air-cooled power plants could be successfully designed to provide equal horsepower at substantially lower weight. He challenged himself to build such an engine.

United Technologies Corp.

LEFT 1/16 FRONT VIEW .R-2800-65   ENGINE NUMBER 11 608   D-5 478

The R-2800 Double Wasp engine was the extremely successful power plant that gave American fighters the punch to defeat Axis aircraft in the air over their own territory. Rated at greater than 2,000 horsepower, with improved supercharging and water injection, the R-2800 produced more than one horsepower per cubic inch.

His search for financial backing ran a straight path from the Niles Tool Works in Hamilton, Ohio, to its corporate headquarters in New York, the Niles-Bement-Pond Company, and finally to its Hartford, Connecticut, tool division, Pratt & Whitney.

On July 14, 1925, a contract was signed incorporating the Pratt & Whitney Aircraft company. Rentschler was given $250,000 to design his engine, plus a promise of $1 million more for production should his prototype be successful.

Recruiting the Best

Rentschler recruited the best for his research and development team. Among those he chose were George Jackson Mead, a brilliant design engineer and MIT graduate; Andrew Van Dean Wilgoos, a man who could "think with his fingertips"; and Dan Brown Sr., who had experience at both Wright-Martin and Wright Aeronautical. The team completed its prototype on Christmas Eve 1925.

It was an air-cooled, nine-cylinder radial engine, developing 425 horse-power with a weight just under 650 pounds. The 1,340-cubic-inch dis-placement power plant employed a revolutionary new design for the crankshaft and master rod assembly, which eliminated what proved to be a weak spot in other engines. Cooling was also enhanced by a new finned cylinder head having integral rocker arm boxes. Each 5.75-by-5.75-inch cylinder was machined from a steel forging with exceptionally thin close-pitch fins.

The cylinder head was fabricated from cast aluminum, screwed and then shrunk onto the cylinder barrel for a pressure-tight fit. Provisions were allowed for a single inlet and exhaust valve with neatly designed tele-scoping covers protecting the pushrods.

The crankcase consisted of two matching aluminum forgings—for high strength—mated together down the centerline of the cylinder openings. The two-piece steel crankshaft, absorbing all the power impulses from the pistons, utilized vibration dampers for smooth operation and was sup-ported by two roller bearings for exceptionally friction-free motion.

The air-induction system was designed by Mead to use a low-pressure blower, thereby enhancing the fuel distribution between the float-type car-buretor and cylinders. All of the engine's innovative features were con-tained within a compact package characterized by a simple design and functional accessibility.

Many names were suggested for the new engine. Eventually Rent-schler's wife, Faye, offered the name that would stick: the Wasp.

The U.S. Navy, in the process of constructing two new aircraft carriers requiring more than 200 planes, consulted with Rentschler concerning the availability of air-cooled power plants exceeding 400 horsepower. Cranking out a decent 415 horsepower, the Wasp easily passed the navy's 50-hour qualification test held in March 1926. By October, 200 engines had been ordered.

The second Wasp engine was tested on May 5, 1926, mounted in a Wright F3W-1 Apache with Lt. C. C. Champin at the controls.

Post-flight evaluation revealed unprecedented performance gains affecting every aspect of the flight envelope, exceeding everyone's expectations.

Wasp's First Flight

The Boeing F2B-1, a carrier-borne biplane, was the first production aircraft to have the Wasp hung from its nose. Employing the 4-1340B model producing 450 horsepower, the little wood-and-rag-winger achieved a remarkable top speed of 158 mph and was so impressive a product that it was selected for use by the navy in its precision aerobatic team: The Three Sea Hawks.

Until the Wasp was developed, airplane engines had been the weak point of aviation. They were temperamental and required frequent overhauls (one every 50 hours of use in some cases). Pratt & Whitney was soon deluged with requests for the Wasp, known as "the little engine that could." About 100 different experimental aircraft were built around the Wasp. The engine remained in production from 1925 until 1960. Engines built in 1930 are still operational today.

THE HORNET

In 1926, Pratt & Whitney completed design on a new engine, called the Hornet. It measured 1,690 cubic inches of displacement and was rated at 525 horsepower. This engine gave power to air transport planes and various military aircraft.

Hobbs Builds a Twin

In 1927, a new member was added to the Pratt & Whitney team. He was research engineer Luke Hobbs. Hobbs developed a twin-row radial engine, the 14-cylinder R-1830 Twin Wasp. The new Twin first yielded 750 horsepower but later, with improvements in fuel chemistry, cranked out a very respectable 1,350 horsepower. To withstand the stresses encountered at the higher rating, a multi-layered master rod bearing was developed that combined a thin layer of lead impregnated with indium over a second layer of silver. This, in turn, was bonded to a copper coating on the hard steel case of the bearing.

In complete harmony with its predecessors, the Twin Wasp distinguished itself as the power plant for the B-24 Liberator and PBY Catalina, as well as the previously mentioned C-47 and F4F. During World War II, a staggering 173,618 Twin Wasp engines were produced, more than any aircraft power plant in history.

Double Wasp

As the 1930s passed and World War II began in Europe, the United States knew that it was going to need a 2,000-horsepower-class airplane engine to equip its land- and sea-based aircraft. Pratt & Whitney was once again up to the task.

It developed the R-2800 Double Wasp, a real powerhouse. This engine, more than any other technological development, helped give Allied pilots the edge in the skies over all of World War II's theaters of operation. Research and development for the Double Wasp began in August 1936. It was to be an air-cooled 18-cylinder radial capable of greater than 2,000 horsepower. The first production Double Wasp was delivered to the army on May 13, 1939. The navy received its Double Wasp on November 22, 1939. The navy's engine, tested in a Vought XF4U-1, boasted a two-stage, gear-driven supercharger for enhanced high-altitude power.

Large orders were placed for the A model of the R-2800 for use in the Martin B-26 twin-engine bomber and the British Vickers Warwick twin bomber, beginning what was to become a great financial and technical success story. All the while a stronger and improved B version was being readied by Pratt & Whitney, Ford, and Nash for utilization in the P-47, F4U-1, F6F, Curtiss C-46, and Northrop P-61 twin night fighter. Chevrolet came on line to aid production of the thoroughly redesigned Double Wasp C, slated to enter service with Grumman's F7F twin-engine Tigercat and F8F Bearcat, as well as Vought's F4U-4 Corsair.

Republic's P-47 Thunderbolt, best described as a flying tank with all its punch and durability, seemed as if it were born to have the mighty and sturdy Double Wasp mounted in its nose. The rugged P-47 airframe, in unison with the capable R-2800 turning the Hamilton Standard Hydromatic propeller, made for quite an able combination.

When the Japanese attacked Pearl Harbor on December 7, 1941, the pace of aviation development greatly accelerated.

CHAPTER 5

THE EARLY YEARS OF WORLD WAR II: THE WORLD ERUPTS

In this chapter, we'll be examining the warplanes flown by Germany, Great Britain, Japan, and the United States during the first years of World War II, the biggest war in history. We'll also look at the birth of the night fighter and the transoceanic bomber.

On October 1, 1938, the Nazis took the Sudetenland of Czechoslovakia. The remainder of that country fell to the Germans in March 1939. On March 13, 1939, Hitler annexed Austria. On September 1, 1939, Hitler attacked Poland. The German generals had learned their lessons from WWI. This time, there would be no bogging down in trench warfare. Speed, dash, and mobility were the order of the day. Blitzkrieg, they called it: lightning war.

Why smash against France's Maginot Line defense when you could go around it and attack from the rear? Air strikes and close support of ground operations were integral to the Blitzkrieg doctrine. Stuka dive-bombers destroyed the Polish air force on the landing fields. Denmark fell, and then Ju 88s helped pound Norway into submission.

JUNKERS JU 88

The Junkers Ju 88, the prototype for which first flew in 1936, was originally intended to be only a high-speed bomber, but it ended up functioning as a heavy fighter, a close-support aircraft, a torpedo bomber, a reconnaissance plane, and a dive-bomber. It had a 65-foot, 7-inch wingspan and weighed slightly more than 10 tons. With a range of four hours, it could climb at 1,655 feet per minute, and was powered by two BMW 801D-2 14-cylinder engines, producing 1,700 horsepower. It was armed with two 30mm and up to six 20mm cannon.

The Ju 88C, which first flew in 1939, was powered by pairs of BMW 801 or Jumo 211 engines. The nose of the plane featured as many as eight cannon. The three-seater 88G was radar-equipped to fight at night. Ju 88s were the menace of incoming Allied bombers during all but the final months of the war.

MESSERSCHMITT BF 109

The Messerschmitt Bf 109 was Germany's premier fighter plane of World War II. An astounding 37,000 of them were produced during the war.

The one-seater could climb higher and fly faster (354 mph) than the British Spitfire, but its low fuel capacity only allowed for 90 minutes flying time. Its range of 400 miles meant, in practical terms, that it only had 20 minutes of "battle time" over England before it had to start the trip back. An external fuel tank was eventually added to improve the plane's range, but the change was made too late to affect the outcome of the Battle of Britain. It was powered by a Daimler-Benz 601N producing 1,200 horsepower and had a range of 460 miles. It had a wingspan of 32 feet, $4\frac{1}{2}$ inches, and was 28 feet, 4 inches long.

The Bf 109, more than any other plane, benefited during the early years of WWII because it gained experience—a dress rehearsal, if you will—during the Spanish Civil War beginning in 1936.

FINGER-FOUR FORMATION

The inevitable encroachment of high-speed monoplanes into the fighter arms of the world's air forces necessitated a change in tactics. The close formations used in WWI became dangerous with the increase in speed.

It was a German, Werner Molders, who developed the loose "finger-four" formation. This comprised two, two-plane elements, with a leader and a wingman in each element. The wingman flew above and behind, guarding the leader.

When the Bf 109 reported for duty in Spain, it had only recently been chosen as the Luftwaffe's primary day fighter. Under the rigors of actual combat, the weaknesses of the C and D models—they were underpowered and had weak landing gear and light armament—were highlighted in time for the Germans to make corrections. The result of those corrections, the Bf 109E was in widespread use by 1939.

THE BIRTH OF RADAR

During the 1930s, Great Britain was aided by a new kind of early warning system, Radio-Direction Finders, now commonly shortened to "radar." By giving advance notice of the raids, it provided invaluable intelligence for the defenders.

Radar was developed into a workable device by Sir Robert Watson-Watt, although early models had limitations. The equipment was not able to determine the number of the enemy force and (which is still the case to a lesser extent) radar had difficulty picking up approaching aircraft that were flying at a low altitude.

BRITISH SPITFIRE AND HURRICANE

By 1940, Britain had developed the world's most sophisticated defense system. This system rested upon two fighters: the Hawker Hurricane and the Supermarine Spitfire. Both were single-engine monoplane designs of the mid-1930s. The Hurricane was somewhat more dated with its steel tube and fabric-covered rear fuselage. The Spitfire, arguably one of the best-looking fighters ever designed, had one curve flowing gracefully into the next.

Military Technical Journal

The Spitfire Mark XIV takes flight during the summer of 1944.

Each warplane was armed with an unheard-of total of eight machine guns. A study by the RAF had concluded that, with the high air speeds of future combat, there would only be a matter of seconds for the fighter pilot to hold a target in his sights.

The true jewel behind the design of these planes was the use of the Rolls-Royce Merlin engine. A milestone in British metallurgy, the block was crafted from an extremely dense alloy, which allowed the same power output as other engines, but did so in a 20 percent smaller package.

The immediate advantage was a reduction of frontal area. This, in turn, produced two benefits:

- Lower drag, contributing to higher speeds
- A smaller target area for enemies to shoot at

THE NORDEN BOMBSIGHT

In the months before the Japanese attack on Pearl Harbor, the United States was struggling with its own vision of strategic bombing. The B-17, which we'll be discussing in Chapter 6, was still in the early stages of development. But the United States had developed one innovation that was to give it a distinct edge: the Norden bombsight.

Subject to high security measures throughout the war, the bombsight was crucial to successful bomb delivery from 30,000 feet, as it incorporated a number of compensation factors necessary to overcome the difficulties of dropping bombs from 6 miles above the target. These difficulties included various erratic motions the aircraft exhibited in flight when releasing its bombs.

SECOND BATTLE OF BRITAIN

England presented a tricky problem for any would-be conqueror. The challenge was in getting troops across the English Channel without meeting resistance—in this case from the British navy, which still ruled the waves in 1940.

Operation Sea Lion was Hitler's grand design for the invasion of England. Air superiority was a prerequisite for success. Thus began what came to be known as the Battle of Britain—the greatest air battle the world has ever seen. The first phase of the German attack was known as Adlerangriff (attack of the eagles). Three great Luftwaffe air fleets were massed on the coast: bombers, fighters, and scouts.

The first phase of the second Battle of Britain (the first occurred during WWI) began with bombing runs, pounding English aerodromes. These first clashes were inconclusive, with each side bloodying the other. Ever impatient, furious at being balked at, Hitler changed plans midbattle. The RAF was no longer the target; he set his sights on London. This would be the first time that a major military thrust would target civilians, an unfortunate precedent that by war's end led to the destruction of many cities in Europe and in Japan.

A 1,000-plane raid with 300 bombers and 600 fighter escorts attacked London on September 4, 1940. It inflicted heavy damage and casualties, but proved to be a bad miscalculation. The British were not cowed, and the diversion had bought the RAF valuable time to rebuild for the coming battle.

Göring vowed to destroy the RAF. The climactic battle came on September 15. From horizon to horizon, the skies over southern England were one tremendous battlefield as swarms of planes dove, banked, crashed, and burned. England held. Hitler soured on Operation Sea Lion, double-crossed his "pal" Stalin, and invaded Russia. This established the Eastern Front.

The RAF had prevented the Luftwaffe from achieving air superiority over Great Britain. The invasion of England would never come.

A Heinkel 115 torpedo plane used by Germany against Allied shipping. The plane carried and launched torpedoes, similar to those fired by U-Boats, designed to strike ships beneath the waterline.

When it came to airpower during WWII, the Germans got back a lot more than they dished out. Their air attacks on Great Britain during the first years of the war had been carried out with short-range fighters escorting medium bombers such as the He 111, Do 217, and Ju 88. Their payloads were limited and for self-defense they had to rely on a handful of 7.9mm machine guns. These attacks would seem minuscule compared to those carried out by the Allies several years later over Germany.

BIRTH OF THE NIGHT FIGHTER: HEINKEL HE 219 "OWL"

When World War II started there was no such thing as night-fighting aircraft. They were considered unnecessary because well-armed, high-flying bombers could, even in broad daylight, fight through any air defense and reach their targets. In daylight, the chances that the bombers would hit their targets was greatly increased.

But that thinking went out the window on December 18, 1939, over the German coast when 22 British Vickers Wellington twin-engine bombers, manned by experienced crews, were sent on an unescorted, armed reconnaissance to Heligoland Bight. Their assignment: to find and destroy German shipping. The British bombers were detected by German radar as they neared the coast.

Thirty-two Bf 109s and 16 Me 110 twin-engine fighters were sent aloft to destroy them. Twelve of the Vickers Wellington bombers were destroyed. Many others were damaged. The necessity of night bombing was now apparent.

Night Bombing: Safer but Less Precise

It was safer to fly bombing missions at night. Darkness provided the best cover. But, in the days before "smart" bombs, hitting targets on the ground at night was very difficult. Safety won out and the British ran more and more nocturnal bombing missions.

In response, the Luftwaffe began developing a night fighter force. The first German night fighter division was formed on July 19, 1940, under Gen. Josef Kammhuber.

Making the force effective would be a challenge. They were attempting things that had never been done before. The early night fighters were simply twin-engine day fighters or bombers—such as the Messerschmitt Me 110 and Junkers Ju 88—that were painted black. Their prime advantage was long range and the ability to carry a variety of heavy machine guns and cannon. The multi-man crew allowed the pilot to concentrate on the attack while others tended to navigation, weapons, and observation.

As the night-fighting force grew and gained experience, these same German aircraft were reworked to accommodate early airborne radar and other homing devices. Locating and destroying enemy bombers at night became much easier. Armament was also increased. Cannon replaced most of the machine guns as heavier weapons were needed to knock the big, sturdy bombers out of the air. These improvements made the aircraft heavier, slower, and less maneuverable. These factors were not great concerns. Expected opposition included only the slow and ungainly enemy heavy bombers.

However, by late 1941, British bombers were getting faster and more maneuverable. The Hadley Page Halifax and Avro Manchester bombers were almost as fast as the He 110. Other new British bombers, then in development, would be faster than any of the German night fighters.

If the bombers were faster than the night fighters, the German pilots would be unable to intercept the enemy aircraft. The best the Germans could hope for was a single head-on pass before the bombers flew off into the night. General Kammhuber and his staff realized that unless they found a new and faster night fighter, the British night-bombing campaign might well destroy Germany.

Fortunately, the Heinkel Aircraft Company was already working on a new aircraft design to satisfy Kammhuber's needs. The new aircraft was originally conceived in April 1940 by Heinkel engineers as a high-speed bomber, bomber destroyer, or torpedo aircraft. The engineers realized that they could easily adapt their new design to the night-fighter role. They showed the plans to Kammhuber, who was so impressed with the new aircraft that he went directly to the führer to get approval to build it. With such high backing, the *Reichsluftministerium* (RLM) accepted the plane as Germany's new night fighter. Construction on the prototypes began in January 1942.

The new aircraft made its first flight in November 1942 and proved to be an excellent airplane. Although it experienced some teething problems, due to the complexity of its design, no problem was great enough to cancel the project.

The aircraft was put into production on August 3, 1943, under the designation Heinkel He 219A "Owl." The initial order called for 100 Owls to be built. Even before series production on the aircraft began, a few pre-production aircraft were completed and available for testing.

These aircraft should have gone to the German air force's test facility at Rechlin, Germany, but Kammhuber insisted they be sent to the air force's principal night-fighter base in Venlo, Holland, for combat evaluation.

First Combat

The night-fighter pilots were impressed with the aircraft. So much so, in fact, that Maj. Werner Strieb, the commander of one of the night-fighter squadrons, flew the preproduction Heinkel He 219 to intercept British bombers on the night of June 11–12, 1943. Strieb shot down five of the attacking bombers.

The first Heinkel He 219As began arriving in operational units in the early winter of 1943. They were put to use immediately destroying enemy bombers, assigned to the most experienced and aggressive units. The plane had a top speed of 348 mph due to its two Daimler-Benz DB 603A 12-cylinder, liquid-cooled, in-line engines. It's range was 1,305 miles.

During one 10-day period, the Owls of one night-fighter squadron flew six sorties and shot down 20 enemy bombers. Among these kills were the same high-speed British de Havilland Mosquito twin-engine bombers that the Germans previously had been unable to intercept.

As effective as the aircraft was, combat experience with the He 219A gave rise to several changes. In addition to the forward-firing guns, two cannon were mounted at an angle in the fuselage behind the cockpit so they could fire forward and upward.

This arrangement allowed the fighter to fly underneath an enemy bomber and destroy it without risk of getting hit by debris. Two more forward-firing Mk. 108 cannon were added and some models were equipped with the Mk. 103 30mm cannon. Later versions of the aircraft were also equipped with the more powerful Daimler-Benz 603G supercharged 1,900-horsepower engines.

Pilots' Choice

The He 219 became the pilots' horsepower choice for a night fighter. Even though the initial order from the air ministry was doubled, production could not keep up with demand. Heinkel could only produce 15 Owls a month. The air ministry's attempts to bring other companies into the construction program were unsuccessful.

Kammhuber did not let production difficulties stand in his way. In order to get more He 219s into battle, he ordered all of the preproduction aircraft, which had finally been sent to the test facility at Rechlin, returned to the operational units.

Despite the success and popularity of the aircraft with the crews, the air ministry did not like the Owl. They considered it too complex and too specialized for the air force's needs. In addition, they were not satisfied with the aircraft's high-altitude performance. Based on these objections, on May 25, 1944, the air ministry decided to phase out the He 219 in favor of the Junkers Ju 388 or Tank Ta 154 aircraft.

According to military aviation historian Timothy J. Kutta, writing in *Warzone* magazine: "The short-sighted policy destroyed Germany's chance to mass produce one of the most effective night fighters of the war and counter the British night bombing campaign. The lack of official enthusiasm for the aircraft ensured that there were never enough Owls to seriously challenge Bomber Command's massive bomber strength."

BRITISH BLACK BOXES

Unlike today's "black boxes" which help determine the cause of plane crashes, the black boxes of WWII were radar devices that helped British night bombers navigate. The first black box was introduced in February 1942 and was called "Gee."

To take advantage of the black boxes, Bomber Command, under the direction of Sir Arthur Harris, formed a specialized Pathfinder Force (PFF) which could locate targets and mark them with indicator (flare) bombs. The PFF units were equipped with the de Havilland Mosquito, one of the most versatile planes of WWII.

THE MOSQUITO

Designed in 1938 as a high-speed unarmed bomber, the de Havilland Mosquito utilized two Merlin engines and lightweight wooden construction to achieve success in all its multiple roles. Generally immune to interception, Mosquitoes bombed strategic targets throughout the war. Other versions of the plane became the leading British fighter-bomber and night fighter.

On January 16, 1943, the PFF used a new weapon called the "Oboe." The device received signals from two ground stations that indicated the target when the plane was at a given distance from each station. Two weeks later, a new invention, known as H2X, debuted. This device generated a radar map of the ground below. Although sometimes hard to read, this gave the British one more advantage in the skies over Europe.

MITSUBISHI G3M AND G4M MEDIUM BOMBERS

In the meantime, on the other side of the world, the Japanese had been busy increasing their airpower as well. One of these advancements involved a bomber-transport plane. Originally designated as Ka-915, the prototype for the Mitsubishi G3M first flew in July 1935. The service trials that followed proved that the plane had great range.

The first production version (G3M1) debuted in 1936. Holding a crew of four, it was powered by a pair of 910-horsepower Mitsubishi Kinsei 3 radial engines. It was armed with three 7.7mm machine guns (two dorsal, one ventral, all retractable).

Thirty-four G3M1s were built when a new, more powerful engine, the Kinsei radial, worth 1,075 horsepower, became available, and production began on the G3M2. It was this version of the bomber, which held a crew of seven, that first saw combat.

First Transoceanic Bombing Mission

On August 14, 1937, a squadron of G3M2s based in Taiwan struck targets in China—1,270 miles away—and returned safely. It was history's first transoceanic bombing mission.

The G3M2 had a 20mm cannon, and there were now four machine guns. More than 1,000 G3Ms were built, some as bombers and some as transport planes. Americans fighting in the Pacific called the bomber version "Nell." The transports were called "Tina." The planes were used throughout WWII, but were relegated to less important missions by the introduction of the Mitsubishi G4M, which we'll be discussing in a moment.

Nells had their greatest victory of the war only three days after the attack on Pearl Harbor, when they sank, using torpedoes and bombs, the British battleship *Prince of Wales* and battle cruiser *Repulse*.

Enter Betty

The Betty was Japan's premier heavy bomber throughout WWII. It made its combat debut in May 1941, bombing China. The plane had huge fuel tanks and little armor, which gave it the range to go on 2,000-mile bombing missions. The Betty was vulnerable to antiaircraft fire because of its lack of armor. And, since its fuel tanks were not self-sealing, it tended to go up in flames whenever it was hit.

Mitsubishi G4Ms were responsible for the attacks on U.S. transport ships following the Guadalcanal landings. The attacks were not effective, however. Many of the Betties were shot down, although one suicide-crashed into the transport *George F. Elliott* on August 9, 1942, destroying the ship. After this, Betties would only attack at night, when it was harder to shoot them down. Betties had a range of 2,262 mph, were powered by twin Kasei-22s producing 1,850 horsepower, and were armed with three 7.7mm machine guns and one 20mm cannon in the tail. They carried a payload of 2,205 pounds of bombs/torpedoes.

Betties, attacking at night, sank the heavy cruiser *Chicago* during the Battle of Rennell Island in January 29, 1943. In February 1944, a Betty torpedoed and damaged the aircraft carrier *Intrepid* during fighting in the Caroline Islands.

Late in the war, in 1945, specially modified G4Ms were employed to carry the Ohka rocket-propelled piloted bomb, which we'll be discussing in Chapter 7. In all, 2,479 Betties were built.

ATTACK ON PEARL HARBOR

Japan and the United States share a common boundary: the Pacific Ocean. It was inevitable that these two dynamic cultures would eventually conflict with one another. So reasoned Japan's aggressive military ruling clique during the 1930s. Since war was inevitable, it was necessary for them to gain the best advantage. The strategic planners were aware of the United States' industrial might, with its capacity to turn out planes, ships, guns, and munitions. The longer they delayed, the better armed and prepared America would be for the conflict. They gambled on a bold thrust to the enemy's heart. A daring gamble, but if successful, one that could destroy the United States' ability to make war in the Pacific.

It almost succeeded and yet, ironically, its near success was the cause of Japan's ultimate defeat. Adm. Yamamoto, chief of the combined fleet, planned the attack. Minoru Genda, the Japanese naval aviator who helped Mitsubishi's designers create the Zero (a plane that will be discussed extensively later), was the architect of the plan. The armada consisted of 31 ships, including six aircraft carriers. There were 423 planes, of which 353 were dedicated to the attack.

On December 7, 1941, the "date which will live in infamy," Japan struck. Three attack waves of Nakajima B5N attack bombers, Aichi dive-bombers, and Zeroes bombed and strafed U.S. naval facilities at Pearl Harbor, Hawaii. They pounded Wheeler and Hickam airfields and torpedo-bombed Battleship Row at Ford Island.

Some U.S. P-40s and P-36s escaped the surprise attack and managed to get aloft. Lt. George Welch downed four Japanese planes. When the smoke cleared and the damage was added up, the battleships *Arizona* and *Oklahoma* had been destroyed. The other six battleships were damaged.

Half of Pearl's military aircraft were wiped out, but the docks and the shipyards were not destroyed. The Japanese had canceled the third attack. This left the fuel tanks intact. Had the fuel tanks been destroyed, the remaining units of the Pacific Fleet would have been forced to return to the U.S. West Coast. Also left intact were the dry docks. The destruction of these would have delayed the repair of the naval vessels damaged in the attack.

Most importantly, America's three aircraft carriers had been out at sea during the attack and survived. And carrier-based airpower would be the key to victory in the Pacific.

Nakajima B5N "Kate" Attack Bombers

The three-seat "Kate," the Nakajima B5N, was Japan's premier sea-based torpedo-bomber at the time of Pearl Harbor, but had been in service with the Japanese navy since 1935. Kates were devastating to the U.S. Navy during the war. The Kate was powered by a Nakajima Hikari 3 nine-cylinder radial, worth 770 horsepower. It had a maximum speed of 217 mph, flew to a ceiling of 25,000 feet, and had a range of 683 miles. It was armed with a 7.7mm machine gun, manually aimed, in the rear cockpit, and had underwing racks for eight bombs.

Not only did they participate in the attack at Pearl Harbor, but B5Ns sank the aircraft carriers *Lexington*, *Yorktown*, and *Hornet* (at the battles of Coral Sea, Midway, and Santa Cruz, respectively). At Pearl Harbor, 40 B5N2s armed with torpedoes and 103 B5N2s armed with bombs decimated the U.S. battle fleet. In total, 1,149 Kates were built. By the end of the war, they were considered obsolete and had been replaced by the Nakajima B6N Tenzan.

Aichi "Val" Dive-Bombers

The top Japanese dive-bomber of WWII was the sea-based Aichi D3A "Val," which was first flown in 1939. At Pearl Harbor, 129 Vals were launched from six carriers. In the Indian Ocean on April 5, 1942, 53 Vals sank two British heavy cruisers in just 19 minutes. Every bomb released was a hit or near miss. By 1944, the low-wing Vals were largely replaced by the D4Y "Judy" bomber. The Val was powered by a Mitsubishi Kinsei 43 14-cylinder, air-cooled, radial piston engine, producing 1,000 horsepower. It was armed with three 7.7mm machine guns, and two wing-mounted and one center-mounted bomb. It had a top speed of 240 mph.

The two-seated and highly maneuverable Val was based extensively on the German Heinkel designs. A total of 1,294 were built.

Mitsubishi A6M "Zero"

The Mitsubishi A6M Zero-Sen was the most famous of Japan's combat aircraft. The carrier-borne fighter was a one-seater manufactured by Mitsubishi Jukogyo KK. It was powered by a 925-horsepower Nakajima NK1C Sakae 12 engine, and had a maximum speed of 346 mph.

The prototype for the Zero first flew in April 1939. When the plane went into production in 1940, it was known as the A6M2 Reisen (Type 00). The 00 signified the year on the Japanese calendar, 5700, and soon the plane began to be called the Zero-Sen. It was armed with two 20mm cannon and two 7.7mm machine guns.

The plane first saw combat in July 1940, over China in the Sino-Japanese War, where it quickly outclassed all other fighter aircraft, including the Curtiss P-40s being used in that theater on December 17, 1941, by the American volunteer force, Claire Chennault's Flying Tigers. (More about the Flying Tigers later.)

At the time of the Pearl Harbor attack in December 1941, more than 400 Zeros had been delivered to the Imperial Japanese navy. In air combat, the United States, to its dismay, quickly discovered that the Zero could outfight the Grumman F4F Wildcat, as well as the American land-based fighters.

That isn't to say that the Zero was perfect. It was poorly armored and, because of its lack of self-sealing fuel tanks, proved to be dangerously flammable. It was constructed of a light alloy that did not stand up well against enemy bullets. U.S. Navy pilots in their F4Fs soon learned that diving through Zero formations while continuously firing at them brought satisfactory results.

The A6M2 was the supreme fighter plane in the Pacific only until the Battle of Midway (discussed in Chapter 6) in June 1942. In the following years two new U.S. planes, the F4U Corsair (first action over the Solomons in February 1943) and the F6F Hellcat (first production delivery in January 1943), gave the Allies air superiority.

To compensate, Mitsubishi developed new versions of the Zero. The A6M5, introduced in August 1943, could dive faster than its predecessor because of a stronger wing—and the A6M5b came with an armored windscreen and fuel tank fire extinguishers.

By June 1944, the Zero was once again lagging behind the new U.S. planes. At the Battle of the Philippine Sea, in what became known as the "Marianas Turkey Shoot," U.S. Navy F6Fs shot down 315 Zeros and lost only 23 aircraft in exchange.

In 1944, Mitsubishi again upgraded the Zero, introducing the A6M5c, which featured pilot armor, larger fuel tanks, and heavier-caliber guns. This model proved too heavy to be effective until the end of 1944, when the 1,130 horsepower Sakae 31 engine was mated with it.

By that time the Zero was no longer a carrier-based plane, for the simple reason that all of Japan's aircraft carriers had been sunk. Continuing as a land-based plane, with experienced pilots becoming fewer and fewer in number, the remaining Zeros were converted into kamikaze planes and, in the spring of 1945, took a horrible toll on the Allied armada off Okinawa. In all, 10,500 Zeroes were built.

THE FLYING TIGERS DEFEND THE BURMA ROAD

The Flying Tigers first entered battle on December 17, 1941, over Kunming, China. Defending China against the Japanese, the Flying Tigers were officially known as the 1st American Volunteer Group. They operated with leftovers and hand-me-downs, often only one step ahead of the Japanese, and in the process they wrote for themselves a gallant chapter in the history of air warfare.

The story of the Flying Tigers began in 1937, when a pilot named Capt. Claire Chennault retired from the U.S. Army and made his way to China. Initially, he was only to conduct a short-term survey on the readiness of the Chinese air force (CAF). He ended up staying for the duration of the war.

It was Maj. Mao-Pang-chu of the Chinese air force who invited Chennault, among others, to become a flight instructor for the CAF. Over the next year and a half, while negotiations continued with the Chinese, Chennault realized he had reached a dead end in the U.S. military and quit.

In a 2003 interview with the author, aviation-historian Philip Semrau said, "The Chinese were looking for help to organize and equip their air force. They turned to America for personnel and weapons. It was not openly admitted, but it was also in America's interest to keep China actively in the war."

Safeguarding the Burma Road

Unfortunately, with the Japanese in firm control of the Chinese coastal areas, something was needed immediately to counter their offensive on the mainland. Something had to be done to safeguard the Burma Road, the lone artery for the flow of Allied war materiel into China.

The United States and China arranged to create an air group to be staffed by American volunteers, and commanded by Chennault. Ideally, this would comprise the core of the re-formed CAF once they had been trained and equipped for battle. Later on, the American brass regarded it as the forerunner of what was to become the U.S. 10th Air Force.

Although Chennault was seen as a maverick in the United States (and not as the best choice for commander), the workings of the arrangement put the organization under Chinese control. And this meant that the operation was to be run by the senior air officer, Claire Chennault. His years of service had proven his value to Chiang Kai-shek but, more importantly, his tactical skills and grasp of the needs of the local situation were invaluable.

First American Volunteer Group

Endless negotiations between the British, Chinese, and Americans resulted in the framework to staff and equip what was now the 1st American Volunteer Group (AVG).

Tacit approval was given, allowing a return to active U.S. service to those who chose to join the 1st AVG. Early in 1941, pilots and service crews recruited from the air branches of all three services began the long trip to China.

The Tomahawk

It wasn't Chennault's first choice, but beggars can't be choosers, and by way of concession (on a plane that was of no use to them in Europe where it was already obsolete), the AVG was allotted 100 Curtiss P-40B Tomahawk fighters.

The one-seater plane, with its snout painted with eyes and toothy mouth to resemble the face of a shark, was manufactured by the Curtiss-Wright Corporation and powered by an Allison V-1710 12-cylinder engine of 1,150 horsepower. The engine bestowed the Tomahawk with a top speed of 352 mph at an altitude of 15,000 feet.

The plane had a wingspan of 37 feet, 3½ inches. On its nose was mounted an 11-foot-in-diameter Curtiss Electric Multi-position propeller.

A Better Diver Than Climber

Without a supercharger, high-level performance was poor and the rate of climb was certainly less than what Chennault wanted for his interceptor. To its benefit, the P-40 could dive like a stone because of its solid construction.

It was armed with two .50 caliber machine guns in its nose and two .30s in each wing. Chennault made the plane work in battle, using his fighting doctrine: Power-dive into the enemy, and then, if necessary, climb away to make a second pass. The light, slower Japanese army planes—the Tigers' usual foe—couldn't be outmaneuvered in a dogfight nor could they follow an AVG fighter through a dive.

Initially opposed by the fixed-gear Nakajima Ki-27 "Nate" (with two light machine guns and a 290 mph top speed), the Flying Tigers often faced Nate's scheduled replacement, the Nakajima Ki-43 "Peregrine Falcon," which was capable of 305 mph and armed with two machine guns.

Tigers versus Zeroes only occurred on a handful of occasions. The AVG was driven inland by the advancing Japanese army and thus had fewer and fewer encounters with Japanese naval aircraft. The lifeblood of the AVG was the Burma Road and the Group's primary goal was to defend its artery supply in the face of Japanese aggression.

The skirmishes were many, often with the Tiger on the run, and yet slowly Chennault's men gained the upper hand, making the Japanese think about their next attack. Chennault had organized an early-warning system composed of local people arrayed in an arc against the incoming raiders.

Three Squadrons

The 1st AVG was split into three Squadrons known as "Adam & Eve," "Panda Bears," and "Hell's Angels." These squadrons were moved around China, Burma, and Thailand as the need arose. Supplying the demands of advanced equipment in a forward area proved taxing for the AVG, and they were constantly short of spare parts. "As soon as a plane became unflyable," points out Philip Semrau, "it was cannibalized to keep the other aircraft going."

The Tigers were the air defense of China, and their primary targets were Japanese bombers. Whenever possible, they tried to ignore the escort fighters and direct their attacks against the twin-engine bombers. Their successes against a superior enemy, almost unstoppable in early 1942, vindicated Chennault's tactics: never let the enemy fight on its own terms.

There usually wasn't enough time to get many AVG planes in the air to intercept, and the few that took off did their damage by driving through the formations straight at a bomber with guns blazing.

At times, when the Chinese or British mounted an offensive strike, the Tigers were called upon to provide escort fighters. On these occasions, the Americans had a tougher go of it. Now they had to mix it up with the Japanese to protect the Allied bombers.

Remarkable Victory Record

The victory record of the Flying Tigers still stands as one of the more remarkable chapters in the history of American aviation. In their fight against the Japanese, the only planes they got credit for shooting down were ones that could be verified by the Chinese. The Chinese paid bonuses for 294 victories.

The Japanese, in turn, caused the loss of only 13 AVG pilots, who were killed or went missing during aerial combat against Japanese planes. The 22-to-1 kill ratio is even more amazing because the Tigers only existed for seven months (at the height of Japanese power), from their first mission on December 20, 1941, to disbandment on July 4, 1942.

The AVG was disbanded to make way for the U.S. 10th Air Force, who would continue the fight in the China-Burma-India theater of operations. It was hoped that the volunteers would transfer en masse but, for most of the group, it was the end. After months of hard fighting in worn-out planes, having to put up with shortages of all types, and being treated as forgotten stepchildren by the U.S. Army, it was time to move on.

Chennault himself served in China until the Japanese surrender in 1945.

OVER THE HUMP WITH THE C-47 SKYTRAIN

From 1942 until the end of the war, one of the most important transport aircraft in the China-Burma-India theater of operations was the C-47 transport plane. It was this plane, along with the C-46, that flew convoy after aerial convoy over the perilous "hump"—the 20,000-foot-plus Himalayas to sustain China's effort against the Japanese. The C-47 had a wingspan of 95 feet. It was 64 feet, $5\frac{1}{2}$ inches long and was powered by two 1,200-horsepower Pratt & Whitney R-1830-S1C3G Twin Wasp radial piston engines. Its maximum speed was 230 mph, and it had a range of 2,125 miles. A total of 13,177 were built.

The plane was also known as the DC-3. According to Canadian pilot Tex Gehman, the plane smelled great. He said, "Probably the most memorable thing about the [Dakota] was the smell. The odor of the leather mixed with hydraulic fluid made a perfume second to none. [The plane] always treated me well, unlike some of the other birds I've flown, and my memories of it are all good."

BIRD OF MANY NAMES

The C-47 had many different names. When used by the RAF it was known as the Dakota. The navy version was called R4D Skytrooper. It was also nicknamed "Gooney Bird."

The plane was originally designed in 1934, as a 24-passenger commercial airliner. The army recognized the plane's potential as a cargo transport plane and some design changes were made for the military version, to be known as the C-47 Skytrain. Those changes included more powerful engines, the removal of airline seating in favor of utility seats along the walls, stronger rear fuselage and floor, and the addition of large leading doors.

P-39 AIRACOBRA

In the years before the United States entered the war, the military knew that it would need a new, fast, heavily armed fighter aircraft that could catch and destroy enemy bombers such as the German Heinkel He 111, Italian Savoia Marchetti S.M. 79s, and Mitsubishi G3M.

Many aircraft designers went to work in an attempt to get the lucrative government contract. Among these designers was Larry Bell of the brand-new Bell Aircraft Corporation. He and two of his designers, Robert J. Woods and Harland M. Poyer, decided to put the Oldsmobile 37mm cannon into a high-speed aircraft, thus giving the army the capability of downing enemy bombers.

The Bell design team quickly encountered problems. Although the massive 37mm weapon provided unprecedented power—it could destroy an enemy aircraft with a single round—the cannon's recoil had to be absorbed by the plane's airframe.

Mounting the gun on the airframe presented the first obstacle. The cannon, as it turned out, had to be mounted in the nose because it was too bulky to mount in the wings. Even then, it filled up most of the nose position, so the engine had to be mounted somewhere else.

The engine could be mounted on the wings—but if that were done, the designers would have to add a second engine to balance out the aircraft. A twin-engine aircraft could not generate the speed necessary, so this idea was scrapped.

The designers finally placed an engine in the center of the fuselage. The next question was how to transfer engine power from the middle of the aircraft to the propeller. The answer was a long shaft built lengthwise through the aircraft extending from the engine to the nose-mounted propeller. The arrangement was odd but made sense in view of what the designer wanted to accomplish.

Where Does the Cockpit Go?

The next problem was where to place the cockpit. The original plan was to put it behind the engine, which would have placed the pilot almost in the plane's tail. The designers decided that a cockpit that far back would limit the pilot's vision. The solution was to place the cockpit between the engine and the nose-mounted propeller, a location which offered the pilot excellent visibility.

Military Technical Journal

The P-39 Airacobra served in every theater of World War II operations.

The radically different design was an extraordinary gamble—especially from the Bell Corporation, which had only designed one other aircraft since it came into being. Bell submitted the proposal for the new plane to the army on May 18, 1937.

The USAAC, uncertain of the design, but intrigued by the heavy firepower, allowed one prototype to be built: the XP-39. Bell had already nicknamed the aircraft the Airacobra.

The prototype emerged from the Bell plant in Buffalo, New York, in early 1938, and was sent to the USAAC test facility at Wright Field, Ohio, for evaluation. The XP-39 was a low-wing, single-seat monoplane. The fuselage, wings, and tail surfaces were made of metal, while the control surfaces were constructed with fabric. The aircraft was powered by a supercharged Allison V-1710-17 engine rated at 1,150 horsepower. The engine drove a three-bladed propeller covered with a streamlined hub.

Teardrop-Shaped Canopy

The canopy was also unusual for the time. Its teardrop shape offered the pilot excellent all-around visibility—but not without a cost. The framework of the canopy was fixed to the fuselage and the pilot was required to enter the aircraft through a door on the left side.

Bell also opted for a tricycle undercarriage, an unusual accessory for a pursuit aircraft, consisting of two single-wheel main gears that retracted inward and a nonsteering nose wheel that retracted to the rear. Once retracted, the gear was fully covered by gear doors, adding to the aircraft's streamlined appearance. The landing gear arrangement, though unique, gave the XP-39 pilot excellent visibility during taxiing and the aircraft great stability on rough runways. Both these traits would be prized by the pilots that operated the aircraft from unimproved airfields during World War II.

The P-39 made its first flight from Wright Field on April 6, 1938, and achieved a speed of 390 mph and an altitude of 20,000 feet. This Airacobra was not equipped with any armor or armament and was substantially lighter than the production model, but the performance was impressive enough to warrant further tests.

During these tests the engine overheated on several occasions. Initially, the army thought that the superchargers were overheating. The Bell engineers modified the air inlets and exhausts but it did not fix the problem.

Wind-Tunnel Testing

After this series of tests was completed, the aircraft was shipped to the National Advisory Committee for Aeronautics (NACA) in Langley, Virginia, where it underwent wind-tunnel testing. The tests resulted in the USAAC requesting several modifications.

The prototype was sent back to Buffalo where the Bell engineers streamlined the fuselage and canopy, reduced the wingspan, and replaced the supercharged engine with the V-1710-39 nonsupercharged engine with a rated altitude of only 13,000 feet. The NACA engineers did not think that the engine contributed that much to the aircraft's performance, and the constant threat of fire made it a liability.

The XP-39 with the high-altitude engine was canceled on the drawing board and the new version was designated the XP-39B. It was ready in a few months and successfully met or exceeded every expectation during testing. With the success of the prototype, the army ordered 13 YP-39 production prototypes in April 1939. The first YP-39 was ready for testing on September 13, 1939.

The new aircraft carried all of the armament and armor that the combat aircraft would carry. A few modifications were added to the airplane. These included a larger tail and an Allison V-1710-37 1,090-horsepower engine. Despite NACA's claim that the YP-39 would not be adversely affected by a nonsupercharged engine, the aircraft could only attain a top speed of 368 mph at 15,000 feet. At higher altitudes the speed and climb dropped dramatically. Still, the USAAC had achieved their goal and an order of 80 production aircraft was awarded to Bell.

First Production Model

The first production model, the P-39C, rolled off the assembly line in the fall of 1940, and flew for the first time in January 1941.

After making only 20 P-39Cs, Bell stopped the production line and re-tooled to make the necessary modifications. The new version, the P-39D, was an impressive aircraft with a wingspan of 34 feet. It was 30 feet, 2 inches long, and stood 11 feet, 10 inches tall. Fully loaded for combat with machine guns and cannon, it weighed 7,650 pounds. It was powered by the Allison V-1710-35 12-cylinder liquid-cooled engine, which generated 1,150 horsepower. The engine could propel the aircraft to a top speed of 360 mph at 15,000 feet with a range of 525 miles.

Staggering Power

The P-39D had a punch. It carried one 30-round, 37mm M4 cannon, which fired through the hub of the propeller. It also carried four .30 caliber machine guns in the wings and two .50 caliber machine guns mounted over the cannon. The P-39D's staggering hitting power could destroy even the most soundly built enemy aircraft with just one concentrated burst of its cannon and machine gun.

Then came Pearl Harbor and everything sped up, production-wise. Even as the P-39Ds were being prepared for combat, the British, desperate for modern aircraft, sent a purchasing committee to America to find and buy the best aircraft available. The committee received a report on the P-39C and ordered 675 Airacobras without seeing or flying the aircraft. The British version was designated the Airacobra I and modified to English specifications. These modifications included replacing the American-made radios and weapons with British versions and several other minor changes.

The British found the production aircraft to be lacking in speed at altitudes above 13,000 feet. After a brief test with four aircraft, the British sent 212 Airacobras to the Soviet Union and another 179 (redesignated as P-400s) to the USAAC. The P-400s and the first of the P-39Ds were shipped to the Southwest Pacific to reinforce the battered army air units operating against the Japanese.

The P-39 in Combat

The 8th and 35th Fighter Groups were the first two U.S. fighter groups to operate the Airacobra in the Pacific. The groups received their aircraft in February and March 1942. After a brief workup, the 8th Fighter Group was sent to defend Port Moresby, New Guinea, on April 26, 1942.

The Airacobras, because of their heavy firepower and poor high-altitude performance, were assigned to strafe enemy airfields. During their first mission over the enemy airfield at Lae, 13 P-39s shot up a number of parked enemy bombers but were in turn attacked by an equal force of Mitsubishi Zeros. The enemy fighters caught the P-39s at low altitude and, in the ensuing dogfight, P-39s shot down four enemy aircraft while losing three of their number.

American pilots quickly found that the Airacobra lacked the speed to fight with the Japanese aircraft on even terms. The best the P-39 pilots could do was make one quick diving pass at the enemy fighters and then try to outrun the pursuit.

As reports of the P-39s' performance in combat reached Bell Corporation, the designers worked to remedy the problems. The propeller was changed. More powerful Allison engines were added. The center of gravity was changed. More armor, shackles to carry bombs, racks to launch rockets, and a host of other changes were incorporated.

The last version, the P-39Q, entered production in 1943, and most of the 7,000 aircraft produced under that designation went to the Soviet Union. Seventy-five P-39Qs were sent to the 332nd Fighter Group operating in Italy. This fighter group included the last Americans to fly the aircraft in combat as they operated the P-39s for two months until transitioning to Republic P-47 Thunderbolts.

The P-39 served in every theater of World War II operations. It was flown by American, British, Australian, Portuguese, Russian, Free French, and Italian pilots during the course of the conflict. A total of 9,558 of all types were produced.

B-25 MITCHELL

In 1937, the U.S. War Department became interested in developing a twin-engine medium attack bomber with the performance of then-existing fighters which that bomber may have to face. In 1938, the major American aircraft companies submitted bid proposals: Bell, Boeing-Stearman, Douglas, Martin, and North American.

North American's proposal was accepted, but without guarantee of production. The resulting prototype, under North American designation NA-40, crashed on March 1, 1939. The follow-up prototype flew on August 19, 1940. There was great urgency for a twin-engine bomber because the war in Europe had already begun.

The medium bomber became known as the North American B-25 Mitchell, named after Brig. Gen. Billy Mitchell, a vocal advocate of airpower before his court martial for criticizing the deplorable state of U.S. airpower.

The 17th Bombardment Group, McChord Field, Washington, in February 1941, received its first B-25B. The B-25C was the first large-scale production variant, starting deliveries in December 1941. B-25 production went through many different variants, showing the wide variety and capabilities of that aircraft. Many were converted to specialized airframes for specific missions. The largest number built in one variant was 4,318 for the B-25J, also the final production version, which first flew in October 1943.

Side view, left side, B-25J, serial number 43-27493. The Plexiglas nose and the rest of the aircraft has been magnificently restored. Aircraft flown at Ellsworth Air Force Base, South Dakota (east of Rapid City, South Dakota, off Interstate 90), at the base's annual open house, Dakota 2002.

The B-25H was an antishipping attack aircraft. Its armament was beefed up: one 75mm cannon in the nose, along with four .50 caliber machine guns positioned in a line across the nose; two .50 caliber machine guns in separate blisters on the right side of the aircraft, forward firing. This armament allowed the aircraft to deliver devastating firepower in a short amount of time. The B-25H could approach an enemy ship at low level, using a skip-bombing technique to drop a bomb into the side of a ship while taking out that ship's defensive guns.

This variant was used in the Pacific against Japanese warships and transports. Eventually, the 75mm cannon was removed, because operational reports indicated .50 caliber machine guns were more effective with their higher rate of fire.

The plane held a crew of six. It was powered by two 1,700-horsepower Wright R-2600-13 Double Cyclone 14-cylinder air-cooled radial piston engines. It had a range of 2,700 miles and a maximum speed of 275 mph. Its maximum take-off weight was 35,000 pounds.

The B-25 was also used extensively by America's WWII allies: Royal Air Force (Britain), Netherlands East Indies Air Force, Royal Australian Air Force, Royal Canadian Air Force, Soviet Air Force, National Chinese Air Force, and French Air Force.

Doolittle Raid

But the most well-known use of the B-25 was the bombing of Japan in April 1942, taking off from the U.S. Navy aircraft carrier USS *Hornet*. President Franklin D. Roosevelt wanted to attack Japan in response to Pearl Harbor. A limited response was developed by U.S. Navy captain Francis Lowe, using twin-engine medium bombers, taking off from the deck of an aircraft carrier to bomb Tokyo.

Adm. Ernest J. King approved the concept under the code name of "Tokyo Project." The plan was passed on to Gen. Henry H. Arnold, commanding general USAAF, who selected Lt. Col. James H. Doolittle to plan and lead the attack against Japan. Lt. Col. Doolittle selected the B-25 for the mission because it had better short field takeoff capabilities than the only other medium bomber available, the Martin B-26 Marauder.

Mission Profile

The mission profile required that ...

- Twenty (eventually using 16 because of deck takeoff space) B-25s would be launched from the deck of a U.S. Navy aircraft carrier, at a range of 500 miles east of Tokyo, Japan.
- The targets selected would be primarily in Tokyo, with four aircraft to strike Yokohama, Osaka, Kobe, and Nagoya.
- The B-25s would fly low-level to their assigned targets.
- The bomb load would consist of one 500-pound incendiary and three 500-pound conventional bombs.
- Once the targets were bombed, the B-25s would fly on to China, land for refueling at four bases, and fly on to Chungking.

To test this concept, two B-25s were loaded onto the deck of the USS *Hornet* at Alameda Naval Base, San Francisco, California, on February 3,

1942. Once out to sea and away from land, the carrier turned into the wind, successfully launching both B-25s.

The mission was given the go ahead, requiring the modification of the B-25s. The B-25B was available, 24 assigned to the 17th Bombardment Group (34th, 37th, and 90th Bomb Squadrons, along with the 89th Reconnaissance Squadron), stationed at McChord Field, Washington. The 17th BG had been flying patrols guarding against a Japanese carrier attack against the Pacific northwest and on down the west coast to important military targets.

The B-25B modifications consisted of ...

- Retractable ventral turret removed (saving 600 pounds).
- Fuel capacity increased to 1,141 gallons; (standard) 646 in wing tanks; 225 gallons in one bomb-bay tank; 160 gallons in collapsible tank, located in crawl space above bomb bay; 160 gallons in ventral turret space; 50 gallons (carried in ten 5-gallon fuel cans, stowed inside the aircraft). Note: before takeoff, an additional five 5-gallon fuel cans were loaded into the aircraft.
- Norden bombsight removed. USAAF did not want the bombsight to fall into Japanese possession. Would not be needed for low-level bombing. Replaced by simple angle metal device, allowing bombardier to sight ahead of the aircraft and release the bomb at that point of intersection.
- Rear twin .50 caliber machine guns removed, replaced by two black wooden dowels.

Intense Training

The B-25 crews went through intense training at Elgin Field, Florida—under the guidance of U.S. Navy lieutenant, senior grade, Henry L. Miller—learning how to take off a fully loaded B-25 in a space of 450 feet. They learned to set the aircraft's flaps at full, engines run up to maximum power, standing on the brakes, releasing, pulling the control yoke back full at the proper time, and lifting off the ground at a speed of 55 to 60 mph.

Despite the fact that only 16 planes would fly the mission, all the trained aircrews would be taken on the mission, providing crew backup once at sea.

On March 24, 1942, 22 B-25s took off from Elgin Field, flying in stages across the United States, at low level, landing at Sacramento Air Depot, California. On April 1, 1942, the B-25s landed at Alameda Naval Base.

Admiral Nimitz Museum

View of how close each B-25B was to another on the deck of the Hornet. *Two navy officers (right in the photo) are talking to two Doolittle raiders, with a third walking away. More Doolittle raiders are visible to the rear of the B-25B, top left center of the photograph.*

Sixteen B-25s were hoisted onboard the *Hornet* and secured on the deck. The aircraft carrier's complement of aircraft was stored below in the hangar deck.

On April 2, 1942, the *Hornet* put out to sea. It was escorted by two cruisers (*Vincennes* and *Nashville*) and four destroyers (*Grayson*, *Gwin*, *Meredith*, and *Monseen*), and supported by fleet oiler *Cimarron North* of Midway. This force was joined by aircraft carrier *Enterprise*, two cruisers (*Northampton* and *Salt Lake City*), four destroyers (*Balch*, *Benham*, *Ellet*, and *Fanning*), and fleet oiler *Sabine*.

At a distance of 1,000 miles east of Tokyo on April 17, 1942, the two oilers refueled the task force, with the two aircraft carriers and four cruisers continuing on to the designated launch point. The B-25s were spotted for takeoff on April 16, 1942. Because of high winds due to the bad weather, the aircraft were subjected to constant vibrations that required continuous maintenance. One engine had to be removed from one B-25, repaired in the hangar deck, and reinstalled on the aircraft. B-25 crews and aircraft carrier deck personnel constantly checked the tie downs to be certain an aircraft did not come loose, breaking away and striking other aircraft on the deck. With the aircraft carefully spotted they took up 293 feet of the deck, leaving a takeoff distance for the first B-25 of 467 feet.

On the morning (7:38) of April 18, 1942, at a distance of 668 miles from Tokyo, the task force was reported by a Japanese picket ship (sunk by the escorts). The decision was made to launch the B-25s, even though they were outside the planned launch range, leaving doubt as to their ability to bomb targets and reach the recovery bases in eastern China.

The *Hornet* turned into the wind, with Lt. Col. Doolittle taking off at 8:25 A.M., and the last B-25 clearing the deck at 9:20 A.M. Thirteen B-25s bombed Tokyo, with three other B-25s (one each) dropping four 500-pound incendiary bombs on Nagoya, Osaka, and Kobe. All B-25s successfully made good their exit from the Japanese home islands.

Not Everything Goes as Planned

But the remaining part of the mission did not go as planned: One B-25, short on fuel, turned away from China and landed at Vladivostok, with the aircraft and crew interned by the Soviet Union (which was, at that time, not at war with Japan).

Four B-25 crews crash-landed their aircraft when low on fuel. Eleven B-25 crews, including Doolittle's, bailed out of their aircraft. Of the airmen on this mission, five were interned by the Soviet Union; two went missing after they parachuted from their aircraft and were not accounted for; five became POWs under Japanese control, with four surviving captivity until the end of WWII; three were executed by the Japanese; one was killed during his parachute descent from the B-25; and 64, including Doolittle and his crew, safely reached China and were transported back to the United States.

Results of the Bombing

Eight B-25s bombed their primary targets. Five B-25s bombed their secondary targets. More significantly, the Japanese military command decided to expand their defensive zone to preclude a follow-up aircraft raid by the United States, leading to the Battle of Midway, which we'll discuss in Chapter 6.

The subsequent U.S. victory at Guadalcanal was a slim one. The Japanese had withheld four fighter groups in Japan for home defense. If used at Guadalcanal, those groups could have given the Japanese the strength they needed for victory.

Lt. Col. Doolittle was awarded the Congressional Medal of Honor, promoted to the rank of brigadier general, and given a new command, creating the 12th Air Force in England. The B-25 continued its brilliant wartime record and many aircraft have been restored and continue to fly under civilian control and are on display in air museums.

P-51 MUSTANG

One of many reasons the Allies won WWII was the high level of cooperation between the U.S. and British war efforts. One of the best examples of this is the P-51 Mustang.

The Mustang was requested by the British Purchasing Commission in 1940. A combined U.S and British effort, the prototype was flown before the year was over—design and construction of the prototype took 117 days—and the first service versions were delivered to the RAF in 1941.

It was a combination of the British Merlin engine and an American (North American Aviation) frame. The plane could carry nearly three times the fuel load of a Spitfire.

The Mustang had a maximum speed of 437 mph at 25,000 feet, flew to a ceiling of 41,900 feet, could climb at 3,475 feet per minute, and was armed with six .50 caliber MG-52 machine guns, up to 1,000 pounds of bombs, or six 5-inch rockets. It went on to become the dominant escort fighter of the war. Although work was put into extending the Thunderbolt's range, the Mustang was the first American fighter to overfly Berlin in May 1944, several weeks before D day.

The Mustang's combat record was extraordinary. It is credited with 4,950 air kills, 4,131 ground kills, and 230 V-1 (German Vengeance Weapon, "buzz bomb") kills.

In total, 15,586 Mustangs were built. There are fewer than 300 Mustangs still in existence. Approximately half of those remain in flying condition.

BRITISH HAWKER TYPHOON

Designed by Hawker as a replacement for the Hurricane, the Typhoon (nicknamed "Tiffy") had some early problems, but was developed into one of the best ground attack fighters of the war. Armed with four 20mm cannon and a 2,200-horsepower 24-cylinder Sabre engine, the aircraft had great speed and could carry bombs or eight 60-pound rockets.

About 3,300 of them were built, both by Hawker Aircraft Limited and the Gloster Aircraft Company. The one-seater was armed with four 20mm cannon, plus 500 pounds of bombs and rockets. Its primary role was ground attack and it first flew on May 26, 1941.

Typhoons first saw combat during the Dieppe operations of August 19, 1942. They were later used to intercept German planes attacking Great Britain and were used extensively against V-1 buzz bombs. In the battle following the D-Day invasion of Normandy, Typhoons were responsible for the destruction of 137 German tanks.

So, as you can see, the Allies and the Axis both had their strong points, as well as their weaknesses, as the world erupted into WWII. It would be the Allies' superior ability to improve their airpower, and to produce warplanes in great numbers, that would result in the air superiority that would eventually destroy the Axis.

CHAPTER 6

TURNING THE TIDE

The turning point of the Pacific War was the Battle of Midway. This pivotal battle, the point at which Japanese aggression was first turned back, featured sea-based aircraft as the primary weapons. In the war in Europe, the beginning of the end for the Third Reich came on D day, June 6, 1944, when Allied troops by the thousands invaded at Normandy, France, and began the process of taking Europe back from the Nazis. D day was a success largely due to the fact that the German air force, the Luftwaffe, had been decimated by Allied airpower. In this chapter, we look at the battle of Midway in the Pacific and, in Europe, the destruction of the Luftwaffe as a dominant airpower—the turning of the tide in WWII.

CONTROL OF MIDWAY ISLAND

During the spring of 1942, the United States was in control of Midway Island, but the Japanese wanted to take it away. In previous months, the Japanese had gotten what they wanted, gaining control of many islands in the Pacific. But that was about to change. There were three U.S. aircraft carriers at the battle, which took place June 3–6, 1942.

There was the *Yorktown*, which was heading up Task Force 17. The *Yorktown* had 75 aircraft aboard. Also aboard was Rear Adm. F. J. Fletcher. This task force also included two cruisers and six destroyers.

Also at the battle was Task Force 16, which featured two carriers, the *Enterprise* and the *Hornet*. Between them they carried 158 aircraft: 54 Wildcats, 75 Dauntless dive-bombers, and 29 Devastator torpedo bombers.

Japanese Order of Battle

The Japanese carriers at the battle were split up among four different forces. The main force, Japan's First Fleet, commanded by Adm. I. Yamamoto, featured one light carrier, the *Hosho*, which had eight planes aboard.

There were also, in the main fleet, two seaplane carriers, the *Chiyoda* and the *Nisshin*, but neither ship carried any seaplanes. They had been converted to accommodate midget submarines.

In the First Air Fleet, commanded by Vice Adm. C. Nagumo aboard the fleet carrier *Akagi*, were four carriers. In addition to the *Akagi*, there were the *Kaga*, *Hiryu*, and *Soryu*. This fleet went to battle with 262 aircraft.

The Second Fleet was commanded by Vice Adm. N. Kondo. This fleet featured the light carrier *Zuiho* and its 24 aircraft, as well as two seaplane carriers (the *Chitose* and the *Kamikawa Maru*) which brought 24 float fighters and 8 scout planes. The Fifth Fleet, commanded by Vice Adm. M. Hosogoya, contained one carrier, *Junyo*, with 45 aircraft, and a light carrier, *Ryojo*, with 37 planes.

The Japanese fleet had hoped to attack Midway by surprise, much as it had at Pearl Harbor six months before. But long before Japanese ships neared Midway, their reconnaissance planes were spotting U.S. submarines and scout planes in the area, indicating that the element of surprise was lost.

There was reason to believe the United States was waiting for the attack. On June 2, Nagumo's ships were closing on Midway from the northwest while the American carrier forces had left Pearl Harbor and were headed to a spot 325 miles northeast of Midway to wait for the arrival of the enemy. The fleet was late in arriving at Midway because of bad weather; a long stretch of thick fog had delayed its progress.

Hostilities Commence

The first hostile exchange between the two sides at Midway occurred on June 3 when nine Army Air Force B-17s attacked the Japanese fleet, which at the time was still 570 miles from Midway. No ships were damaged. As June 4 began, both task forces were 200 miles north of Midway Island. The first aircraft to be sent aloft were 10 Dauntlesses from Task Force 17 at 4:30 A.M., which went on a search 100 miles to the north. At the same time, Nagumo, his forces 200 miles south of the island, sent his planes aloft.

One hundred and eight planes headed for Midway. There were 36 level bombers from the *Hiryu* and *Soryu*, 99 dive-bombers from the *Akagi* and *Kaga*, and 36 fighters from all of the carriers. First contact between the enemy forces came shortly after dawn when a U.S. PBY reconnaissance plane spotted Japanese carriers. Soon thereafter, radar picked up the Japanese planes heading for Midway.

Within minutes, every U.S. plane available was in the air. The fighters took the lead to engage the incoming Japanese planes. Adm. Raymond A. Spruance's group headed southwest to engage the enemy. Fletcher's forces picked up their scout planes and headed in the same direction. From an airstrip on Midway, six new Avenger torpedo bombers and four Marauders took off, heading for the Japanese carriers. As the U.S. bombers approached, antiaircraft guns fired from the ships below even as Zeroes attacked from above. Five Avengers and two Marauders were shot down. One of the Avengers hit the *Akagi* on its way down, but bounced off without doing any damage. None of the U.S. torpedo bombs found their mark.

The pilots of American Wildcats and Buffalos tried to intercept the Japanese bombers, but never had the opportunity because they were too busy fighting attacking Zeroes. Seventeen American pilots were shot down.

Things were not going well that morning down on the island either. The bombers made it through and successfully dropped their bomb load.

Destroyed in the run was the U.S. Marine command post. Antiaircraft fire on the island managed to down only five bombers. However, the bombing did not put out of action Midway's runway. The Japanese strike leader recommended a follow-up air strike to be certain the carrier force could not be attacked from the island. But the recommendation was not taken. The failure of the earlier bombing raid upon the Japanese fleet had convinced the admirals that no second attack on Midway would be necessary.

U.S. Goes on the Offense

Instead it was the United States that went on the offensive. Spruance decided to attack the Japanese carriers from afar, a dangerous decision because pilots were bound to run extremely low on fuel on the return trips to their carriers. Spruance hoped that the element of surprise would make up for these risks. He held back only 36 planes to protect his own fleet in case of a counterattack.

At 7:55 A.M., 16 U.S. Marine dive-bombers arrived in the skies above the Japanese carriers. But again the Japanese got the best of it. Eight of the planes, fully half, were shot down. Of the eight that returned only two were in good enough shape to ever fly again. One plane made it back to its ship with 259 bullet holes in it. Minutes after the failed Marine raid, 15 USAAF B-17s dropped their bombs from 20,000 feet up, but no Japanese ship was struck. When the Japanese force realized that the U.S. ships were approaching as fast as they could, they were startled.

Nagumo's Choice

The Japanese leaders now had a problem. As West Point historian Thomas E. Griess explained in his book *The Second World War: Asia and the Pacific*, "[Nagumo] could launch the 36 dive-bombers which were ready on the *Hiryu* and *Soryu* and the torpedo bombers on the *Akagi* and *Kaga*, most of which had bombs on them; but if he did send them off immediately to attack the American carrier force, he could not send fighters to escort them. (Nagumo had sent his standby and second-wave fighters aloft to engage the American aircraft which had just attacked him, and they would have to be re-armed and possibly refueled before they could be used to escort the bombers.)" As Nagumo was trying to figure out what to do, a further complication arrived in the form of crippled Japanese planes returning from the Midway bombing. Only after recovering these aircraft did Nagumo again consider his options regarding the advancing U.S. Navy. At 9:18, Nagumo ordered the First Fleet to change course 90°.

By this time, Fletcher's task force had arrived and launched 35 planes. Eight Wildcats circled above Task Force 17 to look out for attackers. These planes missed their target, however, because of Nagumo's evasive move. Some of the planes managed to refuel on Midway Island but others crashed into the sea. The first U.S. planes to reach the Japanese fleet were 16 Devastator torpedo bombers from the USS *Hornet*. These pilots knew that they were virtually on a suicide mission. They had no margin for error when it came to fuel. They came in at sea level to make a run at the Japanese ships when they were attacked and wiped out by Zeroes. Only one American pilot survived, Ens. George Gay.

A Turn of Luck

A group of bombers from the *Enterprise* attacked the *Soryu* but 11 of the 14 were shot down. A third attack from the *Yorktown* was equally disastrous, with 13 of 14 aircraft being lost. Things looked plenty bleak, but then luck turned when a pilot from the *Enterprise*, Lt. Comdr. Clarence McCluskey, spotted four Japanese carriers sailing in a diamond formation.

At 10:20 A.M., McCluskey and a squadron of Dauntlesses attacked the *Kaga*. The Zeroes were all far below, still at the proper altitude to wipe out more torpedo bombers. The U.S. bombers dove at the *Kaga* and *Akagi* at a 70° angle. Three bombs hit the *Akagi* and four struck the *Kaga*. Aboard the *Kaga*, the captain and most of the officers were killed when a bomb struck the bridge.

Eight minutes later, Dauntlesses from the *Yorktown* hit the *Soryu* with three bombs. All three Japanese carriers were destined to sink. Nagumo got off his ship via rope. The captain of the *Soryu* went down with his ship. Yamamoto, who was nearby aboard the battleship *Yamato*, ordered his Japanese naval forces to continue attacking, despite their huge losses. They still had four light carriers afloat so the battle could continue.

Sinking of the *Yorktown*

At 11:00 A.M., 24 planes from the *Hiryu*, the lone remaining Japanese fast carrier with Rear Adm. Tamon Yamaguchi in command, were launched. These planes attacked the carrier *Yorktown* and their bombs caused severe damage. Because of this success, and knowing that there were other U.S. carriers in the area, Yamaguchi launched a second attack at 12:45 P.M. This time the Japanese pilots only had enough fuel remaining for a one-way trip.

So this second attack was the last for the Japanese pilots, but it was also enough to finish off the *Yorktown*, the ship known as "Waltzing Matilda." The order to "abandon ship" was given by the captain at 3:00 P.M. The attack might have finished the *Yorktown*, but it had also supplied the United States with the precise location of the *Hiryu*. Spruance ordered 24 dive-bombers to launch immediately and head toward the *Hiryu* without fighter escort. (Technically, another attack, a submarine torpedo on June 6, actually sank the *Yorktown*, but it was dead in the water at that point.)

Those bombers arrived in the skies over the *Hiryu* at about 5:00 P.M. Aboard the *Hiryu*, preparations were being made for another attack, one that would never occur. Four bombs hit the *Hiryu*, causing fatal damage. An hour later, B-17s from Midway tried to dish out the death blow, but their bombs missed. As it turned out, no further blow was necessary. The *Hiryu* was done, the fourth Japanese aircraft carrier to be sunk during the "Battle of Midway." Both Yamaguchi and the ship's captain tied themselves to the bridge of the sinking ship to make sure that they went down with their vessel.

As midnight approached on June 4, Yamamoto ordered Nagumo to continue to fight, but Nagumo refused. He was instantly replaced. While this was going on, the United States continued to fly planes off of their carriers to attack and destroyed a Japanese heavy cruiser, the *Mikuma*. And so ended the phase of the war in which the Japanese could be said to be "winning."

DOWNFALL OF THE LUFTWAFFE

Now we switch our attention back to the European Theater of WWII, and the turning of the tide in that hemisphere. Some historians believe that the ultimate defeat of the Luftwaffe by the Allies was assured even before WWII began, in 1933, with the appointment of Hermann Göring as *Reichskommissar* for air.

That's because Göring, a former WWI flyer, viewed the complexity of the upcoming air war as taking a back seat to the pageantry and politics of his position. His divide-and-conquer style of management left Germany's air tacticians unable to bring their expertise to the aid of the Third Reich.

The command structure created several opposing factions that spent more time courting Göring's favor than promoting the state of the Luftwaffe. Hitler's limited understanding of the use of airpower and his use of cronyism to fill Luftwaffe command positions were to haunt him in the last years of the war when thousands of Allied planes filled the skies over Germany.

Hindered by lack of foresight, the German High Command began the war equipped for tactical warfare. Political payoffs made by Hitler, in return for his rise to power, had put incompetents in many of the high-level positions. Their lack of understanding left Germany ill-equipped to fight the war it had started.

The belief in the success of Blitzkrieg (lightning war) led them to think their objectives could be won if a long war were avoided. In this scenario, the Luftwaffe was little more than flying artillery, blasting a hole in the enemy's front lines to allow passage of the Panzers (tanks) on the ground.

ERNST UDET

Perhaps no one person hindered the Luftwaffe's chances of staying ahead of Allied airpower during WWII more than Ernst Udet, another WWI flyer. He was so enamored with the concept of dive-bombing that he decided all German planes needed to have the ability to attack in a vertical dive, even those planes that obviously had too large of an airframe. The He 177 Grief, a late-war design, might have been an effective bomber had Udet not demanded that it have dive-bombing capabilities. As engineers puzzled over that one, the Allies marched into Berlin.

One of the few Germans to understand the potential of strategic bombing, Gen. Walter Wever, was killed in May 1936, and many believe all hopes for the Luftwaffe died with him.

Hitler Misses the Point

The German High Command made its greatest blunder of the air war with its handling of the Messerschmitt Me 262, the first operational turbojet to engage the enemy. Used as a fighter, it could have done much to hand air superiority back to the Germans. Upon seeing a demonstration of the sleek fighter, however, Hitler was concerned only with how many bombs it could carry as a vengeance weapon—in other words, as a weapon to be used against British civilians. Willy Messerschmitt had to redesign the Me 262 to Hitler's specifications. This cost time, a commodity that was gradually being taken away from the Germans.

Germany's war against the Soviet Union had turned into a war of attrition, which diverted aircraft away from the Western Front. Against the growing numbers of Allied aircraft production, the Germans had just squandered their one plane that could beat anything in the sky.

U.S. Redefines "War Production"

Germany so underestimated the Allies that it did not even begin full-time war production until 1943. By that time the United States had converted many of its factories into war production facilities and were producing war materials enough for its own forces, as well as for much of its Allies' needs. The U.S. automotive industry now made planes, tanks, and jeeps, for example.

The United States had been gearing up for higher production since 1939, when the British and the French had placed large orders for aircraft and other war materiel. During peak production, Boeing made up to 16 B-17s a day. In comparison, Focke-Wulf in Germany could produce only eight Fw-190s on a good day. Usually, that number was less.

HAWKER TEMPEST

The Hawker Tempest Mk V was used by the RAF and New Zealand air force in April 1944 to fly many cross-channel sorties before and after D day. It was one of the few fighters that could successfully chase the German V-1 flying bomb and either blast them out of the sky or flip them out of control.

By D day (June 6, 1944) the Luftwaffe was overwhelmed by the number of Allied aircraft being built. The Luftwaffe flew few sorties to attack the Allied armada, and these were easily driven off by the thousands of Allied planes flying cover for the beach landings. After D day, Mustangs began to provide bomber escort. Thunderbolts and British Typhoons flew over Europe destroying anything of value to the Germans.

SBD-1 DOUGLAS DAUNTLESS

We discussed the birth of dive-bombing as a technological achievement and strategy for attack back in Chapter 4. Now let's take a look at some of the top U.S. dive-bombers used during WWII.

The navy's first dive-bomber was conceived in 1934, when the U.S. Navy Bureau of Aeronautics invited several aircraft manufacturers to submit proposals. The job finally went to the Northrop Aircraft Company, which designed the XBT-1. When the head of Northrop, John K. Northrop, sold his company to Douglas Aircraft in 1938, the dive-bomber became known as the SBD-1 Douglas Dauntless. It was powered by a Wright R-1820-32 nine-cylinder air-cooled radial engine producing 1,000 horsepower. It had a maximum speed of 253 mph and a range of 1,165 miles.

The design innovation that allowed the Dauntless to dive was the inclusion of perforated diving flaps on the wings. The result was a bomber that handled like a fighter. The windshield was bulletproof. The landing gear retracted hydraulically. Two versions of the Dauntless were built, the SBD-1 and SBD-2. They were very similar. The SBD-2 had a machine gun in its rear cockpit, whereas the -1 did not. The -2 also had armor plate for the crew, self-sealing rubber-lined fuel tanks, and two 65-gallon fuel tanks in the outer wing panel. Thus, the -2 had greater range than the -1. The -2 also had added to its design an outer wing panel for 100-pound bombs.

The Dauntless became the workhorse of the Pacific War, and participated in every major engagement against the Japanese.

CURTISS SB2C HELLDIVER

Plans were to replace the Dauntless with a newer dive-bomber called the Helldiver. The Curtiss SB2C Helldiver was a two-seat carrier-based dive-bomber. The prototype flew for the first time on December 18, 1940, and the navy ordered them into large-scale production before the year was out. They were assigned to the new Essex-class carriers.

Although the Helldiver was intended to replace the Dauntless, the Dauntless was the better plane. The first Helldivers did not see action until late in 1943, when they flew from the deck of the *Bunker Hill* for a raid over the major Japanese base of Rabaul.

Problems with the Helldiver, in particular with the handling, revealed themselves during the Battle of the Philippine Sea. The plane had poor low-speed stability, and its stability during high-speed dives was not great either.

The Dauntless was the more accurate of the two bombers. The navy stuck with the Helldiver despite its shortcomings and it ended up dishing out a whole lot of damage against the Japanese.

REPUBLIC P-47 THUNDERBOLT

The rugged Republic P-47 Thunderbolt was originally designed to be a lightweight interceptor, but developed into a heavy fighter. In combat, it proved that it could sustain heavy damage and still fly its pilot safely home. It first flew on May 6, 1941. The first production model was delivered in March 1942, and it first flew in combat in April 1943, over Western Europe. It was used as a high-altitude escort fighter as well as a low-level fighter-bomber. More than 15,600 Thunderbolts were built during the war, and they served in every theater of combat. The -B, -C, -D, and -G models were built with metal-framed cockpit canopies. The -M and -N models had "bubble" canopies that offered the pilot better vision to the rear. Nicknamed "Jugs," Republic P-47 Thunderbolts, with their ability to dive at 680 mph, made their largest effect on the war on March 8, 1944. On that day heavy bombers of the 8th Air Force laid siege to Berlin.

While this was going on, red-nosed P-47 Thunderbolts of the now-legendary "Wolfpack" 56th Fighter Group swept the skies clean of determined German interceptors. The P-47 was one of the most famous fighter planes of the war.

In dogfights against Bf 109s and Fw 190s, the Wolfpack scored 27 victories. Those victories made the 56th Fighter Group the first in the European Theater of Operation to destroy 300 enemy aircraft in the air.

One of the reasons for the success of the Thunderbolt was its R-2800 Double Wasp engine, which we discussed in detail in Chapter 4. The Thunderbolt's engine employed a single supercharger operating at a constant speed ratio with the crankshaft. The Thunderbolt had a maximum speed of 433 mph and a range of 1,030 miles.

General Electric, pioneers in turbocharger technology, installed one of its units in the P-47's rear fuselage area to sustain high-altitude performance.

A water-injection system was incorporated in the -63 series of the R-2800 to enable the pilot to operate the engine at the "best power" setting without burning excess fuel or overheating the engine. The engine would come in very handy whenever a pilot needed an extra kick to overcome unfavorable circumstances.

AMERICA'S WORKHORSE BOMBER: B-17

The single most important warplane to fly during WWII was the B-17 Flying Fortress. Although it was used in every theater of combat during the war, B-17s of the Eighth Air Force became famous as the planes that, in broad daylight, made daily strategic bombing runs over Germany.

Because the B-17 had such tremendous range, it could take off from England, bomb sites in Germany, and return to England. That meant that raids could be flown before D day, when much of the continent of Europe was under German control.

Because escort fighters—Mustangs and Thunderbolts—did not have the B-17's range, escorts were not available to the Flying Fortresses until after D day, when Allied troops regained control of land areas closer to Germany.

Until then, the B-17s were on their own. They were frequently attacked—and shot down—by German fighters during the earlier bombing runs. The B-17s defended themselves with gunners who were positioned in turrets, firing machine guns. The plane was equipped with thirteen .50 caliber machine guns in chin, top, ball, and tail turrets.

Even after the escorts joined the B-17s, the danger was only diminished slightly. The escorts did nothing to protect the Flying Fortresses from antiaircraft fire from the ground, the dreaded German flak. Flak shot down more B-17s than German fighter planes did.

One third of all the B-17s to fly in combat over Europe were shot down—4,732 of them. B-17s often made it home safely despite getting hit repeatedly by flak or gunfire from German fighter planes. It was not uncommon for B-17s to return from missions with more holes than Swiss cheese.

But the B-17s dished it out, too. Their bombing raids destroyed countless German industrial sites, and crippled Germany's ability to keep its army, spread out over multiple fronts, freshly stocked with fuel and equipment.

Missions over Germany lasted longer than eight hours. The B-17s flew so high that their crews had to wear oxygen masks and frequently suffered from frostbite. Crewmen learned to shave before missions to keep the irritation from the oxygen mask to a minimum.

Battle fatigue became a problem with B-17 crews. So a rule was made that an airman had to fly only 25 missions. If he survived, he got to go home. This rule helped keep crewmen sane—despite the fact that the life expectancy of a B-17 crewman was only 15 missions.

Boeing's research and development of the B-17 started during the early 1930s, with the prototype (YB-17) first flying on July 28, 1935. There were only a few B-17s in service before Pearl Harbor, but after that factories in the United States began to crank them out at an amazing clip. By the time the war was over, 12,726 B-17s had been built.

Military Technical Journal

A B-17 Flying Fortress takes off from a British airport during the summer of 1941 for an air raid on the harbor of Brest, France, and the German battleship Gneisenau.

Combat experience led to improvements being made on the B-17 throughout the war. The final version was the B-17G. Nearly two thirds of all the B-17s built were the G model. This version had a wingspan of almost 104 feet and was 74 feet, 4 inches long. It was armed with 13 .50-cal. machine guns with normal bomb load of 6,000 pounds, and powered by four Wright "Cyclone" R-1820s of 1,200 horsepower apiece. It had a maximum speed of 300 mph and flew to a ceiling of 35,000 feet. The plane held a crew of 14 (pilot, copilot, navigator, bombardier, radio operator, engineer, right and left waist gunners, ball turret gunner, tail gunner, nose turret gunner, cheek gunner, top turret gunner, and radio room gunner).

Although the B-17 was one of the most technologically advanced aircraft in the world during WWII, it became obsolete soon after the war ended. The reason: jet power. The Flying Fortresses that survived the war were cut up for scrap or sold on the surplus market. Today fewer than 15 B-17s are in flying condition.

GRUMMAN FIGHTERS

After Pearl Harbor, the United States was faced with an enemy whose major targets were far from Allied air bases. Between Hawaii and Japan were many islands, most of which were controlled by the Japanese.

Before the United States could attack Japan directly, American soldiers and Marines would have to "island hop." That is, they had to fight a series of increasingly difficult battles, to kick the Japanese out of the Pacific.

Many of those islands—Guadalcanal, Midway, Saipan, Guam, Iwo Jima, just to name a few—are famous in the United States because of the battles that were fought there. The United States won each and every one of those battles, and one of the reasons was air superiority.

The company that created the carrier-based fighter planes that helped win back the Pacific was Grumman. The planes most responsible for giving our troops support during those long and bloody battles were the Wildcat, the Hellcat, and the Avenger. In our next few sections, we'll look at those aircraft.

HELLCATS OF THE NAVY

One of the United States' premiere carrier-based planes during World War II was the Grumman Hellcat F6F. It flew for the first time on June 30, 1941, five months before the United States entered the war. Grumman delivered the first Hellcats to the military in October 1942, and in January 1943 they were assigned to the aircraft carriers *Essex*, *Yorktown*, and *Independence*. It had a maximum speed of 376 mph, and a range of 1,090 miles. It was armed with six .50 caliber Colt-Browning machine guns, and was powered by one R-2800 Double Wasp engine, producing 2,000 horsepower.

The Hellcat got off to a late start in the war. By 1945, however, it was one of the United States' most valuable carrier-based planes. A total of 2,545 of them eventually went to war. The plane was upgraded in 1944 to the Hellcat FF6-5, which had a stronger engine and additional armor installed behind the pilot. The new version could carry a ton of bombs, and in dogfights proved itself again and again to be superior to the Japanese Zero.

Marianas Turkey Shoot

The F6F was the American plane involved in the famous Marianas Turkey Shoot, the most one-sided large-scale dogfight in the history of combat.

On June 19, 1944, a nine-carrier Japanese task force headed toward the island of Saipan in the Marianas Islands to stop the island-hopping advance and, hopefully, flush out and destroy the U.S. Pacific fleet.

Contact was made and the ensuing air battle reached epic proportions as Hellcats smashed the enemy attacks. The battle only lasted a few hours. Only 30 Hellcats were shot down. A total of 346 Japanese aircraft were destroyed in the air.

THE AVENGERS

The Grumman TBM Avenger was originally designed to be a torpedo bomber. However, during its extensive use in WWII in the Pacific Theater, it was used predominantly as a glide bomber. In that capacity it attacked Japanese ships and provided air support for U.S. troops on the ground. It also searched for enemy submarines in the Pacific and Atlantic, where it was used by both the United States and Great Britain.

During the years leading up to America's entrance into World War II, the primary U.S. torpedo bomber was the Douglas TDB Devastator. But after only a few short years of operation, the Devastator proved to be obsolete.

Grumman won the contract to design its replacement. The navy ordered its first Avengers in December 1940. During the summer of 1941, the prototype made its first test flight. A little more than a month after the Japanese attacked Pearl Harbor in December 1941, the Avenger was operational. Her crews more frequently referred to it by its affectionate nickname, "Turkey." The three-seated Avenger was powered by a Wright R-2600 Cyclone producing 1,900 horsepower, and armed with three

.50 caliber machine guns and up to one ton of ordnance. It flew at a maximum speed of 276 mph and had a range of 1,130 miles.

Grumman production of the Avenger continued until 1944, and it made a total of 2,293. The Avenger could carry bombs in an internal bomb bay and could carry depth charges and rockets under its wings. More than 150 Avengers per month were produced by Grumman during 1943. Later, Grumman was kept busy building Hellcats, so the production of Avengers was switched to Eastern Aircraft, the airplane-producing wing of General Motors. By the end of the war, almost 10,000 Avengers had been built, about three quarters of them by Eastern.

Although the majority of Avengers were TBF-1 (Grumman) and TBM-1 (GM) models, there were numerous variants and modifications. When the APS-20 radar was added, the designation was TBM-3W. These models were paired with the TBM-3s to become the first hunter-killer types, remaining operational until mid-1954. Other postwar variants included the target-towing TBM-3U, the TBM-3N for night operations, the TBM-3Q featuring radar countermeasures, and the seven-seat COD TBM-3R.

Avengers in their many variants served the Royal Navy, the Royal Canadian Navy, the Royal New Zealand Air Force, the Royal Netherlands Navy, the French Aeronavale, and, as late as 1962, the Japanese Maritime Self-Defense Force.

An indication of the strength and longevity of the Grumman "Iron Works" products was the usage of Avengers as fire bombers into the 1970s.

WILDCATS

The Grumman F4F Wildcat was first designed in 1935. It was the first all-metal, carrier-launched monoplane fighter ever to be used by the U.S. Navy. This was the U.S. Navy's and Marine Corps' primary fighter plane when America entered WWII. The plane had a reputation for seldom having mechanical difficulties and when it did it could be repaired, as they say, with a Band-Aid and some bubblegum.

This plane was originally designed as a biplane. The U.S. Navy didn't go for the original design, choosing instead the Brewster Buffalo. But

Great Britain and France both liked Grumman's design and so the first Wildcats (although it wouldn't get that name until later) were shipped to Europe. When France fell to Germany, the planes were moved to England. The plane, known then as the Martlet, scored its first victory on Christmas Day, 1940.

The Wildcat was powered by a Wright R-1820-56 engine developing 1,350 horsepower. It flew to a maximum speed of 322 mph and had a range of 1,350 miles. The carrier-based version, the one with the folding wings, debuted in time for the attack at Pearl Harbor and first saw action for the U.S. Navy at the battle of Wake Island. The plane was upgraded several times during the war, with the FM-2 being the most abundantly produced (4,777 of them were made). As would later be the case with the Avenger, the manufacturing of the plane was shifted from Grumman to General Motors.

The FM-2 had a lighter, yet more powerful Wright R-1820 radial engine. Additionally, the plane carried four rather than six .50 caliber machine guns and was often fitted with *HVARs* (High-Velocity Aircraft Rockets) for use against ground targets, ships, or surfaced submarines. The FM-2 also had a larger tail than the standard F4F to counter the increased torque produced by the Wright engine.

In the Pacific, the Wildcat was perfectly suited for use on escort carriers. It won numerous dogfights against Japanese Zeroes, and sank several Japanese submarines and one cruiser. The Wildcat was America's primary naval fighter through the end of 1942. However, during 1943, most Wildcat squadrons were reequipped with either the larger Grumman F6F Hellcat or the Chance-Vought F4U Corsair.

CHANCE-VOUGHT F4U CORSAIR: WHISTLING DEATH

Though the great majority of Corsairs were land-based and supported the Marines, they were also the United States' most successful carrier-based fighter plane. The one-seater had a kill ratio of better than 11 to 1.

The first germ of an idea regarding the Corsair came about almost three years before the United States entered WWII, in February 1938. It was then that the U.S. Navy Bureau of Aeronautics requested proposals from aircraft manufacturers for a high-speed, single-engine fighter with a stalling speed not higher than 70 mph.

JOHN GLENN

One of WWII's top American flying aces, flying an F4U Corsair, later went on to even greater fame—as an astronaut! John Herschel Glenn Jr., born on July 18, 1921, in Cambridge, Ohio, won his wings and lieutenant's bars in 1943 as a Marine. During WWII, he flew 59 combat missions in an F4U Corsair over the Mariana Islands and Marshall Islands in the South Pacific.

After the war, Glenn trained other pilots and did some test-pilot work. During the Korean War, Glenn flew 63 ground-support missions in an F9F Panther jet. He was credited with shooting down three North Korean MiGs in nine days. During his military career he won the Distinguished Flying Cross six times.

When the conflict in Korea ended, Glenn was accepted at the Navy Test Pilot School.

While working as a test pilot, he was asked to help design what would become the Mercury capsule. He became involved in the program when he agreed to test the centrifuge and other equipment that NASA would use to simulate the g-forces an astronaut would have to endure to reenter the Earth's atmosphere from orbit. When Glenn became a candidate to be one of the Mercury 7, he had already tested and contributed to the design of the same equipment that would be used to test *him* during the selection process.

Less than two years after his historic space trek, Glenn realized that his age was apt to keep him from ever walking on the moon. Glenn resigned from the Manned Spacecraft Center in January 1964, and a month later announced his plans to run for the Senate in Ohio. He dropped out of the race after a fall left him with a concussion and a lingering inner ear problem. He again ran for the Senate in 1970, but was defeated. He tried again in 1974, and the third time was the charm.

In 1998, Glenn became the oldest man ever to orbit the Earth.

The request specified that the plane should have a range of 1,000 miles, four guns, and provisions under the wings to carry antiaircraft bombs. The winning design came from Chance-Vought. The wings were bent to resemble those of a sea gull. The plane, which came to be known as the Corsair, was the first U.S. fighter to fly faster than 400 mph.

The Chance-Vought F4U Corsair became legendary during the Pacific war, striking fear into the hearts of Japanese pilots, who called the aircraft "Whistling Death." It was powered by a Pratt & Whitney R-2800-18W engine producing 2,100 horsepower. It was armed with six .50 caliber machine guns. It had a maximum speed of 446 mph and a range of 1,005 miles.

The Corsair was not immediately assigned to the navy's carrier fleet, however. Because of its long nose, which restricted pilot visibility, especially during takeoff and landing, it was considered unsuitable as a carrier craft. That's why the Corsair's earliest victories were in support of the Marines, who used them to replace their Wildcats.

As it turned out, Corsairs worked fine off aircraft carriers. They came in particularly handy during the final weeks of the war, as they could out-duel kamikaze Zeroes before the Japanese suicide pilots could reach U.S. ships.

CHAPTER 7

THE FIERY END OF WORLD WAR II

In this chapter, we look at how U.S. warplanes brought about the end of World War II. We examine the P-38 Lightning, the plane that established air superiority for the Allies over Europe. We see how what was left of the Japanese air force self-destructed in desperation. And we look at the history of the B-24 Liberator, which became the most extensively built U.S. plane of the war, and the B-29 Superfortress, which was used to incinerate Japanese cities.

P-38 LIGHTNING

The story of the P-38 Lightning began in 1937 when the army sent out a request for information to several regular defense contractors, to build a high-speed, twin-engine air superiority fighter.

The competition was won by Lockheed and its model number 22. The plane was designed by Hal Hibbard and Kelly Johnson. The most unusual thing about the design was its twin fuselages— one fuselage per engine. Behind each engine were twin General Electric turbochargers. The plane also had contra-rotating propellers, each prop turning inward, which eliminated the torque effect (pulling to one side). So the P-38 was part jet and part prop plane.

The plane didn't get an A during its flight tests, but it passed. The USAAC ordered 13 of the new aircraft to be built. These were different from the prototype in that they featured outward-turning rather than inward turning propellers. The armament consisted of four .50 caliber machine guns and a 37mm cannon.

These 13 performed well and the USAAC ordered 20 more from Lockheed. These were known as P-38s and were delivered in March 1941, three months before the USAAC had a designation change of its own, changing its name to the U.S. Army Air Force (USAAF) on June 20, 1941.

The British version of the P-38, called the RAF Lightning Mk I, was delivered in December 1941. It had a less powerful engine than the American version and did not have contra-rotating propellers.

By the time the Japanese had attacked Pearl Harbor on December 7 and drawn the United States into the war, the USAAF had received the latest version of the P-38, the P-38Es. These featured improved propellers, avionics systems, a pressurized cabin, and a 20mm Hispano cannon, which replaced the 37mm Oldsmobile cannon.

There were a total of 1,849 Lightning fighters delivered to the USAAF, with the last versions known as P-38G. There were also 300 Lightnings built as photo reconnaissance planes. Some P-38s were equipped with radar and thus could serve as night fighters.

Lightnings Go to War

Lightnings went into action immediately upon America's entrance into the war. Within hours of Franklin Roosevelt's declaration of war, a Lightning based in Iceland shot down a German patrol bomber. Before the war was over, the P-38 had served on every front of the war. As fighters, the Lightning flew combat air patrols, enemy fighter interceptions, bomber escorts, ground-troop support missions, and missions to strafe enemy ground troops.

Other P-38s served as fighter-bombers. In 1944, some P-38s overflew Germany carrying as much as two tons of bombs apiece. These bombing missions were efficient because the Luftwaffe was depleted by 1944 and attacked only bombers. They thought the P-38s were fighters and left them alone. A great deal of damage was caused before the Germans caught on.

Military Technical Journal

Note the strikingly clean, aerodynamic lines of the XP-38, secretly constructed between June and December 1938.

The P-38's most famous mission came on April 18, 1943, when it caused the demise of Adm. Isoroku Yamamoto of the Imperial Japanese Navy, the man who had planned the Pearl Harbor attack and was the engineer behind Japan's success early in the war. Historian John D. Cugini described in *Military Technical Journal* what happened: "[Yamamoto] found his Betty Bomber besieged upon by Lightnings of the 12th, 70th, and 339th Fighter Squadrons. Yamamoto's bomber was hit and set afire by P-38 .50-caliber machine-gun fire. Trailing thick black smoke, the Betty slowly descended and crashed into the jungles of Bougainville killing Yamamoto—a severe psychological blow to the Japanese people."

The limited numbers of P-38s available to the USAAF during 1942–1943 meant that, during those years, the planes went to where they were needed most. That meant the Southwest Pacific and North Africa.

On these fronts, the Lightnings proved valuable in tactical operations. The three Lightning groups in North Africa (1st, 14th, and 82nd) suffered heavy losses in the early months of that campaign but the aircraft showed up well in combat with Focke-Wulf 190s and Messerschmitt Me 109s.

At low and medium altitudes, where most combat took place, the P-38—in spite of its larger size—was able to turn with the enemy aircraft, could usually outclimb it, and had a faster top speed. Although the attrition rate was high, the P-38 proved its worth in North Africa equally as well as against the Japanese in the Southwest Pacific.

Trouble over Europe

By the autumn of 1943, the Luftwaffe had approximately 800 fighters ready in France to meet the Eighth Air Force bombers as they headed toward their targets to the east. The toll the German fighters were taking on the U.S. bombing missions was high so it was determined that the bombers needed increased protection.

The answer was the long-range fighter, the P-38. The plane could both protect the bombers and take a toll on the attacking enemy fighters. The P-38, fitted with drop tanks for extra endurance, was given priority for the Eighth Air Force during that autumn. P-38s escorted B-17 and B-24 heavy bombers to some of the toughest targets in Germany. Bomber crews called the Lightnings their "Little Friends."

The first escort missions for the Lightnings were troubled by mechanical failures. The low temperatures at 20,000 feet over Europe had, along with giving pilots frostbite, caused engine problems. There was also trouble with the P-38's turbo-supercharger regulators. For a time mechanics and engineers couldn't figure out why the superchargers were malfunctioning, but they eventually determined that the problems were caused by moisture from the plane's vapor trail gathering behind the engine exhaust stubs, getting into the balance lines, and freezing. The vapor trails were also a tactical handicap. Their twin trails could be seen up to four miles away.

The standard P-38 armament consisted of one 20mm cannon firing 150 rounds per gun and four .50-caliber guns with 500 rounds per gun. P-38L models could also carry ten 5-inch rockets slung under the wings. The

Lightning's firepower caused great damage to both enemy planes and ground targets.

In Europe alone, USAAF Lightnings flew 129,849 sorties. They shot down 1,771 enemy aircraft, and dropped 20,139 tons of bombs. When the United States entered the war, there were 96 P-38s in service. By December 1944, that number had grown to 2,759.

The United States' number-one flying ace of World War II was Maj. Richard Bong, who shot down 40 Japanese aircraft in his P-38, which he had named "Marge" after his wife. Three out of America's top ten World War II flying aces flew Lightnings.

The one-seater had a 52-foot wingspan and was 37 feet, 10 inches long. It was powered by two Allison V-1710-89/91 Turbo-supercharged engines. It had a maximum speed of 414 mph and a range of 2,600 miles. In combat, flying below 18,000 feet, the P-38 was superior to the Me 109 or FW 190. Above that altitude it lost its superiority, and could become inferior.

In the first year after the war, the USAAF scrapped most of the P-38s. By December 1946, only 113 remained. They were redesignated as F-38s when the USAAF became its own branch of the military, the U.S. Air Force (USAF), in 1947. The last Lightning was taken out of service in 1949. Most of the surplus Lightnings were sold for scrap, but many were abandoned on Pacific islands. Of those still in flying condition, some were used by the Chinese Nationalist air forces in the 1946–1949 civil war. Others were used by Italy and several countries of Central America. It is a testament to the P-38 that the *Luftwaffe* called it *der Gabelschwanz Teufel*, or the Fork-Tailed Devil.

B-24 LIBERATOR

Let's take a look at the developmental history of the B-24. The War Department signed a contract with Consolidated to design and build a long-range strategic bomber with a top speed of 300 mph, round-trip range of 3,000 miles (combat range of 1,500 miles), and a maximum service ceiling of 35,000 feet. The aircraft had a tricycle landing gear, outward and upward retracting roller-shutter bomb-bay doors, and an 8,800-pound bomb load stored vertically on each side (separated by a metal crew catwalk).

It was powered by four 1,200-horsepower Pratt & Whitney R-1830-33 Twin Wasp radial engines, giving it a top speed of 273 mph. Even though its speed was below design specifications, it was sufficient to meet the first test flight performance goals. These engines were replaced by super-charged R-1830-41 engines, which increased top speed to 303 mph.

Military Technical Journal

The B-24 Liberator was the workhorse bomber of World War II.

The XB-24 prototype first flew on December 29, 1939, beating the War Department's contract first flight deadline by two days. The War Department ordered only 7 production aircraft, but the French government ordered 139. Besides the French order, the British Royal Air Force (RAF) also ordered the bomber. But after Germany conquered France in August 1940, the RAF took possession of the French order.

Consolidated Aircraft Corporation named the aircraft the Liberator, because it would carry the air war to the center of Germany, liberating conquered European nations from the Nazi war machine.

The British Ferry Command used the first 26 unarmed Liberators for nonstop, trans-Atlantic flights. Flights from England carried ferry pilots and crews to the United States and returned with high-priority war cargo. Liberators first entered Atlantic combat in an antisubmarine warfare role. RAF Bomber Command's first use of the Liberator resulted in heavy losses from attacking Luftwaffe fighters and it was withdrawn from combat. Additional guns, armor protection, and self-sealing wing fuel tanks became standard on following production models.

C and D Versions

The B-24C had upgraded Pratt & Whitney R-1830-41 exhaust drive turbocharged engines to accommodate the aircraft's increased weight. They were unarmed, did not fly in combat, but were used to train crews.

The B-24D was the first production model delivered to the U.S. military in quantity, with 2,738 built. It was powered by four R-1830-43 supercharged radials, housed in elliptical engine nacelles, which became standard on future Liberator models.

The Liberator had a crew of 10: pilot/aircraft commander, copilot, radio operator, navigator, bombardier, and five gunners (nose, ball, tail, and two waist of beam). It could carry a larger bomb load than a B-17 (12,800 versus 6,000 pounds) and was faster (303 versus 287 mph). But it was harder to fly in formation and dangerous to belly-land or ditch. Its most dangerous design deficiency was the complex wing design. If a flak burst or cannon shells from an attacking fighter hit the shoulder-mounted wing root, one or both wings would fold upwards, causing the fuselage to burst into flames as it plummeted to the ground.

The Liberator was built in greater numbers than the Flying Fortress, becoming the most extensively built U.S. World War II aircraft. Five production facilities built 19,203 Liberators until production ended on May 31, 1945.

The B-24G/H/J models differed from each other only slightly. The B-24J had a wingspan of 110 feet, fuselage length of 67 feet, 2 inches, cantilever monoplane tail with twin fins and rudder, tricycle landing gear, and was powered by four 1,200 horsepower Pratt & Whitney Twin Wasp R-1830-65 14-cyclinder two-row radial air-cooled engines. It was protected by a twin .50 caliber machine gun nose turret, a twin .50 caliber machine gun dorsal turret, a retractable twin .50 caliber machine gun ball turret, a single .50 caliber machine gun waist position on either side of the fuselage aft of the wing, and a twin .50 caliber machine gun tail turret.

The B-24J had a maximum speed of 297 mph with a 12,800 pound bomb load at 25,000 feet, maximum combat range of 1,540 miles at 237 mph at 25,000 feet, and a maximum operational ceiling of 28,000 feet.

Flew in Every Theater

The Liberator flew in all World War II combat theaters. It fought German U-boats in the Atlantic, flew high-altitude strategic bombing missions against Nazi Germany, bombed the Aleutians in the Northern Pacific combat zone, and served in the China-Burma-India (CBI) theater.

Regardless of where the Consolidated B-24 Liberator fought, it proved its versatility. During World War II, it earned recognition and respect as a long-range bomber, dropping over 635,000 tons of bombs, and destroying approximately 4,000 enemy aircraft.

KAMIKAZES OFF OKINAWA

It was the steady advancement of the United States across the Pacific that led the Japanese to make Okinawa, an island just south of the Japanese mainland, a stronghold. In September 1943, the Japanese leaders had drawn a line across the Pacific and Asia and called it the "Absolute National Defense Zone."

That line encompassed the Kuriles to the north, the Marianas, the Bonins, the Carolines, western New Guinea, the East Indies, and Burma. By the end of 1944, the Americans had broken out of Absolute National Defense Zone and so, after a change in power, the Japanese regrouped.

By the spring of 1945 the Japanese had formulated the plan *Ten-Go*, the defense of Japan's most vulnerable neighbors. These included Formosa, the island of Hainan between China and Indochina, the coast of China and, in the Ryukus, Okinawa.

The defense of Okinawa would be accomplished at sea by 4,800 specially prepared Japanese aircraft. Each would have enough fuel for a one-way trip to the China Sea off Okinawa; from each, the landing craft was removed. The planes would be loaded with enough heavy explosives to single-handedly sink an American destroyer and be piloted by a man ready to commit suicide for his country. These were the kamikazes.

The word *kamikaze* means "heavenly wind." It was a term first used in 1570 to describe a typhoon that saved Japan by destroying an invading Chinese fleet. The kamikazes were recruited by Capt. Jyo Eiichio, appealing to the pilots' spirit of *bushido*, a concept of martial arts whereby a man is willing to sacrifice his life for a glorious cause.

Kamikazes did not strike at Allied ships until the aftermath of the Battle of Leyte Gulf, in the Philippines, on October 25, 1944. In a span of four hours on that day, kamikazes sank one American aircraft carrier and damaged four more.

By December 12, 1944, the toll from kamikazes had risen to seven ships sunk, seven heavy carriers damaged, and another 16 ships damaged. On January 9, 1945, 100 kamikazes sank another aircraft carrier and damaged four others.

The kamikaze attacks off Okinawa started on March 25, when 26 kamikazes attacked at once. Eight hit their mark. The battleship *Nevada*, a survivor at Pearl Harbor, took a direct hit. Five days later the cruiser *Indianapolis* was struck and badly damaged. But on April 6, so went the plan, the true deluge of kamikazes would begin, and the carnage would be the worst the U.S. Navy had ever known.

On April 6, the U.S. Fifth Fleet was attacked by 900 Japanese aircraft, one third of which were kamikazes. During the first 24 hours of the attack it looked like Japan's plan might work, as ship after ship received direct hits. In addition to other damage, three destroyers, two ammunition ships, and a landing ship tank were sent to the bottom of the East China Sea.

The kamikaze offensive was one of diminishing returns, however. As time went on, through April and May and into June, and the battle at Okinawa grew older, the kamikazes came fewer in number—attrition being the obvious factor here—and fewer got through to their targets due to the increased ability of the navy's antiaircraft gunners to shoot them down before they could do any damage. The sailor gunmen were learning on the job. One thing they learned was that, in combat, a man who wants to live has a great advantage over an enemy who wants to die.

To further reduce the threat of kamikaze disaster, the U.S. fleet repositioned 16 radar-picket destroyers to better supply early warnings of kamikaze attacks. Although the strategy was a sound one from the viewpoint of the entire fleet, it was hell on the men on those destroyers, whose ships now became targets themselves for the kamikazes.

President Franklin Delano Roosevelt died on April 12, placing a further somber cloud over an already bleak Fifth Fleet. He was replaced by his virtually unknown vice president, Harry S. Truman, whose job it would be to end the war as quickly as possible.

Several days after FDR's death, one American destroyer, the USS *Laffey* was attacked simultaneously by 20 kamikazes. Some missed and the *Laffey*'s gunmen shot down most of them, but six got through and made direct hits upon the ship. The damage was extensive. Three after-crew compartments were flooded. The rudder was jammed and massive fires blazed aboard. Still, the ship continued to steam and its guns continued to fire back at the Japanese attackers.

In a ship full of heroes, none was braver than surgeon Mathew Driscoll. Though wounded in the hand by bomb fragments, Driscoll continued to treat 60 wounded sailors in the ship's wardroom. Operating with his good hand, he shouted instructions to his assistants for the treatment of other casualties.

In the East China Sea the final tally of death and destruction was a gloomy one, despite the impending Allied victory. The 1,900 kamikazes that had attacked the fleet had sunk, between April 6 and July 29, 14 destroyers and 17 other ships and boats. Only four ships, however, were sunk after June 1.

The damage done couldn't be measured merely in numbers of wounded and dead. Many of the sailors who survived the two months of kamikaze attacks intact would remain forever emotionally scarred by their experience. Military psychiatrists agreed that the cases of battle fatigue were more numerous and severe among the sailors in the East China Sea than in any other theater of war. These men were on alert for attack in the face of agonizing death 24 hours a day for more than two months.

The British ships of Task Force 57, also off Okinawa, fared much better than the American ships—in particular the aircraft carriers. Their decks were armored to prevent damage from shellfire, such as a ship might encounter in narrower European waters, and therefore sustained only minor damage, even when suffering a direct hit from a kamikaze.

Among the U.S. ships heavily damaged were the aircraft carriers *Enterprise*, *Hancock*, and *Bunker Hill*, flagship of Admiral Raymond A. Spruance, commander of the Fifth Fleet. On the *Bunker Hill* alone, where two kamikazes had made direct hits within the space of one minute on May 11, 396 crewmen were killed. More than 5,000 American sailors died from kamikaze attacks and another 4,824 were wounded. Thirty-two U.S. ships were sunk and another 368 were damaged. It was the bloodiest battle in the history of the U.S. Navy.

Despite this, the Japanese plan had failed miserably. The U.S. fleet remained. The invading troops were not stranded and the Japanese forces on Okinawa were slowly vanquished in blood.

When the war ended, it was discovered that the Japanese had developed a new "plane" designed specifically for kamikaze missions. It was called the Yokosuka MXY7 Ohka 11, and was basically a flying bomb designed to be flown by its pilot directly into its target.

It was given the nickname *Baka* by the Japanese, meaning "cherry blossom." It had to be carried by a twin-engine Mitsubishi G4M Betty bomber (see Chapter 5), nestled partially in the bomb bay, to the target area. At that point it would be released, with the pilot igniting the three solid-fuel rocket motors, diving, picking up speed to 560 mph, picking out a ship, and slamming into the target, detonating the 2,640-pound warhead.

The Cherry Blossom was to be first used on March 21, 1945, when 15 Betties with Bakas were shot down by American Hellcats. The first Baka success was on April 1, 1945, when one damaged the battleship *West Virginia*. By the end of the war, Bakas had also sunk one destroyer and had damaged three destroyers, one minesweeper, and two transports.

Now, for the U.S. military leaders, came the grim task of plotting a strategy for the invasion of mainland Japan. Taking into consideration the intensity with which the Japanese defended Iwo Jima and Okinawa, U.S. generals and admirals knew that the taking of Japan would result in greater loss of life than any other battle in the history of warfare.

These men did not know that the atomic bomb being developed by Robert Oppenheimer and a team of scientists in the United States would soon be ready, and would, in turn, render the invasion of Japan unnecessary.

Massive Firestorms

The absolute self-destruction of the Japanese air force resulted in absolute air superiority for the United States. Since the Marines had taken Iwo Jima and the Marianas, airstrips had been constructed on those islands long enough for U.S. heavy bombers to fly over Japanese cities and return safely. More than 60 cities were bombed, many with M-69 jellied gas (napalm), which caused massive firestorms.

In Europe, the same thing was happening. Allied air superiority had all but destroyed the Luftwaffe and bombers were causing massive destruction—including the almost complete destruction of the German city of Dresden on February 13–15, 1945.

The firebombings were accomplished by dropping the napalm, followed by fire sticks to ignite it. The resulting blazes would create a self-sustaining firestorm with temperatures as high as 1,500° C.

In Dresden, as many as 100,000 died. The same number perished in the Japanese capital of Tokyo on March 13, 1945, where the crowded wooden buildings burned so hot that the river that flowed through the area boiled dry.

B-29 SUPERFORTRESS

The plane most responsible for ending World War II in the Pacific was the Boeing B-29 Superfortress. Research and development for the United States' best strategic bomber began in 1937.

The first definitive design came about in 1940, and the first prototypes were ordered to be built by Boeing in 1942. The prototype first flew on September 21, 1942. Fourteen pre-series models were built. These were known as YB-29s.

The USAAF was so pleased with the models that it put in an order for 1,500 more. This was so many that Boeing couldn't handle all of the production alone, so some models were built by Bell Aircraft and others by the Glenn L. Martin Company. Production began in 1943.

The first B-29s arrived in India and China to fight the Japanese during the spring of 1944. Bombing missions over Japan started in June 1944 and continued through the end of the war. The B-29 was, up to that time, by far the most expensive warplane ever built. Each plane cost $600,000, three times as much as the B-17, the previous record holder. In all, 3,970 B-29s were built—but by far the most famous of these were known as *Enola Gay* and *Bockscar*, the two Superfortresses that dropped atomic bombs on Hiroshima and Nagasaki.

A long chain of circumstances culminated in *Enola Gay*'s historic mission. As we've seen, the bombing of Japan had grown increasingly vicious, as the United States desperately tried to break Japan's morale and convince its leaders that surrender was their only choice. The first air raids were carried out against the home isles by the carrier-based U.S. bombers. Later, Chinese airfields served as staging areas for bomber attacks upon Japan. By the summer of 1944, B-29 airfields were built on Tinian Island, in the Marianas. Raids against Japan revealed the weakness of the army's doctrine of daylight high-altitude "precision" bombing against enemy targets. Simply put, the bombs were not hitting their targets.

Strategic airpower calls for destroying the enemy's ability to make war by eliminating the "sinews of war"—that is, factories, bridges, ports, railroads, and so on. High-altitude bombing couldn't do the job. There were alternatives. Gen. Curtis LeMay commanded a B-29 fire raid against the Japanese-occupied Chinese port of Hangchow. Incendiary bombs turned the target into an inferno.

When the failure of precision bombing against Japanese industry reached the crisis point, LeMay was tabbed to get results. LeMay changed tactics. He switched the missions to low-level night bombing in March 1945. The B-29s were stripped of their defensive weapons, so that they would be able to carry more bombs and fuel. LeMay gambled that Japanese antiaircraft fire, set to counter high-altitude bombers, would be unable to hit the bombers when they came in low during a surprise attack.

He was right. On March 29, 282 B-29s dropped 2,000 tons of M-69 jellied gas incendiaries on Tokyo, reprising the Dresden firestorm, gutting the heart of the city, and leaving many thousands dead. The new pattern was set. In the following months, city after Japanese city would be reduced to scorched ruins.

The B-29 had a 141-foot, 3-inch wingspan. It was 99 feet long and had a range of 6,700 miles. It could carry 10 tons of bombs. Its 12-man crew consisted of the pilot, copilot, bombardier, flight engineer, assistant engineer, navigator, radio operator, radar operator, radar countermeasures officer, electronics test officer, weaponer, and tail gunner.

Reasons for Using the Bomb

The Japanese believed in *bushido*, which means fighting to the death. President Truman took that into consideration when he decided to use the atomic bomb against Japanese cities. The alternative was the continued bombing of Japanese cities and the invasion by U.S. troops of mainland Japan, with possibly 1,000,000 American casualties as a result.

The Allies' ultimatum, the Potsdam Declaration of July 26, 1945, demanded Japan's unconditional surrender, threatening "prompt and utter destruction" should Japan refuse. The ultimatum was rejected by the war group of generals Anami, Umezu, and Tyoda—along with Premier Susuki. It was considered an insult to *kokutai*, the mystic national essence. Japan would fight on.

Gen. Curtis LeMay suggested using a single plane to deliver the bomb upon Hiroshima, the city chosen as the site of the first atomic attack. A large flight would attract attention, LeMay pointed out. A single plane, on the other hand, would be mistaken for a weather or reconnaissance flight, which were being flown daily over Japan by the 20th Air Force.

The 509th Composite Group was formed in 1945 with 1,767 men and a single combat squadron, the 393rd Bombardment Squadron. The men were kept isolated on Tinian's North Field, where—starting in May 1945—they trained in 15 specially modified B-29s. One of the maneuvers the pilots practiced again and again was a steep diving turn of 158°, enabling the plane to travel eight miles in 42 seconds.

LeMay, meeting with Group commander Paul W. Tibbets to finalize personnel for the big mission, said, "I want the best crew you've got …

and that doesn't necessarily mean you." Tibbets thought otherwise and picked himself to lead the mission.

On July 16, during the Potsdam conference, Truman was notified that the United States had successfully detonated an A-bomb at Trinity, New Mexico. On July 26, last day of the conference, USS *Indianapolis* delivered bomb materials, including radioactive U-235, to Tinian. (The *Indianapolis* was torpedoed and lost 4 days later, losing all but 316 of its 1,916-man crew.)

The Story of the *Enola Gay*

In the early morning hours of August 6, 1945, on a Pacific island in the Marianas, the heavily laden B-29 Superfortress named *Enola Gay* lumbered down a runway, struggling to take off. Crosswinds and heavy-loaded B-29s made the site hazardous. Four B-29s had crashed in succession the previous night while trying to take off with similar combat weights.

Enola Gay must not fail. In her belly was an atomic bomb. The pilot was Col. Paul W. Tibbets, commander of the 509th Composite Group, the Army Air Force's atomic bomber wing. The copilot was Capt. Robert A. Lewis. The plane had a specially modified bomb bay to accommodate "Little Boy," as the uranium-gun type atomic weapon was familiarly known.

LITTLE BOY SPECIFICATIONS

Little Boy was 120 inches long and 28 inches in diameter, and weighed 9,700 pounds. Outwardly, it resembled a standard-issue aerial bomb. If it worked as expected, it would yield an explosive blast equivalent to 20,000 tons of TNT.

The bomb would not be fully armed until the plane was in the air so there would be no atomic explosion should the plane crash upon takeoff. The plane rolled along the runway at 180 mph, seeming earthbound to the white-knuckled observers in the air control tower. A witness, Gen. Thomas Ferrell, later recalled, "I never saw a plane use that much runway. I thought Tibbets was never going to pull it off." There was only a few feet of runway to spare when the *Enola Gay* became airborne at 2:45 A.M.

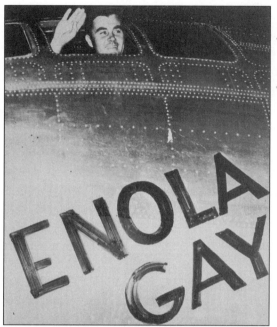

Military Technical Journal

*Col. Paul Tibbets waves goodbye from the cockpit of the
Enola Gay, the B-29 that dropped the bomb on
Hiroshima.*

It was not literally a one-plane mission, as LeMay had suggested, however. Two other planes were on the mission, and these were filled with sci-
entific observers and monitoring devices. The accompanying aircraft were
344-27291, piloted by Capt. George W. Marquardt; and a plane named
Great Artiste, piloted by Maj. Charles Sweeny, who three days later would
be the pilot of *Bockscar*, the B-29 that dropped the final bomb of the war
on Nagasaki.

As the *Enola Gay* began its final run-up to the target, the crew donned
special arc-welder's type goggles—all but the pilot, copilot, and bombardier Maj. Thomas Ferebee.

In the plane's nose, Ferebee handled the delicate task of keying in the
Norden bombsight (see Chapter 6). The Norden worked by literally taking over the plane, via the intermediary Minneapolis-Honeywell C-1
autopilot, which transformed every turn of the bombsight's knobs into
corresponding responses from the B-29's control surfaces.

It was a mathematical operation: The bombardier directed aircraft and bomb to the point in the sky from which the bomb must hit the target. The rest was done by the bombsight's mechanical analog computer.

The plane would be on autopilot during the final two-minute run. Ferebee adjusted the crosshairs over the target site, the Aioi Bridge, over the Ota River. The final approach came at 8:09 A.M., Hiroshima time.

At 8:13 plus thirty seconds, Tibbets turned control over to Ferebee's Norden.

The bombing alert radio-tone sounded through the intercom. The plane was 6 miles up, with an airspeed of 328 mph. When the plane reached the right spot, the Norden mechanism automatically released the bomb.

In a sense, the first A-bomb attack was launched by a machine. Auto-drop occurred at 8:15, plus 17 seconds. Radio tone stopped. The shackles opened, and the bomb dropped bottom first, flipped, and fell nose down. Forty-three seconds later, it exploded. The bomb detonated in midair and the resulting blast, which destroyed the city of Hiroshima, caused a mushroom cloud that rose 50,000 feet into the air. When the dust cleared, Hiroshima was gone. A few days later a second bomb was dropped on the medium-size Japanese city of Nagasaki. The Japanese, facing extinction, surrendered.

B-32 DOMINATOR

The least remembered of the U.S. bombers during World War II was the B-32 Dominator. And there was a good reason for this: Its history was problem-filled. One hundred fifteen Dominators were used by the USAAF. One more problem and it might have missed the war altogether. As it was, it saw action only during the last days of the war against Japan, and its use was quickly discontinued when the war ended. The remarkable thing is, considering how long it took to actually see action, when it finally got its chance it stepped up to the plate. Rugged and dependable, it fought and won the final aerial battle of the Second World War.

The plane was originally intended to be a sister bomber to the B-29. It originated on January 29, 1940, when "Request for Data R 40B" was circulated among America's plane-building defense contractors.

Consolidated, builder of the B-24, won the contract with its XB-32 design.

XB-32 first rolled off the San Diego assembly line on September 1, 1942, and flew for the first time on September 7. There were difficulties during the flight tests, during which time the plane was given the optimistic nickname "Dominator." Problems included a malfunctioning rudder, an inadequate tail, high flight-deck noise levels, poorly sited instruments and controls, and, most serious, severe engine nacelle design deficiencies that resulted in power plant fires. It would be the spring of 1945 before the plane would be ready to see action.

WAR SKIES GROW LESS CROWDED

The number of fighter planes that can go into combat together has decreased over the years. The faster and more powerful a fighter is, the fewer of them can go on a mission together. All that speed and power increases the risk of friendly aircraft colliding with one another.

That's why, during World War I, the entire sky over France could be filled with planes, circling each other wildly, looking for a clear shot at one another. By World War II, no more than a squadron went up at once. By the Korean War, and the introduction of jet aircraft, the number of fighters that flew together into combat was rarely greater than four.

B-32s: First Real Bombing Mission

On May 29, 1945, three B-32s struck out against the Japanese for the first time, taking off from Clark Field in the Philippines and bombing a supply depot on the island of Luzon. The mission was not flawless. Problems started right away. One of the three B-32s had trouble on the runway and aborted upon takeoff. The other two planes, which were nicknamed *Hobo Queen II* and *Lady is Fresh*, dropped their bombs from 10,000 feet, took photos to verify they had hit their targets, and returned to Clark Field.

Forty-eight hours later the B-32s were moved to the 386th's home base at Floridablanca, Luzon. On June 12 all three B-32s took off for a bombing mission. Between June 13 and June 25 nine more missions were flown, for a total of 11. The missions struck again at Luzon, and also at Japanese military sites in Formosa and against Japanese shipping in the South

China Sea. The only opposition the B-32s faced was over Formosa, where they encountered some flak but were not hit. The success of the combat test led USAAF headquarters to move ahead with plans to convert the entire 386th Bomber Squadron to B-32s.

Crew conversion training was speeded up, and the 386th was scheduled to get six more B-32s through July and August. The 312th Group was to move to Okinawa as soon as the 386th's conversion was completed, and then participate in the final aerial offensive against Japan. (Although the war was almost over, the USAAF could not assume that was the case. As we've seen, it was the atomic bomb that brought an end to hostilities with Japan. But the success of the bomb could not be assumed, and an invasion, with its accompanying bombardments, would have been the alternative had the atom bomb been a failure.)

The personnel of both the B-32 test contingent and the 386th BS spent most of July 1945 preparing for the move to Okinawa. The atomic bombing of Hiroshima followed on August 6, but no immediate surrender from Japan came. On August 9, Nagasaki was also destroyed, but there was still no immediate surrender. So the B-32s were moved to Okinawa as scheduled. Four of the six promised B-32s were delivered to the 386th on August 12. The fifth showed up the next day, and the sixth was so delayed that it missed the war and flew no missions.

On the night of August 14–15, one B-32 attacked a small ship during a sweep of the South China Sea, and a second vessel was sunk during a two-plane sweep on August 15. That evening two Dominators set out to patrol over Korea and Honshu but were recalled when the Japanese agreed to an official cease-fire. The B-32s did not stay on the ground for long, however, for FEAF directed the 386th BS to conduct daylight reconnaissance missions over Tokyo to monitor the cease-fire.

The first of these reconnaissance flights was flown by *Hobo Queen II* and another Dominator on August 16. The planes made their photo runs and returned without incident. The next day things did not go as well. *Hobo Queen II* and two other Dominators again flew over Tokyo. This time the planes were fired upon by Japanese fighter planes and took several hits. Things got worse on August 18, when the B-32s were involved in the final air battle of the war. *Hobo Queen II* and one other Dominator flew over

Tokyo and were again attacked by Japanese fighter planes. Several of the fighters were shot down but the unnamed B-32 was shot up. One of her crew was killed and two were wounded.

The Dominator had one more mission to fly, however—and once again it would be tragedy marred. On August 28, 1945, a Dominator lost an engine on takeoff, skidded off the runway, exploded, and caught fire. All 13 aboard died. Not a single B-32 was preserved for posterity. The only known remaining B-32 artifacts are a nose turret belonging to the National Air and Space Museum, another on display in a Minnesota museum, an instrument panel held by a private collector, and a single wing panel used as a monument to aviation pioneer John J. Montgomery in San Diego.

CHAPTER 8

THE KOREAN WAR

In June 1950, the forces of Communist North Korea invaded democratic South Korea in an attempt to unify the Korean peninsula by force. The United Nations (UN) Security Council ruled that the North was the aggressor. A UN force was raised. It was composed of U.S. and allied troops and was commanded by Gen. Douglas MacArthur.

During the next three years, the front line moved back and forth, from South Korea into North Korea. At first Chinese and North Korean forces pushed into South Korea. Eventually, the battle lines stabilized at the 38th parallel. After three years of fighting, the border was reestablished where it had been before hostilities began and, in 1953, the war was called a draw.

In this chapter, we will be hearing from a few American pilots, who experienced warfare over Korea firsthand. We'll also look at the war's primary dogfight, that of the U.S. F-86 versus the Soviet-built MiG-15. We'll then take a detailed examination of the U.S. night bomber used over North Korea, the B-26 Invader.

F-86 SABRE VERSUS THE MIG-15 FAGOT

At the end of WWII, Russian aviation engineers began development of a turbojet-powered fighter. The days of the prop fighter were officially numbered. The Mikoyan-Gurevich (MiG) Design Bureau was assigned responsibility to produce a new generation of turbojet-powered aircraft, beginning with a single-seat fighter.

During WWII, German aviation engineers recognized that a swept-wing design was more effective for high-performance turbojet aircraft. Soviet army troops captured German Messerschmitt ME-262 twin-engine turbojet fighters, along with engines, aircraft design specifications, German aviation engineers, and technicians. However, the ME-262's power plant, the Junkers Jumo 004b axial flow turbojet engine, did not produce the desired thrust for the new proposed Soviet fighter. Its primary weakness was a low weight-to-thrust ratio.

The first series of Soviet MiG fighters were a transition from WWII piston engine–powered aircraft. Mikoyan-Gurevich Design Bureau was given specific performance guidelines for the high-performance turbojet fighter:

- Operate and be highly maneuverable at high-altitude (minimum of 50,000 feet).

- Operate from short and rough airfields (as the Soviet air force did during WWII).

- Carry heavy armament.

- Remain airborne on internal fuel, for one-hour duration.

Its design was inspired by the German ME-262 and TA-183. The lack of a suitable turbojet engine technology hampered series production of the fighter. But an unusual event, in 1946, an Anglo-Soviet trade agreement, provided the engine for the Soviet air force fighter.

The British Labour government, under an export agreement, shipped 25 Rolls-Royce Nene turbojet engines, blueprints, and specifications to the Soviet Union (without a manufacturing license). One of these engines was installed into the I-130 (first MiG-15 prototype). The I-130 made its first test flight on July 2, 1947. The British-supplied Nene turbojet engine went into series production at Number 45 Production Factory (Moscow), under a designation of RD-45, later upgraded to the RD-45F.

Lt. Col. George A. Larson, USAF (Ret.)

A restored MiG-15 on display at Hickam AFB, Hawaii.

Aerodynamic Changes

I-130 test flights demonstrated that aerodynamic changes to the aircraft were required. These changes included …

- Adding boundary layer fences to the wing.
- Changing the wing shape from anhedral (slightly downward angle of the wing in reference to the level) to dihedral (upward inclination of the wing).
- Shortening the rear fuselage's length.
- Shortening the tailpipe length to fit into the modified rear fuselage.
- Lowering the horizontal tail.
- Modifying the fin and rudder design to swept-back configuration.

The resulting aircraft, S-01 (the final MiG-15 test prototype), flew December 30, 1947, equipped with the more powerful RD-45F engine. By 1950, the MiG-15bis variant was equipped with the 6,614-pound thrust Kilmov VK-1 engine. The S-01's first test flight took place after that of North American Aviation's XP-86 (October 1, 1947). Once introduced into combat during the Korean War, the MiG-15 first was given the code name designation of "Falcon" by the North American Treaty Organization (NATO), and was later changed to "Fagot."

Designed by Spies

Interestingly, recently declassified documents in Moscow revealed the MiG-15's design process was assisted by technical information offered by Soviet spies operating in the United States who provided ...

- Aerodynamics of American turbojets under development.
- Cockpit pressurization systems.
- G-suit designs for pilots (important for pilots in high-speed aerial dogfights).
- Powered flight controls (to overcome high-speed air pressure on control surfaces).

The MiG-15's design resulted in the production of a remarkably advanced turbojet fighter. It was a single-seat day fighter, with wings at 35° swept-back configuration. It had swept-back tail surfaces, a single turbojet engine, a nose air intake for the single engine, a bubble canopy, tricycle landing gear (strong for rough field operations), aft fuselage mounted speed, and air brakes. There was cockpit pressurization, a G-suit air source and attachment for the pilot. There was an ejection seat (taken from the British equipping of their fighters). The craft had small size (making it more difficult to locate when airborne), light weight, and a subsonic airframe.

The First MiG-15 Attack

The MiG-15 first entered combat on October 18, 1950, when six Fagots (flown by Soviet air force pilots) attacked a flight of F-15s near Sinuiju, North Korea, beginning a new phase in aerial combat, turbojet versus turbojet. The MiG-15 was a considerable shock to Far East Air Force (FEAF) pilots and aircrews (especially to the B-29 Superfortress aircrews).

MIG-15 SPECIFICATIONS

Manufacturer: Mikoyan-Gurevich Design Bureau
Wingspan: 33 feet, 1 inch
Length: 36 feet, 4 inches
Tail height: 11 feet, 1¾ inches
Empty weight: 8,320 pounds
Gross weight: 11,268 pounds
Maximum weight: 12,566 pounds
Power plant: One RD-45F 5,005-pound-thrust, single-shaft, centrifugal turbojet engine.
MiG-15bis: One Kilmov VK-1 6,614-pound-thrust turbojet engine.
Maximum speed: 668 mph
Cruising speed: 525 mph
Initial rate of climb: 3,200 feet per minute
Service ceiling: 51,000 feet
Maximum ceiling: 55,000 feet
Internal fuel capacity: 321 imperial gallons
Maximum range on internal fuel: 600 miles
Maximum range with slipper tanks: 885 miles
Electronics: HF radio; homing receiver
Gun sight: Copy of British GGS MK2
Armament: One 37mm cannon mounted on right side of aircraft's nose; one 23mm cannon mounted on left side of aircraft's nose
Added armament: Two underwing hard points, maximum capacity, 1,102 pounds

After the signing of the armistice to the Korean War, a MiG-15 flown by No Kum Sok, North Korean Air Force (NKAF), on September 21, 1953, landed unannounced at K-14 (Kimpo) airfield, near Seoul, South Korea. The aircraft was test flown later at Kadena Air Base, Okinawa, by Chuck Yeager and Tom Collins. Their combined test flight report confirmed what pilots who flew against the MiG-15 reported during after-action combat mission debriefings: The aircraft had a tendency to go into a spin. MiG-15 pilots were told to eject after three spins (because the aircraft would not recover at this point). The Fagot would stall and the pilot had no warning light to provide indication. There were oscillation problems. The aircraft frequently pitched up unexpectedly. It had bad cockpit pressurization. Pilots were warned not to turn on the emergency fuel pump because of problems with fumes igniting and blowing off the tail section. The aircraft also suffered from a slow rate of fire from the cannons, and there was room only for limited cannon ammunition.

Regardless, the MiG-15 was a highly successful fighter, with production in the Soviet Union reaching 7,000 and through licensed production in Czechoslovakia, Poland, Hungary, and the People's Republic of China adding another 8,168, bringing the total production run to 17,616. The MiG-15 equipped more than 30 air forces.

Jumped from Above

On October 18, 1950, a flight of North American F-51 Mustangs were attacking ground targets in northwest North Korea, directed by an airborne liaison aircraft, when they were jumped from above by six sweptwing turbojet fighters, later identified by FEAF intelligence as MiG-15s.

At this point in the air war, FEAF F-80Cs and Republic Aviation F-84E Thunderjets, among the first U.S. jets to be used in combat, were below the performance demonstrated by the MiG-15, with the primary effect that the FEAF Bomber Command's Boeing B-29 Superfortress medium bomber operations had to be restricted. The B-29s could no longer operate whenever and wherever they wanted over North Korea, even with much close-in fighter support (F-80C and F-84E). The North American F-86 Sabres (which we'll be discussing later) provided aerial counter air cover in front of the B-29 bomber stream as well as high-level close air patrol (CAP) over the B-29s.

Even with this coordinated air cover, a determined attack by large numbers of MiG-15s could get through to the bombers. With the introduction of the MiG-15 into the air equation over North Korea, the USAF began shipping F-86s to air bases in South Korea, although in nowhere near the numbers to match the quantities of MiG-15s appearing at air bases in Manchuria.

The Last Link

According to NASA historian Dr. Michael H. Gorn, the F-86 Sabre was the last link between WWII and the modern air force turbojet fighters.

It brought up to date the piston-powered North American Aviation P-51 Mustang. The F-86 began as a day fighter with a straight-wing configuration.

North American engineers conducted wind tunnel tests on the straight wing design that revealed the wing was not practical. At the same time, an examination of the WWII German swept-wing ME-262 indicated the effects of air compressibility at high Mach levels was reduced. North American engineers selected a 35° swept wing, which allowed a 670 mph speed. Still, there were problems with instability.

The F-86 went into production prior to the instability problems being satisfactorily solved, but proved itself in combat against the MiG-15. The F-86 suffered buffeting in transonic speeds, resulting in loss of elevator control as well as pitch-up (nose control problems). Engineers at Langley AFB suggested a means to maintain elevator control, by allowing the horizontal stabilizer to move freely. Later, the F-86D had an all-moveable horizontal stabilizer. Further testing and use indicated this was positioned too high in relationship to the fuselage, so it was set lower. The tendency to pitch up was related to the swept-wing configuration. A series of wing fences and leading-edge wing slats installed on the wings improved control. This eventually led to a full-length leading-edge slat system.

The F-86 had a maximum service ceiling of 51,000 feet with the MiG-15 able to climb up to 55,000 feet (allowing it to dive down from altitude on FEAF aircraft). The MiG-15 possessed a greater engine thrust and acceleration than the F-86 (corrected by following Sabre variants). The MiG-15 had an initial higher rate-of-climb and more firepower with its three cannons. But at high Mach levels (as initial flight tests revealed on the F-86), the MiG-15 was susceptible to buffeting and loss of elevator control.

General Brown's Tale

According to Lt. Gen. William E. Brown Jr., USAF (Ret.)—who flew 125 combat missions in Korea in the F-86 and was assigned to the 4th Fighter-Interceptor Wing, speaking at the Korean War Air Power Symposium— "I was a 24-year-old second lieutenant in 1951. Basic flying school was completed in propeller aircraft. I went to Williams AFB for 20 hours of transition flying in the F-80. I learned to use the aircraft's speed brakes—which helped slow it down. We were taught to use the aircraft's entire flight envelope, from the slowest to the highest. Then I went on to Nellis AFB for combat training in the F-80. I would say this training was divided into three distinct areas.

"First, we were given proficiency in using the extreme edges of the envelope. These were defined as fighter pilot problem areas—either at the fastest or slowest speed.

"Second: flying in formation. This consisted of tactical formation flying, in finger-four tip formation, so we had to be a wingman—told and trained never to lose sight of our leader. This was taught as an offensive formation. The leader stalked, and it was the wingman's obligation to fly, sticking with the leader, while constantly looking to the rear to be certain an enemy did not attack from this position. We were trained to stay with the leader, no matter what.

"Third: releasing weapons and air-to-air combat. To hone our skills, another F-80 towed a cloth target sleeve, usually following a precise route, and we fired colored .50 caliber machine gun bullets so once the sleeve was on the ground the number of hits by the various color bullets could be counted and scored. This was necessary to prepare us for aerial combat. We also trained in air-to-ground weaponry, using guns, 2.75-inch unguided rockets, as well as skip-bombing."

Soviet air force (including North Korea Air Force [NKAF] and Communist Chinese Air Force [CCAF]) pilots used the MiG-15's performance in altitude to their advantage, combined (whenever possible) with the safe sanctuary of Manchurian air space. MiG-15 pilots took off from the various Manchurian air bases and climbed to maximum altitude, directed to FEAF formations by ground radar operators (the primary target FEAF Bomber Command B-29s and escorting fighters). They would dive at the B-29 formations from above, continuing on through those formations, or engaging fighters (usually selecting the most favorable tactical situation from which to engage). Otherwise, they avoided air-to-air combat, and turned toward the Yalu River at maximum speed.

Yet the F-86 pilots prevailed, says Brown: "Without exception, the F-86 aces were trained to be Tigers! But, more importantly, they had exceptional eyesight, seeing the enemy first, and went on the offensive. These pilots were filled with an exceptional urge for aerial combat, which they sought out. They were thrilled to be in combat against the enemy. These pilots aggressively flew to the sounds of the guns!"

Says Brown: "I was wingman to Major Frederick 'Boots' Bleese [a double ace, signifying ten kills]. As his wingman, I watched him latch on to [on one combat sortie] a MiG-15 with a very talented and apparently experienced pilot, then stayed with him during exaggerated rolls, twists, dives, climbs, eventually hitting the enemy aircraft's wing. The MiG-15 then began to lose altitude, dropping into a rolling dive [apparently out of control]. However, this did not convince Major Bleese, who took up a wide circling descent around the dropping MiG-15, always watching for any change, and at an altitude of 10,000 feet, the MiG-15 pilot leveled out. Major Bleese was faster than the MiG-15 pilot. He positioned himself behind the aircraft, and shot down the MiG-15. This was the special tactics of an aggressive pilot."

Lieutenant Colonel Abbott's Tale

Lt. Col. Dean E. Abbott—who during the Korean War was assigned to "D" Flight, 39th Fighter-Interceptor Squadron—was wingman for Capt. Joseph McConnell, including the mission flown on May 18, 1953, during which McConnell became a triple ace.

Speaking at the Korean War Air Power Symposium, Abbott said: "In the USAF, I was doing exactly what I wanted, an F-86 fighter pilot assigned to the 51st Fighter-Interceptor Wing at K-13 (Suwon Air Base), 'D' Flight, with Capt. Joseph McConnell. Capt. McConnell had exceptional eyesight. At this time, we were flying the F-86F. On one very memorable sortie, we spotted two MiG-15s going across the Yalu River. We chased them. We could hear them on the radio calling for help. I was on McConnell's right wing, as he raised his nose to fire at the lead MiG-15, hitting him. I did the same, but missed! Help then showed up for the two MiG-15s. There must have been 30 MiG-15s, and McConnell said: 'We got them all to ourselves!' Four MiG-15s flew underneath and we turned, four more behind. McConnell shot down his fourteenth MiG-15. We broke again, with McConnell shooting down number 15 (making him a triple ace). The MiG-15s were all over us! With so many, they got in each other's way. By now, we were almost out of fuel and we broke off the engagement, heading for home. As soon as I landed, my engine flamed out."

Even with the large numbers of MiG-15s across the Yalu River in Manchuria, the Communist (CCAF and NKAF) pilots could not win aerial superiority over FEAF F-86s. There were three reasons:

- Soviet pilots were rotated home as complete units, without leaving experienced pilots behind to teach new pilots (interestingly, a policy that the CCAF also followed with its fighter squadrons).

- CCAF and NKAF pilots demonstrated poor flying skills, although there were many individual exceptions.

- The political decision not to widen the air war, not wanting to risk an air attack by the FEAF on Manchurian air bases.

F-86A SABRE SPECIFICATIONS AND PERFORMANCE

Wingspan: 39 feet, 1 inch
Length: 37 feet, 6 inches
Tail height: 14 feet, 8 inches
Wing area: 288 square feet
Power plant: One General Electric-5,200-pound-thrust J-47 turbojet engine
Maximum speed: 685 mph
Cruising speed: 540 mph
Range on internal fuel: 920 miles
Range with drop tanks: 1,200 miles
Service ceiling: 49,000 feet
Maximum ceiling: 51,000 feet
Initial rate of climb: 9,300 feet per minute
Empty weight: 10,600 pounds
Maximum weight: 13,791 pounds
Armament: Six .50 caliber machine guns
Ground attack: Eight 5-inch unguided rockets, or 2,000 pounds of conventional bombs
Production totals: More than 9,000

Kill Ratio

There are various estimates as to the F-86 versus MiG-15 success rate in the Korean War (kill ratio). The FEAF shot down about 800 MiG-15s, and lost about 80 craft in return—for an approximate kill ratio of ten to one. The success of the FEAF in Korea was remarkable.

Gen. Matthew B. Ridgeway best commented on this success: "No one who fought on the ground would ever be tempted to belittle the accomplishments of our air forces there. Not only did airpower save us from disaster, but without it the mission of the United Nations' forces could not have been accomplished."

THE DOUGLAS B-26 INVADER: NIGHT BOMBER OF THE KOREAN AIR WAR

We've discussed the fighter versus fighter situation over Korean skies. Now let's talk about bombers.

The Korean War has been referred to as the "Forgotten War." Little is remembered, for example, about the night air war fought by Far East Air Force (FEAF) aircraft over South and North Korea. The primary night bombing and attack intruder aircraft used was the Douglas B-26 Invader.

The B-26 was pressed into combat service and used in an effort to slow the transport of military supplies and replacement troops by North Korea (later, by Chinese Communist military units) to the front lines. The primary targets were Communist locomotives and railroad cars, railroad tracks (including the bridges over which Communist trains and trucks crossed moving to the front lines), and trucks. It was extremely dangerous for Communist troops to move supplies on the roads during daylight, subject to the superiority of the UN airpower with the number of aircraft that could rapidly be vectored to targets of opportunity. Communist troops quickly learned to dig into the hills, hiding supply dumps and troops from the prowling UN aircraft.

Wanted: A New Medium Bomber

The story of the B-26 Invader aircraft, used in the air war over Korea, begins in the fall of 1940 when the USAAF requested a design for a new medium bomber to replace the existing twin-engine North American B-25

Mitchell, Douglas A-20 Havoc, and Martin B-26 Marauder. (The apparent double designation of the B-26 ended after the Marauder was dropped from active inventory and the Invader replaced it in June of 1948, with the A-26B becoming the B-26B and the A-26C becoming the B-26C.)

In 1939, the USAAC published a design requirement for a low-level medium bomber, which was won by the Douglas Aircraft Company, with its A-20, nicknamed the Havoc. By the time production ended on September 20, 1944, the Douglas Aircraft Company had built 7,385 aircraft. This was a successful design, meeting a requirement for a medium bomber to supplement the heavier B-24 and B-17 strategic bombing operations by the 8th Air Force in Europe.

The Douglas Aircraft Company modified its A-20 and developed a prototype, with the designation of the XA-26 Invader. Design work began during January 1941, with advanced military capabilities built into the aircraft. The aircraft had a mid-mounted wing, with a laminar flow aerofoil, fitted with electrically operated double-slotted flaps. It was powered by two 2,000-horsepower Pratt & Whitney R-2800-77 air-cooled radial engines.

The aircraft was designed to carry an impressive amount of armament: an internal bomb bay able to hold a maximum of 4,000 pounds of bombs or two torpedoes (in a side-by-side configuration), and external under-the-wing hard-mounted ordnance racks. Two .50 caliber machine guns were mounted in remotely controlled dorsal and ventral turrets. Both guns were operated by a gunner, located behind the bomb bay. One version would be a solid nose, two-seat fighter with forward firing .50 caliber machine guns and Air Intercept (AI) radar, with the model referred to as the XA-26A-DE.

The prototype's first test flight was on July 10, 1942. Test flights indicated the aircraft's performance and handling exceeded design specifications. However, a series of changes were made on follow-on production aircraft. Engine cooling was improved by removing the propeller spinner from each engine. Two forward-firing .50 caliber machine guns were mounted on the left side of the nose. The two twin .50 caliber machine gun turrets could be locked into the forward-firing position to increase the aircraft's firepower. Bomb-bay capacity was reduced to 3,000 pounds, but compensated for by the addition of two 500-pound bomb capacity racks under each wing (a total of 2,000 pounds).

The production variant consisted of two types, either a solid or transparent nose. The A-26B was the basic solid-nose variant.

A total of 1,150 A-26Bs were built at the Long Beach, California, plant with 205 produced at the Tulsa, Oklahoma, plant. The decision was made by Douglas executives to shift all Invader production at the Tulsa, Oklahoma, plant to that of the A-26C beginning in January 1945.

DOUGLAS A-26B INVADER SPECIFICATIONS

Designation changed to B-26B during the Korean War.

Wingspan: 70 feet

Wing area: 540 square feet

Length: 50 feet, 8 inches

Tail height: 18 feet, 6 inches

Power plant: Two 2,000-horsepower Pratt & Whitney R-2800-79 air-cooled radial engines. Note: With water injection (full-power takeoff setting for maximum weight), power increased to 2,350 horsepower.

Maximum speed: 355 mph

Cruising speed: 284 mph

Maximum range: 3,200 miles

Combat range: 1,400 miles (with 4,000 pounds of bombs)

Empty weight: 22,362 pounds

Maximum weight: 26,000 pounds

Combat weight: 41,800 pounds

Service ceiling: 31,300 feet

Armament: Eight forward-firing .50 caliber machine guns (solid-nose variant) mounted in two parallel vertical rows of four each; three .50 caliber machine guns mounted in each outer wing panel, outboard of each engine (total of six guns); two .50 caliber machine guns in a dorsal turret, remotely controlled; two .50 caliber machine guns in ventral turret, remotely controlled

Bomb load: 4,000 pounds of bombs in an internal bomb bay; also hard points on each wing for a maximum 1,000-pound bomb per hard point.

Crew: Pilot, navigator, bombardier, gunner (depending on the mission flown)

Designation: Light bomber

Nickname: Invader

Number built: Long Beach, California: 1,150; Tulsa, Oklahoma: 205

The variant with a transparent nose was designated the A-26C, with 1,086 built at the Tulsa, Oklahoma, plant and five development aircraft built at the Long Beach, California, plant. The A-26C had a transparent nose (allowing better forward vision and improved bombing accuracy), dual-flight controls for the navigator/bombardier (referred to as the second pilot), with the eight nose guns removed. The primary resulting variant is the A-26C-30-DT.

Both the B-26B and B-26C were used over Korea. On June 25, 1950, the FEAF had two squadrons of B-26s, assigned to the 3rd Bomb Group, operating from Iwakuni Air Base, Japan. By November 1950, B-26 strength increased with the arrival in the Far East of the 452nd Bomb Group based at Itazuke Air Base, Japan. It did not take long for the B-26s to be committed to the defense of South Korea. B-26s from the 8th Bomb Squadron were assigned to provide continuous air cover for a sea evacuation of U.S. citizens from Seoul before the city was captured by the advancing NKPA, with evacuations beginning on June 27, 1950. Aircrews from the 8th Bomb Squadron maintained air cover over the converted evacuation ship Reinholte as it sailed for Japan.

Lieutenant General Greenleaf's Tale

Lt. Gen. Abbot Greenleaf, USAF (Ret.) flew B-26s during the Korean War. He was assigned to the 452nd Bomb Group, at K-9 (Pusan) Air Base, South Korea.

He says, "I flew B-26s from the summer of 1951 to May 1952. Initially, B-26 air attacks were conducted in daylight, but I was switched to night-intruder missions, flying these for a period of 10 months. Our secondary mission was bombardment of bridges, airfields, or designated military facilities. Initially, the 3rd Bomb Wing did not have enough aircrews or support personnel to fill out one of our three squadrons.

"By May 1952, we were filled up. The attrition in the 3rd Bomb Wing was high. There was no Escape and Evaluation (referred to as E & E) reports from those who did manage to escape capture. It was considered too classified to provide to the aircrews as later given to the aircrews in the last part of the war.

"When we began night-intruder operations, we had no documentation for night operations until receiving some from the British War Records Office in London, which sent a copy to the 3rd Bomb Group. We also modified our B-26s with the British M-5 bomb release instead of using the Norden bombsight. This improved bombing accuracy when the pilot only had a short time to line up on a ground target.

"It is interesting to note, when operating out of K-9 (Pusan East) Air Base, Korea, our commander frequently improvised operational tactics to meet tactical contingencies. Marine Corps aircraft were unable to suppress Communist flak guns. We carried more firepower: bombs, fourteen 5-inch unguided rockets, six Mark-5 flares, eight to sixteen .50 caliber machine guns. We got 20mm cannon for our aircraft from the U.S. Marine Corps and they kept us supplied with ammunition.

"We modified our radios with Marine Corps radio crystals so we could talk to the Marine Corps ground troops. Both those on the ground and in the B-26s could talk to each other. In unique coordination, U.S. Navy B-24s dropped flares at night, our B-26s attacked the Communist flak batteries, while U.S. Marine Corps aircraft shot up any trains caught moving out in the open. This worked good for six to eight months until we were told by 5th Air Force Command to stop this type of unauthorized cooperation. But, it was very effective innovation, and everyone was willing to make it work."

Colonel Harris's Tale

Col. John W. Harris, USAF (Ret.) was assigned to the 13th Bomb Squadron, Kunsan Air Base, and flew the B-26. He says, "The Douglas B-26 was not designed as a night attack airplane. It was well suited for the job in Korea, but such things as the instrument lights were really bad. There was one World War II–type fluorescent light on the glare shield and one on the control column that caused the instruments to glow. When they worked properly—and the rheostats (which regulate currents with variable resistances) actually rheostatted—they weren't too bad.

"Typically, they would rotate around from vibration, such as on takeoff or when firing the nose guns. The covers would fall off, and leave your eyeball vibrating and half-blind for a few minutes. The cover on the light held a filter that removed most of the visible light. Without it, there was a bright purplish light that was particularly hard on your night vision.

"Takeoff was probably the worst time. With the short runway (4,200 feet) at Kunsan Air Base, South Korea, everything was critical, and to suddenly have the lights point somewhere else, especially right into your eyes, or turn off just as you were trying to get the overloaded monster into the air, was a real thrill. Once, both lights went out on takeoff at the most critical time and the navigator saved the day with his flashlight. I didn't have to ask. The flashlight just came on instantly. It was so dark it probably would have been impossible to see."

Training in Enemy Territory

Flying night missions over Korea involved some special horrors for the normal pilot. Everything he had ever learned about flying at night told him to keep sufficient altitude to clear all terrain for a great distance around. You can't see, so you have to stay high enough so you won't hit the ground.

The only flat ground in Korea, except for some small exceptions, was along the coast, and there wasn't much even there. Dive-bombing and strafing had to be done at low altitude if you expected any results other than frightening the enemy. At least, the mountains made the roads easier to find. These were mostly down in the valleys.

Says Harris: "Nobody liked working under flares. I had my switches all set up and was ready to go. We spotted a vehicle's headlights. It was still light enough to see the big terrain features, hills, coastline, and roads. It was wide open and my approach would be to seaward with no obstructions.

"I started to dive from about 8,500 feet with the power back, open the bomb bay early to increase drag, and keep speed in the proper range over the target because I thought the range was great. Apparently, it was short. It sure looked different under those conditions. *Different* probably isn't the right word, because I had never done it before. The armor-piercing incendiaries tore up the rice paddy right where the pip (a gunnery term indicating a small hole in the reticle of an optical sight or computing sight) said. What to do? I aimed lower and missed again, short.

"All of a sudden I realized I was out of time and in very close to the vehicle. I pulled up hard and thought, maybe this 500-pound bomb will get him and salvage the pass and my ego.

"Too late, I realized minimum drop altitude was a long way above me. While all puckered up, waiting for the explosion to blow the airplane out from under me, I became aware of a great, bright light behind me. I hadn't changed my bombs/rockets switch to bombs (the flares were on the rocket rails). The flare was a big relief to me and, I'll bet, the Communist truck driver, too.

"Sometime later I found out that maximum release airspeed for the flares was about 190 mph. We were doing about 300 mph. It should have shredded the flare's parachute, but it didn't. Embarrassing! Nobody hurt. This is still training, but in enemy territory."

Remarkable, but Not Perfect

The B-26 night attacks never completely stopped the flow of supplies to Communist front-line troop positions. A report completed by the FEAF in September 1952 said that the B-26 Wings were attempting to develop effective night attacks, without possessing any effective means of assessing the results of their missions.

Harris says, "The B-26 aircrews in the Korean War performed remarkably, but at great cost, losing 210 aircraft. B-26 squadrons contributed significantly to the air war during the Korean War, especially the night-intruder missions, taking away the Communists' complete freedom of movement at night, although not stopping the flow of supplies, which often were carried on the backs of Communist troops to the front lines."

CESSNA L-19 BIRD DOG

The Cessna L-19 Bird Dog was a civilian light plane, a four-seater called the Cessna 170, converted to military use in 1950, just in time to see service in Korea. During the conversion, it was given a larger power plant, and its power output was increased from 145 to 213 horsepower.

The original defense contract with Cessna called for 418 aircraft. (Eventually, more than 3,400 would be built.) The plane now only held two passengers and was nicknamed the Bird Dog. The back of the plane was redesigned for the military to provide the pilot with a better rearward view.

To accomplish this a see-through panel was placed in the wing. So that a stretcher could fit inside, the door was widened. The plane was used for artillery-spotting in Korea and again in Vietnam until it was replaced by the OV-10 Bronco.

This pattern would be repeated during the Vietnam War, where the Communist North Vietnamese and their allies were always able to supply their troops operating in South Vietnam.

B-26 aircrews flew more than 60,000 combat sorties during the Korean War, dropping approximately 112,000 tons of bombs, nearly equaling the 168,000 tons of bombs dropped by the larger medium bombers, the FEAF Bomber Command's B-29s. Interestingly, a B-26 dropped the last bombs in the Korean War, in a radar-guided close-air-support mission. Also, after this mission, an RB-26 from the 67th Tactical Reconnaissance Wing completed the final combat sortie over North Korea.

This was not the last war for the B-26. It served in the Vietnam War as well.

CHAPTER 9

THE COLD WAR

Within two years of the end of World War II, America found itself in a "Cold War," a long struggle for control of the world between democratic nations and those under communist rule. The army during this time served to stop the Communists from expanding their territory. The Korean Conflict (see Chapter 8) was one such struggle.

In this chapter, we cover the development of warplanes from different nations during the period from the end of the Korean Conflict to the beginning of American involvement in Vietnam.

1950s WARPLANES: AN OVERVIEW

British aviation got off to a strong post–World War II start with such jets as the Gloster Meteor and the de Havilland Vampire. After a shaky start, the Hawker Hunter developed into a superior fighter that flew in Korea and became a staple export for more than 20 years. The Canberra, Britain's first jet bomber, also enjoyed notable success. But a succession of Labour governments slashed funding, crippling the British aerospace industry and fizzling away a promising opportunity to remain in the forefront of military aviation.

The Nazis had condemned French aviation engineer Marcel Dassault (originally named Marcel Bloch) to death for refusing to collaborate, but Allied troops liberated his concentration camp before the sentence could be carried out. Dassault survived to become the leader of French postwar aviation and jet technology. In 1948, Dassault smuggled BMW Air's top designer out of Germany and put him to work. The result was the Dassault MD 450 Ouragan jet, followed over the next few years by different series of the Mystere. A careful man, Dassault's policy was never to combine a new engine with a new body design. Rather, he built slowly on technology that had a proven track record. In 1955, Dassault unveiled the culmination of that model, the Super-Mystere. During the Suez crisis of 1956, an Israeli strike force of Mysteres caught the Egyptian air force napping, and destroyed more than 100 MiG-15s on the ground.

Then came the French-constructed Mirage III, specifically built to counter the Soviet MiG-21. Mirage III's innovations included a delta wing and optional rocket booster. It could fly at Mach 2, twice the speed of sound. Successive models included the Mirage F-1 and the Mirage 2000, with nuclear capacity. History repeated itself in June 1967, during the Six Day War, when Israelis in Mirages blitzed Egyptian airfields, destroying 300 MiGs on the ground. The Egyptians finally returned the favor in the 1973 Yom Kippur War, when they caught the Israelis napping.

One of the most unusual warplane designs of the 1950s was the Northrop B-35 and B-49, brainchild of aviation great Jack Northrop. This was a long-range flying wing jet bomber with no fuselage. It looked like a giant steel boomerang with small stabilizers. Prototypes were built; they flew, but the line was cancelled. Today's B-2 Stealth bomber has many features similar to this revolutionary design. During the 1960s, Northrop offered the two-engine Tiger, which could fly at Mach 1.4 and reach an altitude of 35,000 feet. It was armed with 20mm guns in the nose and wingtip missiles. Later models included the Tiger II and the F-5E. It was adopted by the air forces of 22 countries.

CONVAIR B-36 PEACEMAKER

Although the B-36 was a Cold War–era aircraft, the story of the world's first ten-engined military aircraft begins before the United States became involved in World War II, when fear that England would be conquered by the Nazis led to speculation that an intercontinental bomber would soon be necessary.

The new long-range bomber would be able to operate from U.S. bases, attack over an intercontinental range, defend itself, and carry a large bomb load to targets in an occupied England or Europe. The War Department released specifications for an intercontinental bomber that could accomplish this mission on April 11, 1941, eight months prior to the Japanese attack on Pearl Harbor.

General Requirements

The general requirements called for an aircraft with a maximum speed of 450 mph. This was a significant increase when compared to the B-17's top speed of 287 mph, the B-24's top speed of 290 mph, and the planned B-29 Superfortress's design speed of 358 mph. The new bomber was required to have a cruising speed of 275 mph, be able to reach a maximum altitude of 45,000 feet, and have a combat range of 12,000 miles at 25,000 feet.

On May 3, 1941, the Consolidated Aircraft Corporation entered its Model 35 proposal. It was a six-engine aircraft, with twin tail fins and rudders—similar to those used on the B-24, but these were much larger. Consolidated's proposal for the new aircraft was preferred over the competition and, on November 15, 1941, the War Department issued a contract for two experimental aircraft, designated as the XB-36. (XB-36 was the first and YB-36 the second test aircraft produced.)

The XB-36 design defined an aircraft with a wingspan of 230 feet, slightly swept back, a wing area of 4,772 square feet, wings positioned high on a circular section fuselage, and six 3,000-horsepower Pratt & Whitney R-4360-25 Wasp Major air-cooled radial engines. Each engine drove a 19-foot, three-blade Curtiss variable pitch propeller in a pusher configuration. The engines were accessible for maintenance by the crew during flight operations through the 7½-foot center wing root section.

The XB-36 had a maximum speed of 346 mph at 35,000 feet, a cruising speed of 216 mph, an initial climb rate of 1,740 feet per minute, a service ceiling of 36,000 feet, and a maximum ceiling of 38,000 feet. It had a combat range of 9,500 miles with a maximum bomb load of 77,784 pounds.

Empty weight for the XB-36 was 131,740 pounds. The maximum takeoff weight was 276,506 pounds. It carried 19,976 gallons of fuel in six-wing tanks, a number subsequently increased to eight for greater range. The aircraft was 162 feet, 1 inch long, with a height at the tail of 46 feet, 8 inches. The forward crew compartment and gunner's weapons sighting station compartment behind the bomb bay were connected by a 25-inch-diameter, 80-foot-long pressurized tube. The aircraft's crew transited through the tube on a roller-supported flatbed crawler.

The XB-36 was designed to carry a crew of 15 (although that number never flew on the test aircraft): pilot, copilot, radar/bombardier, navigator, flight engineer, two radio operators, and eight gunners—three in the forward and five in the aft compartment. Reconnaissance versions carried up to 22 crew members. Gunners operated four remote-controlled, retractable turrets, plus nose and rear guns. No guns were on the two experimental aircraft or on the production "A" models.

On July 20, 1942, Consolidated's XB-36 design proposal was accepted by the USAAF and the War Department.

Low Priority

Design work on the B-36 was slow because of Consolidated's existing contracts and was relegated to the bottom of the War Department's priority list. As the war progressed, it became obvious that the United States would be able to use England to launch bombing missions against Nazi Germany, so the immediate need for an intercontinental bomber was gone.

But work never stopped completely. In spare moments the company's engineers rearranged the B-36's forward compartment, replacing the twin tail arrangement with a single tail like that of the B-32, and set the location for defensive armament.

The most unusual feature of the XB-36 was its 110-inch wheels. However, the XB-36's load-to-wheel weight limited the aircraft to three U.S. runways that were thick enough to handle it. These runways, built of reinforced concrete and 22 inches thick, were at the Consolidated factory at Fort Worth, Texas; Eglin Air Force Base (AFB), Florida; and Fairfield-Suisan AFB, California, which is now called Travis AFB.

Speculation about the B-36's future ended on June 15, 1944, when the War Department issued a contract intent letter to Consolidated. XB-36 was rolled out of Consolidated's Fort Worth factory on March 25, 1946.

Testing the XB-36

Consolidated's chief test pilot, Beryl A. Erickson, copilot G. S. Green, and a crew of seven began ground tests on June 12, 1946. Erickson was Consolidated's chief test pilot for the B-24 Liberator and B-36 Peacemaker, and later Convair's chief test pilot for the supersonic B-58 Hustler.

When the XB-36's engines were tested for the first time on the airframe, turbulence was so bad that the B-36's wingtips had to be redesigned and enforced. Consequently, it was not until July 21, 1946, that taxi tests began.

On August 8, Erickson and his flight crew took the XB-36 airborne for the first time, flying for 37 minutes, but keeping the landing gear extended for safety reasons. Erickson's 7,000 hours flying the various models of the B-36, including three flights of more than 10,000 miles each, made him the aircraft's most experienced pilot.

That first flight identified some problems. Among these were the plane's slow-activating wing flaps, inadequate engine cooling, turbulent wing airflow, high fuel consumption, and lower-than-anticipated speeds. The XB-36 returned to its hangar for those problems to be corrected. The USAAF Air Material Command then took control of the aircraft for a 160-hour XB-36 flight test program, which was followed by Consolidated's 117 hours of flight tests.

Erickson, as team leader of a group of pilots and technicians, put the XB-36, YB-36, and operational models of the B-36 through thousands of hours of exhaustive tests to develop it into a formidable weapon.

On June 19, 1948, the XB-36 was turned over to the Strategic Air Command (SAC) as a crew trainer. That first prototype, the XB-36, ended its service life in 1957 as a derelict hulk at Consolidated's Fort Worth plant, where it was repeatedly set on fire and extinguished to train air force firefighters.

The YB-36

The second experimental prototype, the YB-36, differed in appearance because of the addition of a high-visibility canopy, with a raised crew cockpit for better visibility. Consolidated engineers redesigned the forward compartment to increase crew efficiency and provide adequate room for personnel on following production aircraft.

The YB-36 retained the large landing wheels. Those wheels were replaced on the production models with four 56-inch wheels, mounted in a dual bogie-type undercarriage.

The YB-36 was powered by 3,500-horsepower R-43660-41 Wasp Major radial engines. The YB-36, with Erickson as pilot, flew for the first time on December 4, 1947. The aircraft was turned over to the air force on May 3, 1949. It was returned to Consolidated Fort Worth in October 1950 and converted into an RB-36E reconnaissance aircraft.

FATE OF THE YB-36

In the spring of 1957, the YB-36 was removed from active inventory, flown to Wright Patterson AFB in Dayton, Ohio, and turned over to the Air Force Museum. Unfortunately, it was scrapped when the first permanent museum building was built. Luckily, the museum later obtained a B-36J for its aircraft collection.

Consolidated's test flights identified additional deficiencies. The aircraft's range of 6,000 miles did not meet the air force's intercontinental bomber specifications, its lower-than-expected speed made it vulnerable to fighters, and inadequate protection for the aircraft's fuel tanks increased fire potential. Regardless, the B-36 was SAC's only heavy, long-range, operational bomber until the B-52 entered service in 1955.

First Flight of the B-36A

The first production B-36A flew on August 28, 1947, even before the second prototype flew. The production model was powered by R-4360-25 Major Wasp radial engines and carried no defensive armament. Twenty-one "A" models were built and used as crew training and flight-familiarization aircraft.

The "B" model differed in that it had R-4360-41 Wasp Major engines. These increased the maximum speed to 381 mph and maximum altitude to 42,500 feet.

But the B-36's performance was still below original design specifications. Consolidated's engineers proposed a power plant augmentation to increase the B-36's speed and altitude, as well as to correct other aircraft inadequacies.

On October 5, 1948, a pair of General Electric J47-GE-19 turbojets were added underneath each wing, outboard of the pusher engines. Each turbojet added 5,200 pounds of thrust to the aircraft's power output. The four turbojet engines increased the B-36's maximum speed to 435 mph, allowed the aircraft to meet a maximum altitude of 45,000 feet, and reduced takeoff distance by 2,000 feet. The addition of the turbojets increased the aircraft's gross weight to 385,000 pounds.

Engineers added the improved K-3A bombing and navigation system, which allowed a single crew member to function as radar operator and bombardier. The AN/APG-32 radar was added for better tail-gun performance, and snap action, quick-closing bomb-bay doors were configured onto the aircraft to reduce the time the plane would have to spend over the target.

Consolidated converted a B-36B into a "D" model to test the new power-plant configuration. It first flew on March 26, 1949. That year SAC converted 64 B-36Bs to "D" models and all subsequent B-36s had a similar power plant configuration. The B-36D also had improved fuel containers and better sealant, which reduced fuel leakage and fire potential. Twenty-six B-36Ds were built from scratch to complete the "D" series.

The turbojet pod arrangement was similar to that used on the Boeing B-47 Stratojet, then under development as SAC's medium bomber replacement for WWII's B-29. Nose doors on each jet engine closed when not operated to reduce drag on long-range flights, only periodically opening to lubricate the jet turbines.

The aircraft flew well on four, or even three engines. This reduced fuel consumption while at cruising altitude on long-range flights. The turbojets were only used for takeoff and during the bombing run.

Consolidated engineers designed a very clean cylindrical fuselage that had a lift-to-drag ratio of 20-to-1. The B-36's small frontal pusher engine area and efficient engine cowlings reduced drag and increased range. The six pusher engines eliminated over-the-wing airflow disturbances associated with propeller aircraft. The B-36D became the world's first 10-engined military aircraft.

A Major Cold War Deterrent

With two auxiliary bomb-bay fuel tanks, the aircraft could remain airborne for up to 48 hours at 45,000 feet. Consolidated (renamed Convair in 1954) built a total of 385 B-36s, in various models, some one-of-a-kind, like the B-36H-20.

At the height of B-36 deployment (reconnaissance and bomber) with SAC in 1955, 10 heavy bomb wings were operational. Also in 1955, SAC equipped its first heavy bomb wing with the B-52B at Castle AFB, California. There are still close to 100 B-52s operational with the Air Combat Command. (We'll learn about the B-52 in Chapter 10.)

On February 12, 1959, SAC retired its last B-36, a "J" model from the 95th Bomb Wing, at Carswell AFB, New Mexico. It was flown to the Convair plant at Fort Worth, Texas, for display. The last Peacemaker to fly, a B-36J, landed at Wright-Patterson AFB, USAF Museum in April 1959. There is also a B-36H on display at the Castle Air Museum in Atwater, California.

Although the B-36 arrived too late to be used in World War II and was considered more firepower than was needed in the Korean War, it was a major deterrent to aggression by the Soviet Union. During the tense days of the Cold War, at any given time there were up to a dozen B-36s airborne, armed with nuclear weapons. They could be diverted, under Presidential positive control release procedures and orders, to strike predetermined targets.

The B-36 was the last of the USAF's long-range, piston-powered bombers. Its smaller cousins, such as the Douglas A-26, served in the Vietnam War, but by that time SAC had become an all-jet force. Fortunately, four of these huge bombers are preserved to remind Americans of the successful mission they accomplished at the height of the Cold War.

U-2 SPY PLANE

Eye-in-the-sky spy systems became necessary because human beings and electronic devices on the ground in the Soviet Union weren't getting the job done. Communist counterintelligence agents rounded up many of the Western intelligence agents and drove the remainder underground.

Reconnaissance planes were needed to fly over Communist bloc nations and determine the extent and location of their defenses, troop movements, industrial might, and thousands of other details.

To solve the problem, Lockheed developed a plane, the U-2, that could take pictures of the Soviet Union, and yet fly so high that the Russians' antiaircraft guns couldn't touch it—or so it was thought.

The U.S. Department of Defense released Design Study Requirement Number 53WC-16507, dated March 27, 1953, to collect intelligence on the Soviet Union by an aircraft with the following specifications:

- Single-seat reconnaissance aircraft
- Subsonic capability
- Payload capacity of 700 pounds for two daylight reconnaissance cameras
- Range of 3,000 miles
- Operational altitude of 70,000 feet
- Unarmed configuration
- No ejection seat (saved weight; also, high-altitude bailout considered fatal to pilot)

Lockheed Aircraft submitted a design proposal, under the designation of model Cl-282, based on the Lockheed XF-104 fuselage, fitted with long wings for high-altitude operations. The aircraft was to be powered by a Pratt & Whitney J57 engine on the production model. The Central Intelligence Agency (CIA), on December 9, 1954, awarded a production contract to Lockheed.

Lt. Col. George A. Larson, USAF (Ret.)

Left side view of the U-2C, clearly showing the wing's thin structure, mid-fuselage mounted. The front landing gear wheels are larger than the rear wheels.

Lockheed's prototype, aircraft serial number 56-6701, took off at 12:26 A.M., August 1, 1955, from Groom Lake, Nevada, piloted by Lockheed's test pilot Tony LeVier. He climbed the aircraft to an altitude of 12,500 feet, remaining airborne for 45 minutes. The air force gave the aircraft the designation of U-2 (Utility-2).

Lt. Col. George A. Larson, USAF (Ret.)

Rear view of the U-2C.

The U-2 operated at altitudes up to 70,000 feet and was thought to be invulnerable to either interception by enemy fighters or destruction by enemy antiaircraft guns and missiles.

U-2s were soon overflying Communist bloc countries with regularity and impunity. The Russians, of course, were upset at these reconnaissance missions and used every means at their disposal to shoot down the U-2s.

U-2 SPECIFICATIONS

Manufacturer: Lockheed Aircraft "Skunk Works," Burbank, California

Classification: High-altitude, strategic reconnaissance aircraft

Wingspan: 80 feet. Thin wings provide unusual lift capability. Built light, four pounds per square foot.

Length: 49 feet, 7 inches. Built out of wafer-thin aluminum.

Power plant: One J57-P13B Pratt & Whitney 17,000-pound-thrust jet engine

Maximum speed: 528 mph

Cruising speed: 460 mph

Service ceiling: 80,000 feet (unclassified)

Empty weight: 13,000 pounds

Gross weight: 17,270 pounds

Maximum weight: 23,100 pounds

Maximum range: 4,400 miles

Fuel: 1,320 gallons in four tanks

Landing gear: Two-wheel tandem

Camera system: One high-resolution, long-focal length. Ground resolution 2–3 feet at 70,000 feet; one marking camera

The U-2 was designed to fly at high altitude over the Soviet Union. The first of 30 overflights occurred on July 4, 1956. Under "Operation Overflight," the U-2 took off from Wiesbaden Air Base, West Germany, flying over Moscow and Leningrad, taking photographs of Russian military installations.

At that time, the Russian military had no aircraft that could climb to the U-2's altitude to intercept and shoot down the intruder. Surface-to-air missiles (SAMs) were still under development.

As these overflights continued, it was only a matter of time before one was shot down. American intelligence had indications of more SA-2 guideline SAMs being constructed around major Soviet military installations. U-2 overflight routes, as best as could be planned, were to avoid these sites.

By the spring of 1958, Russian antiaircraft missiles had gotten dangerously close to several of the spy planes. It wasn't going to be long before a new and better spy plane would be needed.

In April 1958, the CIA assigned Richard M. Bissell, special assistant for planning and coordination of the U-2 spy missions, to find a replacement for the U-2. It was because of Bissell's foresight that a replacement for the spy plane (the SR-71, to be discussed in the next chapter) was already under development by the time the U-2 became obsolete.

The Powers Incident

U-2 pilot Francis Gary Powers was shot down during a U-2 mission over the Soviet Union, causing the Cold War to suddenly heat up.

POWERS'S SCHEDULED FLIGHT

Francis Gary Powers's scheduled reconnaissance flight for May 1, 1960, was to take him through the following flight plan:

1. Begin at Peshawar Air Base, Turkey.
2. Fly northwest, over Afghanistan.
3. Cross into the Soviet Union near Dushambe.
4. Overfly Soviet territory toward Sverdlovsk.
5. Fly west to Kirov.
6. Fly northwest to Murmansk.
7. Exit Soviet air space.
8. Fly out into the Barents Sea.
9. Fly around Finland and Sweden.
10. Land at Bodo, Norway (completing a flight of 3,800 miles, flight duration nine hours).

Powers's twenty-eighth reconnaissance mission was to be the longest yet for the U-2, cutting across the central section of the Soviet Union from south to north, covering the top-secret intercontinental ballistic missile

(ICBM) facilities located at Plesetsk and Sverdlovsk, on May 1, 1960. Powers was based at Incirlik Air Base, Turkey, assigned to Detachment 10-10, flying U-2 aircraft serial number 56-6693.

Everything remained on schedule until Powers neared Sverdlovsk. In an attempt to shoot down the U-2, Soviet air force MiG-19 Farmer fighters attempted zoom-climb maneuvers to reach the spy plane's altitude, but they flamed out, unable to shoot down the aircraft. However, Soviet ground radars locked on and tracked the U-2, feeding estimated position information to SA-2 sites. At a predetermined time, 14 SA-2s were launched to simultaneously reach the same position, exploding around the U-2. One explosion knocked off the U-2's right horizontal stabilizer, forcing the aircraft onto its back, overstressing the wings, which separated from the fuselage. Powers bailed out of the aircraft.

Both the pilot and the aircraft were taken by the enemy. The United States at first tried to deny that it was a spy plane, saying that it was merely a plane that had wandered off course. After the Soviets found the complex photographic equipment aboard, the United States was forced to admit that Powers had been on a spy mission.

Powers was held in a Soviet prison for two years. He was released in 1962 when President Kennedy agreed to a spy swap. The United States got Powers back in exchange for captured spy Col. Rudolf Abel. To make sure that neither side got burned during the spy swap, the exchange took place on Berlin, Germany's, Glienicke Bridge, which spans the river Havel. Powers stood on the east side of the bridge and Abel stood on the west side. At a signal, both prisoners were allowed to walk across the bridge simultaneously. They passed each other at the center of the bridge silently, offering only a barely perceptible nod as they passed.

Powers was not received warmly by his CIA comrades when he arrived back in the United States. His assignment had been to make sure the plane was destroyed in case it was shot down so the Soviets would not be able to learn anything from it. He had also been trained to take a suicide pill if he were captured, so he would not be able to talk.

On May 1, 2000, U.S. officials presented Powers's family with the Prisoner-of-War Medal, the Distinguished Flying Cross, and the National

Defense service medal during a 30-minute ceremony held at Beale Air Force Base.

The Cuban Missile Crisis

Even after the Powers incident, the U-2 continued to play an important role. On January 1, 1959, Fidel Castro completed a successful six-year revolution against the Batista government, which had been supported by the United States.

National Security Archives, Washington, D.C.

In order to better determine the construction status and operational readiness of Soviet missiles in Cuba, President Kennedy ordered the flying of low-level reconnaissance over the missile sites. This photograph of the San Cristobal site shows the missiles on transporters and associated missile equipment.

After shipping military equipment to Cuba, on April 1, 1962, Soviet premier Nikita Khrushchev decided to ship offensive missiles to Cuba to counterbalance U.S. missiles deployed around the Soviet Union, keep the United States from conducting a large-scale invasion against Cuba, and force the United States to withdraw its missiles deployed around the borders of the Soviet Union. The U-2 revealed what the Soviet Union was deploying to Cuba.

The 4028th Strategic Reconnaissance Squadron (SRS), Strategic Air Command (SAC), based at Laughlin Air Force Base, Texas, monitored events in Cuba, looking for visible evidence of offensive missiles. At 7:37 A.M., October 14, 1962, USAF major Richard Heyser, flying on a course 60 miles west of Havana, took 928 photographs from high altitude. The photographs were rushed to the Naval Photographic Interpretation Center at Suitland, Maryland. The detailed examination identified a medium-range ballistic missile (MRBM) site under construction at San Cristobal, with missiles on transporters. These were identified as the SS-4 Sandal missile, with a range of 1,100 miles.

Medium-range ballistic missile launch site under construction at Sagua La Grande. Missile transporters are visible in the photo. One of the most interesting is the launch pad with a missile erector. These missiles were soft sites (not in protective silos) and were therefore considered as a first strike weapon against the United States.

On October 17, 1962, a U-2 identified an intermediate-range ballistic missile (IRBM) site under construction at Guanajay, along with the SS-5 Skean missiles on transporters, with a range of 2,000 miles.

JFK SPEAKS

On October 22, 1962, President John F. Kennedy made a national television broadcast. He said: "Good evening, my fellow citizens. This government, as promised, has maintained the closest surveillance of the Soviet military buildup on the island of Cuba. Within the past weeks, unmistakable evidence has established the fact that a series of offensive missile sites is now in preparation on that imprisoned island. The purpose of these bases can be none other than to provide a nuclear strike capability against the western hemisphere."

The U-2 continued to monitor the offensive missile facilities and launch site construction in Cuba. On October 27, 1962, at approximately 12 noon, USAF major Andersen's U-2 was shot down by an SA-2, killing him. Two other U-2s were lost to unknown causes during monitoring flights over Cuba, but not shot down over Cuba. On October 28, 1962, Premier Khrushchev agreed to remove the offensive missiles from Cuba.

On November 1, 1962, U-2 reconnaissance confirmed the MRBM sites had been bulldozed, with associated missiles and equipment crated for removal to the Soviet Union. Construction on IRBM sites had ceased, with missiles and equipment removed. The 4080th SRS U-2s flew 102 reconnaissance flights over Cuba between October 14, 1962, and December 16, 1962.

THREE WAYS TO PREVENT CAPTURE

If the problem is the risk that your surveillance plane will be shot down and its pilot and crew captured, there are three things you can do:

1. You can build a plane that, for some reason, is beyond the enemy's capability to shoot down.
2. You can put your cameras higher than a plane can go. In other words, you can attach your camera to a satellite that is orbiting the Earth.
3. You can build your spy planes so that they run on remote control, and therefore do not need a pilot and crew.

During the latter stages of the Cold War, U.S. intelligence services tried all three.

The U-2 continues to fly today, long after its replacement—the super-sonic Lockheed SR-71 Blackbird—has been retired from active duty (it was too expensive to operate). As of 2003, the USAF maintains a fleet of 30 single-seat and five two-seat U-2s. Since 1994, these 35 aircraft have been continuously upgraded, at a cost of $1.5 billion.

F8U CRUSADER

The F8U-1 Crusader, to be built by Vought, became the navy's new carrier-based fighter jet in 1953. Vought won the contract to build the jet over seven other aircraft companies.

It made its first flight in 1955, successfully breaking the sound barrier. In 1956, the jet broke the 1,000 mph mark for the first time and set the American speed record in the process.

F-8 CRUSADER SPECIFICATIONS

Manufacturer: Chance-Vought Aircraft, Inc.
Type: Carrier-based fighter
Crew: One
Power plant: Pratt & Whitney J-57-P-4A with afterburner
Wingspan: 35 feet, 8 inches
Wing area: 375 square feet
Length: 54 feet, 3 inches
Height: 15 feet, 9 inches
Tread: 9 feet, 8 inches
Weight empty: 16,483 pounds
Weight maximum combat: 24,475 pounds
Maximum takeoff: 27,938 pounds (catapult)
Maximum landing: 22,000 pounds (arrested)
Speed: Mach 1.5+
Range: 1,195–1,295 miles
Armament: Four 20mm aircraft guns front fuselage and 500 rounds; 32 2.75-inch rockets carried internally or in rocket pack, centerline fuselage or two AIM-9 missiles externally on pylon each side of fuselage

The following year, Maj. John Glenn set a transcontinental speed record in a Crusader, flying from Los Angeles to New York. The flight's average speed was greater than the speed of sound despite the fact that the jet had to slow down to below 300 mph three times for in-flight refuelings.

During the Vietnam War, the Crusader led all navy aircraft in kill ratio. Over Vietnam it earned the nickname "MiG Master." There were eventually 1,263 F8Us built. Although it ended its service with the navy before 1970, the Crusader continued to serve the Navy Reserve until 1987 and the French navy until 1998.

LOCKHEED F-104 STARFIGHTER

One of the planes that was ready for action if the Cuban Missile Crisis had led to war was the Lockheed F-104 Starfighter. Research and development for the Starfighter, however, had begun many years earlier.

The design for this superior air fighting machine started in the brain of Clarence "Kelly" Johnson, the man who had designed the F-80, a jet that was rapidly growing obsolete in the skies over Korea. He started out his research into the next generation of fighter jets by asking the greatest experts in the world: fighter pilots.

In the autumn of 1951, Johnson went to Korea to talk to air force pilots to determine what would be needed in Lockheed's next product. He learned that the pilots needed an aircraft that traded off excess weight and complexity in favor of superior speed, maneuverability, and high-altitude performance.

After a month in Korea, Johnson returned to Lockheed and went to work. His proposal called for an advanced yet lightweight super-high-performance fighter that would be cheap but keep fighter pilots happy. The resulting streamlined design had a slender missile-like fuselage with a reduced frontal area. It had low-aspect ratio wings that were thin and trapezoidal in shape.

Now Johnson needed an engine that could supply the necessary speed for the new craft. This turned out to be a difficult task. Johnson wanted his jet to go Mach 2, but engines then available could only propel their craft to Mach 1.5.

The two engines then under development that had the potential to make a jet go twice the speed of sound were the Pratt & Whitney J-75, an upgraded and much more powerful version of the very successful J-57, and the General Electric J-79, a radically new and advanced power plant that would eventually produce thrusts up to 18,000 pounds without using its afterburner.

LaPierre's J-79 Project

The J-79 project was begun in 1952 by a team led by C. W. "Jim" La-Pierre, who insisted that the new engine have good fuel economy even when flying as fast as Mach 0.9. The engine, he demanded, also needed to have the strength and thrust power to take a jet to Mach 2. Plus, he said, it needed to be low in weight. Gerhard Neumann, GE's greatest power plant engineer and leader, determined that the only way to meet all of LaPierre's specifications was to increase the engine's pressure ratio. Neumann's team employed a novel variable-stator type compressor. This consisted of having most of the compressor's stator blades mounted in rotary bearings to facilitate movement of the blades to the best angle for changing engine operating conditions. This was comparable to having a constant speed of variable-pitch propeller on a piston engine.

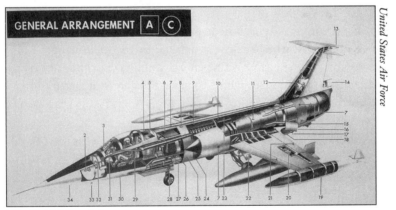

The F-104 Starfighter.

The J-79 concept was accepted by the USAF and the first flight was made in a retractable pod underneath the belly of a B-45 over

Schenectady, New York, on May 20, 1955. It was a resounding success. Since 1955, more than 17,000 J-79 engines have been built.

In January 1953, Lockheed's proposal was chosen over competitive entries by Northrop, North American, and Republic for a fighter to replace the North American F-100 Super Sabre.

First Prototype

Construction began on the first prototype in July 1953 at Lockheed's Burbank plant. This project ran better than expected for such a ground-breaking model of aeronautical innovation, with the completed XF-104 secretly being rolled out on February 23, 1954.

Because the J-79 was not yet ready for implantation into the XF-104, a less-powerful Wright J-65 engine was used. The XF-104 sported two distinct features not found on any other fighter aircraft: a downward firing ejection seat and a "T" tail with the horizontal stabilizer mounted atop the vertical fin.

The downward-operating ejection seat was incorporated by Lockheed engineers who feared that a pilot ejecting at supersonic speed would not clear the tail assembly. Ironically, this was not the case, and the downward-firing system proved more dangerous because it could not be used on takeoffs, landings, or at low altitudes. More conventional upward-firing ejection seats were used on later versions of the F-104.

The all-moving stabilator was positioned at the top of the vertical fin to be free of the disturbed airflow generated by the main wings. This offered greater response and better lateral stability. Lockheed also slated the stubby, trapezoidal main wings to have a negative dihedral (downward slant) for exceptional roll control during high "G" maneuvers and to enhance stability at high speeds and altitudes.

The F-104 was also the first warplane to be armed with the GE M-61 20mm Vulcan cannon, which could shoot 6,000 rounds per minute.

Thumbs Up

Following almost two years of testing, the USAF gave Kelly Johnson's XF-104 a thumbs up. It was deemed worthy of serious consideration for incorporation into its inventory.

Up until this time, all development and testing of the XF-104 had been held in secret. On February 16, 1956, the USAF finally went public with information regarding the new warplane. A ceremony was held at Lockheed's Burbank, California, facility. The public, as well as aviation authorities, registered wondrous admiration at the craft. It was called "the missile with a man in it."

On February 28, 1956, the F-104 became the first fighter to achieve Mach 2 in level flight with its new GE J-79 engine. On March 2, the USAF procured from Lockheed 146 F-104A Starfighters.

Although the F-104 was designed to be an air superiority fighter, it really possessed the potential to assume all of the roles—fighter, attack, bomber, and reconnaissance—executed by the Tactical Air Command (TAC). The Starfighter was a well-rounded weapons platform, capable of carrying conventional and nuclear bombs and missiles, auxiliary fuel tanks, and photographic equipment.

There were, however, operational problems with the M-61 Vulcan cannon. Excessive vibration and premature detonation of its 20mm shells forced Lockheed to delete the Gatling gun from its early model F-104s. By 1964, GE had produced a vastly improved version designated the M-61A1, which would render illustrious service in a variety of U.S. aircraft.

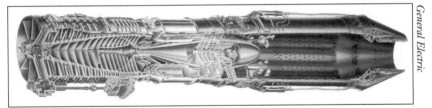

General Electric

Cutaway of the GE J-79 shows its dual-spool compressor (left), can-annular combustor (center), and long afterburner (right). Although its contemporary, the Pratt & Whitney J-75, produced higher thrust, Lockheed chose the J-79 because of its lower specific fuel consumption and lighter weight.

Constantly changing TAC requirements and the many competing aircraft produced by rival manufacturers led to a review of the F-104 program by the USAF and an unfavorable decision. By December 1958, the USAF drastically reduced its contract (at one point orders for 722 Starfighters had been placed) and Lockheed went on to produce only 296 of its jets for the air force.

A Popular Plane with Allies

The United States' allies had other opinions of the Starfighter. They appreciated its great value and cheap price. Major foreign acquisitions boosted Lockheed's Starfighter production to 741, and added 48 co-produced aircraft and 1,789 licensed-built aircraft, for a total of 2,578.

The substantial multinational F-104 program had its origins in a Luftwaffe requirement for a supersonic fighter to supplant its Canadair F-86 Sabres and Republic F-84Fs. At least nine types of aircraft were considered for German reequipment—including the Dassault Mirage III, the Convair F-102 and F-106, and the Republic F-105. The competition narrowed down to a hard choice between the Mirage III and the Starfighter.

The competition was won by Lockheed in October 1958 when the F-104G (G for Germany) was declared the winner. A contract for 66 F-104Gs was awarded to Lockheed on February 6, 1959.

The European production program was enlarged during 1960 by the addition of the Netherlands, Belgium, and Italy. Meanwhile, Canada and Japan adapted the Starfighter for their own air forces, with Norway and Denmark using ex-Canadair F-104s modified to G-model specifications. Spain, Turkey, Pakistan, Taiwan, Greece, and Jordan also modernized their inventory with the Starfighter.

F-104 STARFIGHTER SPECIFICATIONS

Manufacturer: Lockheed

Length: 54 feet, 9 inches

Wingspan: (without tip tanks) 21 feet, 11 inches; (with tip tanks) 26 feet, 3 inches

Height: 13 feet, 6 inches

Weight empty: 20,900 pounds

Maximum takeoff weight: 27,000 pounds

Crew: One

Power plant: General Electric J-79 Turbojet

Maximum speed: Mach 2.2

Maximum climb rate: 40,000 feet per minute

Absolute ceiling: 90,000 feet

The "A" model of the F-104, assigned to the Air Defense Command, had two drawbacks: lack of all-weather capability and a relatively short range. This undesirable situation was remedied somewhat with the introduction of the F-104C, which incorporated a removable probe-and-drogue aerial refueling system and auxiliary fuel tanks fitted to underwing pylons.

Also new were two extra AIM-9 Sidewinder air-to-air missiles mounted under the fuselage centerline and the ability to carry a single nuclear store. It also sported the more reliable and higher-thrust GE J-79-G.G.-7A turbojet that delivered 10,000 pounds military thrust and 15,800 pounds afterburning thrust.

F-104Cs were assigned to four squadrons of the 479th TW at George Air Force Base, California, in September 1958. That same year the warplane won the Collier Award for jet of the year. During the Cuban Missile Crisis, they were deployed to forward bases in Key West, Florida. The F-104 finally saw combat during the Vietnam War, which we'll be discussing in our next chapter.

CHAPTER 10

VIETNAM AND OTHER WARS

Ten years after the Korean War ended, the United States found itself involved in a similar conflict in Asia. Just as had been the case in Korea, this war was basically a civil war. Once again, the northern half of the country was controlled by Communists, while the southern half was a democracy that the United States had sworn to protect.

F-4 PHANTOM II

The U.S. Navy's McDonnell Douglas F-4 Phantom II debuted in 1953 for the navy, a multipurpose attack fighter for carrier and fleet defense. Ten years would pass before the F-4 came into its own as a premier fighter during the Vietnam War. The jet was originally designed as an attack aircraft (bomb dropper) but ended up becoming the United States and its allies' number-one air-to-air fighter. Although it was designed as a carrier-based jet, two out of every three built ended up being land-based aircraft. The F-4 ended up enjoying an operational longevity matched only by the F-86 Sabre.

The F-4 was born out of studies held by McDonnell Aircraft designed to improve its F3H Demon. The performance numbers resulting from that study looked so good that in September 1953

McDonnell made an unsolicited proposal to the navy's Bureau of Aeronautics.

"CHAPPIE" JAMES

One of the most famous American pilots during the Vietnam War was Daniel "Chappie" James Jr., an African American. He was born February 11, 1920, at Pensacola, Florida. He learned to fly while attending the Tuskegee Institute.

He graduated in 1942 and was appointed as a cadet in the USAAF in 1943. He was commissioned later that year and spent the remainder of the war training pilots for the all-black 99th Pursuit Squadron.

He flew 101 combat missions during the Korean War. He flew 78 combat missions in an F-4C Phantom over Vietnam in 1966–1967. By that time he had been promoted to colonel.

In September 1975, he became the first black officer in the history of the U.S. military to become a four-star general. He retired from the air force in early 1978, and died only weeks later, on February 25, 1978, following a heart attack.

There were versions designed with large search radars, missile fire-control systems, mapping radars, cameras, electronics reconnaissance equipment, four 20mm guns, and retractable two-inch FFAR rocket pods. Nine weapons stores stations were provided that could alternatively carry bombs, rocket pods, nuclear weapons, missiles, or external fuel tanks.

The navy liked what it saw and encouraged McDonnell to further develop its Model 98B version, a twin-engine supersonic fighter with large wings. By the time McDonnell had built a full-size mockup, the navy had already committed itself to Grumman's F8F-9 and Vought's F8U-1 fighters.

So McDonnell submitted a proposal for a single-seat, twin-engine, all-weather attack aircraft. This design beat out the competing designs by Grumman and North American. The navy procured two prototypes designated YAH-1. But as the navy reviewed its requirements, it decided it really needed an all-weather interceptor, and so the single-seat, cannon-armed YAH-1 was redesignated to be a two-seat, missile-armed, all-weather interceptor.

The mission requirements also stipulated a capability to patrol at a distance of 250 nautical miles and stay on station—that is, remain at its assigned location—for two hours, with the ability to stay airborne, without refueling, for two full deck cycles (more than three hours).

Blistering Performance

The contract for what was now known as the YFAH-1 was awarded in July 1955. The configuration consisted of two GE J79 turbojets with afterburners, fixed geometry cheek-mounted air intakes, a delta wing with 45° of sweep, and armament consisting of four Sparrow III radar-guided missiles semisubmerged on the lower portion of the fuselage. No gun was provided, making this the first U.S. all-missile fighter.

Extensive wind-tunnel testing uncovered several problems that required significant redesign. The outer wing panels were canted upward 12° and enlarged, which resulted in a dog-tooth leading edge and wingtip dihedral. The single-piece tail plane needed to be lowered, and since that was impossible without a major redesign of the entire tail section, it was canted downward 23°. The fixed intake ramps were redesigned with a combination of variable and fixed ramps, and bleed vents were added to the fixed section. While they were at it, McDonnell engineers incorporated a system that used engine compressor air to provide boundary-layer control over the wing's leading and trailing edges. The first flight was in May 1958. Performance was called "blistering"—in the best sense of the word.

MCDONNELL DOUGLAS F-4C PHANTOM II SPECIFICATIONS

Length: 12 feet, 10 inches
Width: 10 feet, 9 inches
Power plant: Two J79-GE-15 engines producing 17,000 pounds thrust
Maximum takeoff weight: 54,600 pounds
Maximum speed: Mach 2-plus
Crew: Two (pilot, radar intercept officer)
Armament: Six AIM-4 Falcon missiles, six AIM-7 Sparrow III missiles, four AIM-9 Sidewinder missiles

While this was going on, Vought, maker of the F-8 Crusader, wasn't standing still. In December 1958, the brand-new Phantom entered competition against the F8U-3 Crusader III. The Phantom won.

The first 45 Phantoms were powered with an early version of the J79 engine and were designated F4H-1F by the navy (the final F indicating a special power plant). Subsequent aircraft were equipped with upgraded engines. The ninth production Phantom was tested with special multiple racks that enabled the aircraft to carry a total of 22,500 pounds of bombs at the inner wing weapons stations and all the fuselage stations.

Commonality and the Future

In 1961, Defense secretary Robert McNamara decided that commonality would be the future of navy and air force aircraft. As a result of the political pressure, but also impressed by the stellar performance of the aircraft, the air force evaluated the aircraft as a possible air force fighter. Its choice was easy. The air force's then-premiere interceptor was the F-106 Delta Dart, and the Phantom could carry heavier loads over a longer distance and had 25 percent greater radar range and only one third of the maintenance man-hours per flying hour (MMH/FH).

The F-105 Thunderchief was the air force's premiere tactical fighter-bomber, and the Phantom could carry similar external loads over similar distances, while being a far better dogfighter due to its greater power and larger wing.

The F-101 Voodoo was the air force's main tactical reconnaissance aircraft, and the Phantom beat that aircraft in almost every performance parameter as well. By January 1962, the air force had decided to buy two versions of the Phantom, a tactical fighter version, designated F-110A, and a reconnaissance version, designated RF-110A.

By that September, McNamara decreed that not only would their hardware be the same, but the navy and air force would share a common designation system. As a result, the first 45 Phantoms with the -2 engines were designated F-4A, the subsequent navy aircraft were designated F-4B, and the air force versions designated F-4C. The Marine Corps' recon versions were RF-4B and the air force's photo birds were designated RF-4C.

The air force's F-4 varied from the navy's only internally. They were equipped with a further upgrade of the J79 engine with integral cartridge starting, wider tread low-pressure tires, larger brakes, a different radar and fire-control system, flight controls in both the forward and aft cockpit (navy F-4s only had controls in the forward cockpit), and a refueling boom receptacle instead of the navy's refueling probe. The folding wings and arrester hook were retained—meaning that the aircraft could still be used off an aircraft carrier if necessary.

All F-4Cs and late-model F-4Bs were equipped with the multiple rack system tested on the F-4A, giving them an extensive air-to-ground capability in addition to their air-to-air role.

As the navy and the air force began receiving their Phantoms in quantity, the Vietnam War was heating up. The air force took delivery of more than 580 C models before switching to the D. From the air force's perspective, the C was still a navy bird with some air force innards, but the D model was a truly air force aircraft, which incorporated more ground-attack avionics. But the definitive Phantom for the air force was the F-4E, which finally incorporated an internal gun. This model also had significantly improved avionics, numerous structural detail changes, more internal fuel, higher-thrust low-smoke engines, slotted stabilator, and no wing-fold mechanism.

But the air force kept the arrester hook. By now, most air force bases had been equipped with field arresting cables, and the arresting system proved to be a significant safety feature. Later models had wing leading-edge slats for significantly improved low-altitude agility. The E model was in production for 12 years, with 959 being built.

The definitive navy variant was the J model. (The H model letter was skipped to avoid confusion with the original F4H designation and the letter *I* is never used to avoid confusion with the numeral 1.) The J incorporated a new radar, fire-control system, new ground-attack computers, new navigation systems, data-link communications gear, more powerful low-smoke engines, drooped ailerons, slotted stabilator, wing slats, and numerous other detail changes.

In the late 1950s, McDonnell marketed the Phantom heavily to many foreign air forces, but all efforts proved unsuccessful. But the Phantom's superlative performance in U.S. Navy and Air Force use in combat over Vietnam proved to be the best marketing tool.

A-7 CORSAIR II

The chief of naval operations ordered an assessment of the navy's future strike aircraft needs in 1963. Could the current navy attack aircraft penetrate enemy air defenses and deliver a potent payload? At that time the navy's attack jets were still derivative from the prop plane A-1 Skyraider, then being phased out of service. These were the A-6 Intruder, A-4 Skyhawk, and A-1 Skyraider.

The A-6 had some things going for it. It was an all-weather attack bomber with sophisticated electronics that was just then entering widespread service.

The A-4 Skyhawk, built by Douglas, was nicknamed "Heinneman's Hot Rod" after its designer. It was a small, single-engine bomber, designed to safely reach its target through its speed and agility—not to mention its diminutive size. Because of this, however, it could not carry sophisticated electronics or a heavy payload. The navy's 1963 study, called the "Sea Based Strike Study," determined that a new navy attack aircraft would soon be needed.

Building on a Proven Design

Because of the growing war in Vietnam, the navy decided not to design a new plane from scratch, but rather to modify a proven design. The navy had four airframes to choose from: the A-4 Skyhawk, the A-6 Intruder, the F-J1 Fury, or the F-8 Crusader.

Each aircraft's manufacturer was asked to submit a proposal for an updated version of its aircraft. Whereas the other manufacturers simply updated their existing airframe, Vought took a different and more radical approach. Vought decided to use the engine originally designed for the F-111. To make this engine fit, Vought's new fuselage was widened and shortened. The wings were made stronger to accommodate six hard points capable of carrying 15,000 pounds of ordnance.

A heavily loaded A-7 heads out in search of the enemy. This heavy bomb load and ability to strafe was appreciated by the friendly infantry on the ground in Vietnam.

State-of-the-art electronics were put into the fuselage: guidance systems, bombing system, and radar. These were placed in one central portion of the fuselage for easy maintenance. The new design surpassed the navy's expectations, with one exception: The empty weight, at 15,036 pounds, was too heavy. Regardless, the design was the best of the competition and was chosen for production. It received the name A-7 Corsair II.

The first squadron to take the A-7 was VA-147. It embarked aboard the USS *Ranger* and flew its first combat mission over Vietnam in December 1967.

VOUGHT A-7E CORSAIR II SPECIFICATIONS

Wingspan: 38 feet, 9 inches
Length: 46 feet, 1½ inches
Height: 16 feet, ¾ inch
Engine: Allison TF41-2
Thrust: 15,000 pounds
Maximum speed: 698 mph

One for the USAF

By that time, however, the A-7 was already destined to be more than just a carrier-based aircraft. Back in 1965, the USAF had decided that it, too, was in need of a new attack aircraft. Because the USAF had been preparing for nuclear war against the Soviet Union, the smaller and more delicate missions necessitated by the war in Vietnam had caught it unprepared. The only light bombers in the USAF's inventory during the mid-1960s were the F-100 Super Sabre fighter-bomber and the B-57 Canberra (a British aircraft purchased by the USAF in small numbers).

In 1965, the USAF asked Vought to modify the A-7 to USAF specifications. The USAF wanted a new engine, electronics, and communications equipment—plus a 20mm cannon mounted on the aircraft. This was easily done. The TF30-P-6 engine used in the navy version was replaced with the TF41-A-1 Sprey engine. The fuselage was already wide enough to accommodate the new engine.

The USAF also mounted the M61 20mm multibarreled cannon below the cockpit. The aircraft carried only 1,000 rounds of ammunition even though the gun could fire 6,000 rounds per minute. In addition, an in-flight refueling probe and an advanced navigation/attack system were added. These allowed the aircraft to carry out low-level, terrain-following attacks without regard to range restrictions.

The air force's version was called the A-7D, but pilots quickly began calling it, and this is the polite version, the "short little ugly fellow," or SLUF. Despite the name, pilots liked the new craft a lot.

90,000 Combat Missions

On a short-range mission without fuel tanks, the A-7 could carry 18 500-pound bombs. It could also carry napalm, 2.75-inch rockets, or cluster bomb units. Even when carrying a full bomb load, pilots could still out-maneuver antiaircraft gunners and then deliver its ordnance on target with pinpoint accuracy. Using the sophisticated bombing computer and on-board navigational systems, the pilot could easily put all his bombs within 10 yards of his target.

The A-7D was assigned to the 354th Tactical Fighter Wing and received its baptism of fire in Vietnam in October 1972. By the time it arrived in combat, the ground war was winding down, although the A-7s did carry out close air missions in support of allied forces. The A-7 proved itself to be an excellent escort for rescue helicopters.

The navy received more than 1,300 A-7s. The USAF received 460 of them. Together, they carried out 90,000 combat missions over Vietnam.

AC-130: EMERGENCE OF THE GUNSHIP

During the Vietnam War, the USAF had hundreds of fast-moving jet bombers—such as the A-7—that could swoop in, deliver a devastating attack on enemy positions, and then return to base to refuel and rearm. These attacks lasted only a matter of seconds.

To counter the jet attacks, small enemy units learned to attack American forces and lure the jets in. Once the air attacks were finished, the main enemy force would attack in force. What the USAF needed were heavily armed aircraft that could stay over the scene of battle for several hours.

To accomplish this mission, the USAF decided to modify the old WWII cargo plane, the C-47, to carry three GE SUU 11A/A 7.62mm Gatling guns. The guns fired out of the starboard windows. The pilot could put the aircraft in a tight turn and blanket a target with fire.

Puff the Magic Dragon

The modified aircraft was known as the AC-47. It could put a bullet in every square inch of a football field in three seconds. Nicknamed "Puff the Magic Dragon," the AC-47 impressed ground troops with its day-or-night precision and firepower. It could loiter over a target for hours, if necessary—but its arrival usually ended the enemy's attack.

The concept of the transport gunship soon became an integral part of USAF and U.S. Army planning. While the concept was sound, the use of antiquated aircraft was not. The AC-47s wore out quickly and spare parts were difficult to find. The air force adapted several other outdated aircraft as gunships but they suffered from the same problems. The air force decided to build a better gunship. In mid-1967 Project Gunboat was instituted to build the ultimate gunship.

The USAF's C-130 Hercules transport was chosen for conversion. The aircraft could carry a 34,000-pound payload; there was plenty of room for weapons, ammunition, and electronics gear. The engineers designing the new gunship intended to use all of it.

The initial AC-130A featured four 7.62mm miniguns, with a rate of fire of 6,000 rounds a minute per gun. The aircraft also had a forward-looking infrared radar and a night observation device or NOD and an image intensifier that magnified moon and starlight to allow the NOD to function. There was a fire control computer linked to the gun sight—allowing for accurate prediction of where the rounds would strike—and a standard searchlight, infrared light, and ultraviolet light to paint the battlefield.

The Spectre

The new gunship, called the Spectre, was an immediate success in Vietnam. It flew interdiction missions along the Ho Chi Minh Trail and flew battlefield support missions. As with its predecessors, when the Spectre arrived on station, the enemy withdrew. The AC-130 was given more powerful armament. Four 20mm M61 Vulcan chain guns replaced the 7.62mm guns—more power at a slightly reduced rate of fire.

After Vietnam, the AC-130A was replaced with the AC-130E, which had improved weapons, better electronics, more powerful engines, and different combinations of weapons. The 20mm chain guns were standardized and several aircraft mounted a 105mm cannon firing out the rear cargo ramp. During the 1970s the USAF began flying the "H" version, which was equipped with four Allison T56-A-15 turboprop engines and had a top speed of 384 mph. It could carry a 45,000-pound payload and had a range of 5,050 miles. This represented a 26-percent increase in payload, an 11-percent increase in speed, and a 52-percent increase in range for the new version.

Grenada and Panama

The gunships next saw action in October 1983 over Grenada, where they supported the U.S. Army Ranger attack on Point Salines airport. One of the AC-130 gunships, using its low light-level television, detected vehicles and obstructions on the runway and warned the army commander.

As a result, army troops did not try to land on the airfield but rather conducted an airborne assault. A gunship also attacked the enemy forces in Camp Calivigny and allowed its easy capture by U.S. forces.

In 1989, the gunships were again in action over Panama. Spectres supported Army Special Forces and Rangers. On December 22 of that year, an AC-130H accepted the surrender of 200 Panamanian Defense Force fighters. The troops realized they were in the sights of the gunship, stood up and awaited the arrival of U.S. forces to accept their surrender.

Five AC-130Hs attacked a Panamanian infantry barracks just before U.S. troops dropped into the area. The gunship remained in the area for an additional two hours providing air support to friendly forces. Two AC-130Hs attacked the La Comandancia, the headquarters of the Panamanian Defense Force. The two AC-130H, flying in concentric orbit with one at high altitude and one lower, attacked and destroyed nine different targets in a short time. The two aircraft used their night vision to concentrate their fire without hitting one another.

Throughout the operation the AC-130s were at the forefront in support of U.S. forces. When Gen. Manuel Noriega was located hiding in the Vatican Embassy, an AC-130H was dispatched to circle the embassy to keep an eye on the compound.

The accuracy of the gunships was instrumental in providing lethal and heavy firepower against enemy positions while avoiding innocent civilian damage.

Gunships at Desert Storm

AC-130 gunships were back in action during Operation Desert Storm. In early 1990 their mission, again, was to support U.S. Special Forces and Army Rangers during their operations against the Iraqis. They were also tasked with providing airbase defense.

In December, AC-130s knocked out two Iraqi radar sites and a Scud missile launcher. When the Iraqis launched their attack upon the Saudi Arabian border town of Khafji, an AC-130H was sent to support American forces defending the area.

The gunship found lots of targets. Within a few minutes the crew targeted and destroyed eight enemy armored vehicles. The arrival of the gunship brought out the Iraqi antiaircraft units. The AC-130H was soon under attack by 23mm, 37mm, 57mm, and 100mm guns. At 2:00 A.M., the first gunship ran out of ammunition and was replaced by another AC-130H. At about 6:00 A.M., the gunship was hit by a ground-to-air missile that ripped off a section of the wing. The AC-130H crashed in the sea with the loss of all its crew.

The loss of the gunship was repaid several weeks later when AC-130Hs attacked and destroyed thousands of Iraqi troops and vehicles on the road leading out of Kuwait City. The road was christened the "Highway of Death."

$72 Million in Bells and Whistles

Based on its combat experience, the air force decided to create the ultimate gunship. In 1989, it began work on a new version that was christened the AC-130U. The new gunship cost $72,000,000 a copy and featured all the "bells and whistles" the air force could ever want.

The Spectre mounts a GAU-12/U 25mm Gatling gun in a nose-mounted traversable turret. This gun is capable of firing 1,800 rounds per minute from altitudes up to 12,000 feet. The aircraft also carriers a 40mm Bofors cannon and a 105mm cannon mounted on the port side of the fuselage. Both weapons can fire high-explosive, incendiary, and armor-piercing rounds.

In order to ensure that the weapons are on target, the Spectre is equipped with the latest and most technologically advanced sighting and target equipment. The aircraft has an all-light level television monitor that allows the gunners and pilot to see targets in any light. Targets are also identified using a laser illuminator, an AAQ-26 forward-looking infrared detection set, and multimode radar target-detection system.

The weapons' firing is coordinated by the onboard battle management center (BMC). The BMC personnel operate all the sensors, locate and identify targets, and select the proper weapon and ammunition to destroy the target. The BMC and the aircraft's weapons are capable of engaging two separate targets simultaneously.

Unlimited Range

The aircraft has a top speed of 300 mph, a service ceiling of 30,000 feet, and an unlimited range because of its ability to refuel while airborne. The aircrew is composed of 14 men. The air force currently has 13 AC-130Us in the inventory.

The new gunship did not have long to get its baptism of fire. Five AC-130s, one or two of which were undoubtedly AC-130Us, were dispatched to Afghanistan. Directed by U.S. Special Forces on the ground, the Spectre gunships launched devastating attacks against the defending Taliban forces. The attacks were particularly effective against the dug-in enemy. Crews were able to pick up individuals and groups of soldiers, clearly visible on the gunships' televisions, as they huddled in their trenches.

There is no doubt that the AC-130 gunship will be involved in any future US combat operations. The aircraft's ability to loiter over a battlefield and deliver a devastating array of lethal fire on multiple targets makes it a favorite of U.S. Infantry.

THE B-52

The warplane that has been in service the longest is the B-52. As this is written, it has been around for five decades. With upgrades, it may be around for another 50 years.

The B-52D was the third production variant to come off Boeing Aircraft's production lines. The "D" model comprised an aircraft production run of 170 aircraft. Boeing Aircraft in Seattle, Washington, built 101, while the Wichita, Kansas, plant built 69. All of the B-52Ds were delivered to the Strategic Air Command between June 1956 and November 1957. With its tall tail and paint scheme, this became the best known of the Stratofortress series. We single out this model because it is the one that saw action in Vietnam.

The B-52D came off the production lines with natural aluminum finish on the upper surfaces and a white underside antiradiation SAC paint scheme. The B-52D remained this color until 1965 when it was repainted black on the underside and tail. Also added in paint, on the top surfaces, was a Southeast Asia camouflage scheme, which came in two shades of green and one of tan.

As with the entire Stratofortress fleet, the B-52D was extensively modified to increase the aircraft's effectiveness and to reduce structural damage from metal fatigue.

One of the hardest problems to fix on the B-52D was leaking fuel tanks. Beginning in September 1957, the Blue Band program was implemented to repair weak sections on the bomber's interconnecting lines between wing fuel tanks. However, this did not completely fix the problem. The final fix, called Quick Clip, installed safety clips on the fuel lines, which finally stopped the wing-leak problem.

The Big Four modification was listed as the Mod 1000. The B-52D had to be able to penetrate heavily defended targets at low-level, under Soviet surface-to-air missile (SAM) defenses and associated early detection and guidance radars.

Not-So-Good Neighbor SAM

SAC's Stratofortresses, beginning in 1959, became vulnerable to Soviet SAMs. This was shown to be a credible concern when Soviet SAMs downed the U-2 spy plane on May 1, 1960. The U-2 was shot down by an SA-2 near the city of Sverdlovsk, deep inside central Russia, while attempting an intelligence overflight for the Central Intelligence Agency. The B-52D was equipped with the AN/ALQ-27 electronic counter-measures unit (ECM).

B-52 SPECIFICATIONS

Wingspan: 185 feet
Length: 156 feet, 6 inches
Height (at highest point, the tail): 48 feet, 3 inches
Weight (empty): 173,599 pounds
Weight (maximum): 450,000 pounds
Engines: Eight J-57-P-43W turbojets
Defensive armament: Four .50 caliber machine guns in the tail
Maximum speed: 636 mph
Service ceiling: 46,000 feet
Range: 6,326 miles
Crew: 6 (pilot, copilot, navigator, bombardier, electronic warfare officer, gunner)

Big Belly Modifications

The most famous upgrade for the B-52D was the 1965 Big Belly modifications, which increased the conventional bomb load capacity. This modification was especially critical for the bombing support missions flown for U.S. ground forces in Vietnam. This program increased the B-52's bomb load from a total of 27 bombs internally to eighty-four 500-pound Mark 82s or forty-two 750-pound Mark 117s in the bomb bay.

These bombs were loaded onto clips that were then hoisted into the bomb bay, decreasing munitions load time. An additional 24 bombs, 12 on each external underwing munitions pylon, were carried. This meant that there were 150 B-52Ds that had the capacity to carry a maximum conventional bomb load of 30 tons.

ARC LIGHT STRIKES

B-52 bombing missions in Southeast Asia were referred to as ARC LIGHT strikes. A B-52D ARC LIGHT strike usually consisted of three aircraft, referred to as a cell. The B-52Ds could drop a huge bomb load into a target box 3,000 feet wide and 9,000 feet long. The destruction on the ground was beyond description or comprehension.

Better Electronic Capabilities

In 1967, Rivet Rambler was implemented to give the B-52D better electronic capabilities to counter Soviet and Chinese radars and SAM equipment. This was called the Phase V ECM upgrade. Installed were one AN/ALR-18 receiving set, one AN/ALR-20 panoramic receiving set, one AN/APR-25 radar homing and warning system, four AN/ALT-6B or AN/ALT-22 continuous wave jamming transmitters, two AN/ALT-16 barrage jamming systems, one AN/ALT-32H (high), and one AN/ALT-32L (low) band jamming sets. The B-52D was also equipped with active defenses: six AN/ALE-20 flare dispensers, holding 96 flares, and eight AN/ALE-24 chaff dispensers, holding 1,125 bundles.

After Vietnam

After the Vietnam War, the B-52D was returned to its primary mission, nuclear deterrence. The 43rd Strategic Wing on Andersen Air Force Base, on the Pacific island of Guam, was equipped with the B-52D, still wearing its Southeast Asia camouflage. The B-52D usually was armed with four B28 nuclear, freefall gravity weapons. The four bombs were preloaded in the munitions area onto a clip, which was then hoisted into the forward section of the bomb bay. There was sufficient room for another weapons clip, but this was not a standard munitions load configuration. The B28 bomb could be dropped from either a low or a high altitude. It was withdrawn from the B-52D when the bomber was retired in 1982, although the weapon was available until 1990.

THE CODED SWITCH

The B-52D was equipped with a nuclear command and control device called a coded switch. Two wing Single Integrated Operations Plan (SIOP) officers (two-man policy for nuclear-related material was always in place) coded the switch in the intelligence facility, transported it to the aircraft, installed it into the B-52 through a side fuselage access door, and went inside the aircraft to the navigator's position where it was disenabled.

Once airborne and on nuclear alert, upon receipt of the proper nuclear command codes (authorized release by the president or surviving national command authority if the United States was attacked with nuclear weapons), the switch was re-enabled, allowing the crew to arm and drop the nuclear weapons on their assigned SIOP targets.

The Busy Observer

Its primary function as a deliverer of doomsday weapons aside, the B-52D became an important conventional weapons platform. The plane was used in the defense of South Korea, not during the Korean War but during the 1960s and 1970s, during the Cold War.

The B-52D was also used as a long-range reconnaissance aircraft. The B-52D, flying from Andersen Air Force Base on Guam, completed Busy Observer missions to the Indian Ocean and the Persian Gulf tracking Soviet freighters and warships during the Iran–Iraq War. These 33-hour missions required multiple air-to-air refuelings, to fly to the patrol area and return. The crew was augmented by two pilots and a navigator, making for crowded conditions. The crew was equipped with motorized 35mm cameras, fitted with telephoto lenses, and fast film to take photos of Soviet ships. Crews were trained in Soviet ship recognition by wing intelligence personnel and on camera operations. The flight profile used three aircraft, two primary and one spare. The spare flew to the first refueling point and then returned to base.

The Buff Bomber

By 1983, all B-52Ds had been retired from active duty and most had been destroyed under the compliance section of the arms reduction treaty with the Soviet Union. Twenty-five B-52Ds are in museums in the United States, South Korea, Guam, and the United Kingdom. They serve as memorials to those who flew the Stratofortress from 1956 to 1983. Today, only 93 B-52Hs continue in service, flying with the Air Combat Command (ACC). The USAF plans to keep 76 B-52Hs in service until 2030, a remarkable length of aviation longevity for one weapons system. The BUFF is a classic American bomber, one with a proud heritage and a remarkable operational lifespan.

OV-10A BRONCO: SPOTTING THE ENEMY OVER VIETNAM

During the mid-1950s it was time for the U.S. military to come up with a new artillery-spotting plane. The Cessna L-19 Bird Dog, which we discussed in Chapter 8, was approaching the end of its service life.

The U.S. Army and the Marine Corps decided to build a specifically designed artillery-spotter to replace the Bird Dog. The new plane would be a two-seat, twin-engine turboprop, capable of carrying light weapons and a small cargo load. It would be able to land on unimproved airfields or an aircraft carrier so it could provide ground support for Marines during an amphibious assault.

American advisers flying artillery-spotting missions over Vietnamese jungles found their Cessna Bird Dogs to be easy enemy targets. Pilots also spotted many enemy targets outside friendly artillery range. Since Bird Dogs were unarmed, they could do nothing to interdict the enemy except plot their position. The enemy realized they had been spotted and moved. Nothing was accomplished.

Birth of the Counter-Insurgency Aircraft

The Department of Defense needed to adapt to guerrilla warfare and so began a search for a new type of aircraft. This multimission aircraft was categorized as a counterinsurgency (COIN) aircraft. It would be designed to conduct short-range reconnaissance, locate enemy units, call in air or artillery strikes, and be armed with sufficient machine guns and bombs to attack enemy units located outside the range of friendly supporting arms. Plus, the aircraft would be armored to survive enemy small-arms fire and operate from unimproved airfields.

The first prototype, built by North American and unveiled in 1965, was an unusual looking aircraft. The YOV-10, as it was designated, was a high-wing monoplane with a 30-foot, 7-inch wingspan. The fuselage was suspended between two tail booms, giving the aircraft an overall length of 40 feet. The twin booms ended in a high-tail plane with a span of 14 feet, 7 inches. The prototype stood 15 feet, 2 inches tall. Power was provided by two Garrett 666 shaft horsepower T76-G-6 turboprop engines which gave the aircraft a top speed of 305 mph in level flight, a service ceiling of 27,000 feet, and a range of 125 miles. The YOV-10 prototype weighed 4,850 pounds empty and could fly a mission weighing as much as 10,550 pounds.

The crew of two sat, one behind the other, under a heavily glazed, bulbous canopy, which extended over most of the fuselage. It allowed excellent visibility to the front and sides for either crewman. Both crewmen could fly the aircraft and both were equipped with ejection seats. The YOV-10 was armed with four 7.62mm machine guns located in two stub wings mounted low on the fuselage. It could also carry a total of 2,400 pounds of ordnance on the various hard points located under the wings and fuselage. An assortment of bombs, napalm, 2.75-inch folding fin rocket pods, missiles, and fuel tanks could be attached to the hard points, depending on the mission.

In addition, there was cargo compartment behind the cockpit, big enough for 3,200 pounds of cargo or six fully loaded combat troops. The cargo door could be opened in flight and the aircraft provided an ideal delivery method for reconnaissance teams.

We Need More Power!

The prototype was tested and proved to be underpowered and unstable at low speeds. The engineers at North American went back to work. The main wingspan grew by 10 feet, and the fuselage by 1 foot, 7 inches. A pair of more powerful Garrett Airresearch 715 shaft horsepower T-76-G-10-12 engines were added. The new prototype (YO-10A) flew on August 15, 1966, and performed flawlessly. It was ordered into production as the OV-10A Bronco in October 1966.

The Marines took delivery of the first batch of aircraft by the winter of 1967 and soon had sufficient aircraft on hand to equip a squadron. After some training and familiarization with the aircraft in stateside exercises, the first six Broncos—under the command of Maj. Simon J. Kittler—were sent to Vietnam for evaluation. They arrived at Marble Mountain, in Vietnam, on July 6, 1969, and flew their first combat mission that same day.

The Marines were immediately impressed. The Broncos were used to find the elusive enemy and call in an array of allied supporting arms. The Marines trained its Bronco crews to call in artillery, air strikes, and naval gunfire. In addition, the aircraft's heavy armament allowed it to strike at any enemy target that presented itself.

The Marines used the versatile Bronco as an airborne tactical air coordinator, flare aircraft, cargo plane, and liaison aircraft, and to drop reconnaissance teams behind enemy lines. By the end of 1968, the Marines had sent two full squadrons of Broncos to Vietnam and the aircraft had flown 3,000 sorties.

USAF WANTS IN ON THE ACT

The success of the Bronco in Vietnam convinced the air force and navy that this would be an ideal aircraft for them as well. The air force purchased 157 OV-10As for use as forward air controllers. These aircraft coordinated attack-jet air strikes. The Broncos marked targets, gave spotting reports, and coordinated the entry and exit of fighters into and from the target area. Later in the war, they were equipped with a laser designator, allowing them to guide "smart" munitions on designated targets.

A total of 271 Broncos were built before the production line was closed in 1969. However, the Bronco's popularity continues. The production line is still periodically opened to build more.

The Bronco still serves the USAF and USMC as well as the military forces of Venezuela, Indonesia, Thailand, and South Korea.

SR-71 BLACKBIRDS

In May 1967, President Lyndon Johnson was told by the National Security Council that the North Vietnamese government had purchased sophisticated surface-to-air missiles.

The new SA-2 missiles represented a serious threat to the United States' aerial bombing campaign against Hanoi. In order to protect the American pilots, Johnson ordered an increase in aerial reconnaissance over North Vietnam.

The problem faced by American military planners was how to get the pictures. If the missiles could shoot down the bombers, they could certainly shoot down the standard U-2 reconnaissance aircraft.

UNMANNED DRONES

It was suggested that the use of unmanned reconnaissance drones in Vietnam might be productive—and, of course, would not put a pilot's life at risk. But in those early days of remote-control flight, drones were of limited value and many were falling prey to the enemy's increasingly sophisticated antiaircraft system.

Unmanned drones have improved greatly since Vietnam days, and have been used successfully in the war against terrorism in Afghanistan. Today's drones, as we'll see in Chapter 12, not only locate the enemy, but can fire upon the enemy as well.

The problem seemed insurmountable until Richard Helms, then director of Central Intelligence, suggested using the new A-12 strategic reconnaissance aircraft.

The A-12, or SR-71 as the later improved version was designated, was an ideal choice. It had been developed during the Cold War when the Americans needed a high-flying, high-speed aircraft to gather intelligence about what was going on behind the Iron Curtain.

The Lockheed SR-71A (strategic reconnaissance) made its first flight on December 22, 1964. The new aircraft—with its long, narrow delta-shaped fuselage—was 107 feet, 5 inches long.

The thin delta wings, mounted well back on the fuselage, had a span of 55 feet, 7 inches. Two inward canted tail assemblies located on the wings gave the aircraft a height of 18 feet, 6 inches.

The SR-71 in flight. The sleek lines of the aircraft are evident.

The aircraft was powered by two Pratt & Whitney J58-1 turbo ramjet engines with afterburners. Each engine delivered 32,500 pounds of thrust. Those engines could propel the aircraft at an astounding 2,193 mph.

The craft had an operational ceiling of 81,000 feet. At top speed the aircraft covered 33 miles a minute. The SR-71 weighed 65,000 pounds when empty. Fully loaded with fuel, surveillance equipment, and a two-man crew, it weighed 170,000 pounds.

The first Lockheed SR-71A was delivered to the 4200th Strategic Reconnaissance Wing stationed at Beale Air Force Base in California. The aircraft arrived wearing a coat of black paint, specially developed for high-altitude flight. The sleek, black aircraft was immediately nicknamed "Blackbird" by the men of the Wing.

Since there were so few of the aircraft and the maintenance and crew selection was so specialized, the air force consolidated all the aircraft into one wing. When missions required, small one- and two-plane detachments were deployed to various bases throughout the world.

President Johnson authorized sending the first two SR-71s to Okinawa, Japan, on May 22, 1967. When the aircraft landed, they were immediately escorted into a hangar. The doors were closed and no information was forthcoming to explain the arrival. Naturally, the arrival of the two aircraft caused a great deal of interest among both locals and military personnel.

Habu

The new secret plane was called the "Habu," named after an aggressive, all-black snake that was native to the island of Okinawa—which was, of course, the site of the largest battle in the Pacific Theater of WWII.

The SR-71A detachment in Okinawa was in precisely the right spot. It was near enough to North Vietnam to conduct the reconnaissance flights and fast enough to elude even the most sophisticated surface-to-air missiles. The base was also far enough away from the enemy as to keep it out of harm's way. The North Vietnamese had no method of attacking Okinawa.

With the SR-71A now available to military planners for use over North Vietnam, the first mission was laid on. On May 31, 1967, an SR-71A, flown by Major Mele Vojvodich, took off from Kadena Air Force Base in Okinawa and headed toward North Vietnam. The aircraft refueled from a KC-135 tanker over the South China Sea and then entered North Vietnamese airspace at 80,000 feet flying at a speed of Mach 3.1.

The aircraft flew across Haiphong and Hanoi with its cameras noting everything on the ground. The pilot noted that enemy fire control radars were tracking his aircraft. However, the speed of the aircraft was too great for the radars and the enemy fired their surface-to-air missiles in salvos in a vain attempt to knock the Blackbird down. None of the missiles got close. The SR-71A exited North Vietnam in the vicinity of Dien Bien Phu. The mission was a complete success. During its brief visit over North Vietnam, the Blackbird had captured on film 70 of an estimated 190 enemy surface-to-air sites.

After the first mission, 15 other missions were laid out, but only seven of them were ever flown. The North Vietnamese continued to try to shoot the SR-71A down, but they were getting no closer.

MURRAY'S ADVENTURE

The Blackbird continued to cause its crews much more trouble than the antiaircraft fire from the enemy did. On one flight, piloted by Frank Murray, the Blackbird's left engine experienced excessive vibration while flying over enemy territory. Murray successfully shut down the engine, but in the process of maneuvering the aircraft, he inadvertently pointed his camera across the Vietnamese border into Red China.

When the aircraft landed back at Kadena and the film was analyzed, it revealed a trainload of 152mm self-propelled artillery pieces preparing to cross into North Vietnam. The unintended intelligence windfall allowed military planners to find, track, and eventually destroy the big guns before they got into operation against U.S. forces.

North Vietnam Asks for Help

The reconnaissance flights had an immediate effect on North Vietnam. The SR-71s were simply too fast. They appeared on the radar and were gone before any kind of concentrated attack could be made against them.

The North Vietnamese asked their Soviet allies for help. Using a system of agents on the island of Okinawa and intelligence-gathering ships off the island, the Soviets were able to track the SR-71s when they took off and then alerted the North Vietnamese as to when to expect reconnaissance flights.

Even with this early-warning information, however, the North Vietnamese defenses were unable to knock down one of the spy planes. By 1968 there were three SR-71As on Okinawa dedicated to making overflights of North Vietnam.

As the war intensified, so did the number of flights. The aircraft flew a mission a week to determine what the enemy was planning and which enemy forces were moving toward South Vietnam.

Bomber Support

During the heavy B-52 bombing raids against North Vietnam, the Blackbirds were given a new mission. Now they flew in support of the big bombers.

Military Technical Journal

The SR-71 even looks fast when sitting on the ground.

On these missions, the SR-71As were sent aloft over North Vietnam while the B-52s were over their targets. The sensors on the reconnaissance plane could detect enemy radar.

The Blackbirds could listen in on North Vietnamese radio transmissions, which proved to be tremendously helpful as they rained bombs onto the enemy. Capturing this data allowed the U.S. intelligence agencies to dissect the enemy's battle plan and give the bomber crews new ways to defeat enemy tracking and firing radars.

The SR-71As also found that their immensely successful electronic countermeasures systems could be used to help shield the B-52s from enemy missile attacks.

The more bombing missions were flown over North Vietnam, the more missions were ordered for the reconnaissance aircraft. By 1970, the Blackbirds out of Okinawa were averaging two missions each per week.

Increased Tempo Takes Its Toll

The increased tempo of operations soon took its toll on the complicated aircraft. On May 10, 1970, after completing one reconnaissance flight over North Vietnam, both engines of an SR-71 flamed out immediately following refueling. Both crewmen ejected safely and the aircraft disintegrated when it plunged into the South China Sea.

The SR-71s were used to gather information on the Son Tay prisoner-of-war camp, prior to the U.S. raid on that facility.

The aircraft's ability to stay high in the air and still bring back detailed photos allowed them to shoot pictures at will without worrying about giving away their target.

In the late spring of 1972, the SR-71s were called upon to carry out one of their most unusual missions. They were ordered to "buzz" the infamous "Hanoi Hilton." The plan was to keep up the morale of the soon-to-be-released American prisoners of war being held there.

On May 2, 4, and 9, two SR-71s left Kadena, flying mission profiles that would allow them to set off two sonic booms within 15 seconds of one another. The twin booms would almost certainly convince the pilots that American aircraft were still out and about over North Vietnam. All three missions were successful.

As the war wound down in Southeast Asia, so did the number of SR-71A flights. When the Paris Agreement was signed on January 27, 1973, the number of flights dropped off radically. The number of SR-71As stationed on Okinawa also decreased.

By the spring of 1973 there were only two Habus left on the island, and they were restricted to standoff reconnaissance of Vietnam. The A-12 and improved SR-71A played an important part in gathering intelligence over North Vietnam during the war.

B-70 VALKYRIE: SUPERSONIC DASH

The SR-71 Blackbird was not the only U.S. aircraft that could routinely fly Mach 3 at 80,000 feet. The B-70 Valkyrie had an endurance of 7,600 miles and could carry multiple nuclear and conventional weapons.

Built by North American Aviation, the Valkyrie was born in a USAF requirement called Weapons System 110A. The requirement called for a subsonic cruise/supersonic-dash flight profile. This meant that the bomber could fly subsonically toward its target area, make a supersonic dash over its target, deliver its bombs, and then fly back home subsonically. The round trip distance, said the early specifications, was to be 7,600 miles. Remarkably, the requirement was laid down in 1954.

Both Boeing and North American studied the USAF requirement and decided that, in order to meet the payload/range specification, the aircraft would have to weigh 750,000 pounds. It would need to carry huge jettisonable external fuel tanks. It was clearly an impractical design so engineers went back to the drawing board. Further study uncovered a possible alternative. By combining a new high-energy chemical fuel then under development, and a new concept in supersonic aerodynamics called "compressive lift," a much smaller aircraft might be able to perform the mission by cruising supersonically over the whole flight.

After numerous cancellations, reviews, and changes in the program's direction, the first XB-70A was rolled out on May 11, 1964, at Palmdale, California. It had a wingspan of 105 feet, a height of 31 feet, 4 inches, and a length of 196 feet. It had a maximum takeoff weight of 530,000 pounds and carried a four-person crew.

The design featured small canard control surfaces near the crew compartment and large triangular wing surfaces. First flight was on September 21, 1964. The prototype flew from Palmdale, California, to Edwards Air Force Base. It was not until the third test flight, on October 12, 1964, that the bomber broke the sound barrier.

MACH 3

Mach 3 was met for the first time on October 14, 1965, on the seventh test flight. The second aircraft was fitted with an extensive instrumentation system to record structural loads, temperatures, aerodynamic pressures, and a host of other parameters. The second aircraft hit Mach 3 for the first time on January 3, 1966. On May 19 of that year, the second prototype flew at Mach 3 for 32 consecutive seconds. That kind of prolonged exposure to that speed was an important test. Mach 3 subjected the craft to aerodynamic stresses (heat soaking) that could not be simulated at lower speeds. The Valkyrie passed all its tests.

Disaster Strikes

Then disaster struck. On June 8, 1966, on a routine photo public relations flight, an F-104 chase plane flew too close to a Valkyrie on a test flight. The fighter became caught in the B-70's wingtip vortex, lost control, and collided with the bomber. The fighter almost immediately turned into a fireball, but the bomber, with its vertical tails sheared off and left wing damaged, briefly continued to fly. Then it began a slow roll, turned upside down, and went into a flat spin from which it did not recover.

The one prototype that had been fitted with all of the test equipment for the research program had been lost. Test flights continued with the first prototype, but the program never fully recovered. The final XB-70 flight occurred in early 1969. That remaining aircraft currently resides at the Air Force Museum in Dayton, Ohio.

Unique Design and Construction

"The Valkyrie was unique, not only for its astonishing performance, but also for its design and construction," writes aviation historian K. V. Horstmanshoff in *Military Technical Journal*. Using 1950s terminology, the Valkyrie was a "large tail-first delta-wing aircraft." The "tail-first" refers to the Valkyrie's canards, which are small wings forward of the main wings and used to control pitch. Pitch control surfaces are normally on the tail.

The wings had an exceedingly thin cross-section and a leading-edge sweepback of 65°. But what really set the wing apart from any other aircraft, before or since, was the fact that the outer third of the wing could be folded down in flight. For subsonic flight the wingtips were kept level, but for low supersonic flight they were folded down 25°, and for Mach 3 flight they were folded down 65°. Not only did this help improve stability and maneuverability, but at Mach 3, the wings helped capture the supersonic shock wave.

WAVE RIDER

At Mach 3, the shock wave interacts with the wing and the engine inlets and creates considerable lift. This significantly increases the lift-to-drag ratio, which accounts for the Valkyrie's exceptional payload/range performance. In effect, the design can be thought of as an early "wave rider," which is a concept again being studied for the hypersonic aircraft of the future.

A wave-rider aircraft operates on principles similar to a surfer riding an ocean wave, except that, in this case, the aircraft actually makes its own wave.

Construction of the Wings

Besides their unique aerodynamic design, the wings were also noteworthy for their construction. Unlike all large aircraft wings before or since, which are primarily constructed of aluminum sections bolted or riveted together, the Valkyrie was constructed primarily of stainless steel.

The wing "skins" were a series of brazed stainless steel honeycomb sandwich panels, welded together, with the leading-edge panels attached directly to the front spar. The canard and vertical tails had similar construction.

Titanium was used to construct the fuselage forward of the wing, with the fuselage sections over the wing also constructed of stainless steel honeycomb.

The entire wing was sealed by welding, since no sealants could survive the heat generated by Mach 3 speeds. Unlike the SR-71 Blackbird, which had a nasty habit of leaking like a sieve on the ground, the Valkyrie was not only fuel tight, but gas tight as well. This was because the fuel tanks were designed to be pressured with nitrogen gas on the ground and in flight.

Other Innovations

The Valkyrie incorporated numerous other innovations as well. Because sustaining Mach 3 flight for such a long period would completely heat-soak the aircraft's structure, fuel, and systems, many of its greatest innovations were in the area of thermal control.

The Valkyrie's fuel got quite hot during flight, which is why the pressurized nitrogen system was developed: to keep the hot fuel bathed in an inert gas to prevent auto-ignition. Thus, the structure was made of a stainless steel alloy that could handle the heat loads without weakening.

The aft-engine bay structure was made of special high-temperature H-11 steel. The areas that contained heat-susceptible components, like the landing-gear wheel wells and braking parachute bays, were equipped with a "water all" cooling system. The landing-gear tires were made of a special high-temperature rubber and painted silver to reflect heat.

The Valkyrie's flight crew needed to survive not only the heat of sustained high-Mach flight, but also the dangers of ejection at high speed and high altitude. The crew compartment was fully air-conditioned and pressurized. Each seat formed a self-contained ejection capsule.

The crew operated in a "shirtsleeve" environment, requiring no pressure suits or even oxygen masks. By contrast, the crew of the Blackbird wears fully pressurized suits and helmets so that they look like astronauts.

CHAPTER 11

SEA-BASED WARPLANES OF TODAY

In this chapter, we look at the modern sea-based warplane. We learn that one of the big differences between land-based and carrier aircraft is that the carrier aircraft needs to be tougher. A plane that lands and takes off with the luxury of a long runway at an airfield will not undergo anywhere near the stress of a carrier plane.

On a carrier, planes don't roll into an easy takeoff or slow to a stop after a smooth landing. Instead, they are thrown into the air when they take off and are jerked to a stop when they land. It has long been said that landings on a carrier are more like controlled crashes.

CATAPULTS

Since planes taking off from a flight deck don't have as much runway as those on a land airstrip, they need a little boost. A catapult, which gives the aircraft the needed momentum to take off, was the answer and was used even in the days of the Wright brothers.

Today's catapults are steam-powered pistons strong enough to throw an automobile 800 yards. The catapult consists of tubes that have been set into the deck, 200 feet long. At the rear of the tubes are pistons, and these are attached to something called a shuttle that runs along the top of the deck. This shuttle is attached to the nose wheel tow bar of an aircraft.

Super-pressurized steam from the ship's power plant causes pressure to build up behind the pistons. When it has built up to a sufficient degree, the pressure is released all at once. The pistons push the shuttle and the shuttle pushes the aircraft down the flight deck. The aircraft is thrown up off the deck. A bar connecting the shuttle to the plane is released and off we go into the wild, blue yonder.

Catapults for the most part have been fairly dependable—although a notable breakdown occurred during the Falklands War when a malfunction aboard an Argentinean aircraft carrier gave Great Britain an ever greater advantage in that short and one-sided conflict.

THE CONTROLLED CRASH

The concept behind landing an aircraft on a carrier is simple. The pilot doesn't land as much as he aims his plane (at speeds of up to 100 mph) at a spot on the flight deck and then allows the carrier to catch the plane. This is "controlled crashing."

Dangling off the back of the plane is a tailhook. Across the deck are stretched a series of (usually four) super-strong steel wires. The plane hits the deck rear wheels first. The arresting hook catches the wires, the nose wheel slams down, and the plane is yanked to a halt.

The wires start close to the stern of the ship and are laid across one every couple of hundred feet. This gives the pilot a margin of error, but not much. And pilots do miss. That is why the landing strip is angled away from the ship's island and other parked aircraft—so that errant pilots will do as little damage as possible.

IF A PILOT MISSES

A pilot who misses the wires doesn't roll off the edge of the ship into the sea. Instead he or she goes full throttle, bounces the wheels off the deck, and flies back into the air. Pilots actually accelerate into their landings so that they will be able to easily take off again in case something goes wrong.

Pilots always aim for one of the two middle wires, as this allows for the most margin of error. Undershoot and the first wire can be caught. Overshoot and the last wire can be caught. Aim for the first wire and you're apt to come up shy of the ship's stern.

RUGGEDLY BUILT

Carrier craft have always been built to be a lot more rugged than land-based craft. This, of course, comes with a price. Fuel mileage is affected. All that reinforcement in the landing system and fuselage is heavy.

Carrier craft do not have the unrefueled range, and generally cannot carry as many bombs, as do their land-based cousins. (Because of tanking, the ability of modern aircraft to refuel while in flight, the actual difference in range, in some cases, no longer exists.) On the other hand, carrier-based aircraft can go places that land-based craft can't get to, and that is their strength. They can go wherever their ship takes them.

It has only been recently that, through the use of new materials, engineers have been able to design carrier aircraft that are strong enough to handle the stresses of launching and recovery, are also light enough to compete with land-based aircraft. The F/A-18 Hornet, to be discussed later in this chapter, fits into this category.

FOLDING WINGS

Not long after carriers first hit the seas, the need for planes with fold-back wings became apparent. Because of their wingspans, too few planes could be stored in a ship's hangar. Design the wings to unlock at a hinge and fold back, like the wings on a fly, and you could fit many more aircraft into the same size hangar deck.

In the early days of naval aviation, a plane's wings were unlocked by hand and manually folded back. The first British plane with folding wings was the Short Folder, which flew in 1914. It had a wingspan of 67 feet. The wings folded laterally 90° until they ran parallel to the fuselage.

Today, the folding wings of modern aircraft are hydraulically controlled by the pilot. After landing, the pilot presses a button and a chain of electronic wiring, electrical cable, and hydraulic tubing does the work.

VECTORED THRUST

The problems of launching and recovering aircraft on a carrier are lessened when that craft has the ability to take off and land vertically.

During the 1950s, technology was developed to allow full-fledged fighter jets to get into the air and return to Earth in this manner. Aircraft that take off and land like helicopters but fly like jets are called Vertical/Short Takeoff and Landing (V/STOL) aircraft. When used on land, these aircraft remove the necessity for an airstrip.

The British have always been at the forefront when it came to developing this technology. They began working on this revolutionary form of aircraft back in the 1950s. The jets used something called "vectored thrust" to not only take off and land vertically, but to hover in place.

The first V/STOL craft, known as the P.1127, was flown in 1960 and it evolved into today's Harrier. Harrier jets are built in England by British Aerospace, and in the United States by McDonnell Douglas Corporation.

The advantages of using V/STOL aircraft off carriers is that they do not need tailhooks and the flight decks they take off from and land on do not need catapults and arresting wires. They also do not need to be reinforced to withstand the stress of catapult launches and arresting wire recoveries.

The disadvantages of V/STOL jets are that they need a tremendous amount of fuel to take off and land. All this vectored thrust makes for one thirsty bird. V/STOL technology is still developing. We are years away from an all-V/STOL naval air force.

Harriers are used on Navy/Marine amphibious ships, where their job is to deliver Marines to the battlefield, but not on U.S. Navy super-carriers.

Harrier II Plus

The most recent American version of the Harrier is the Harrier II Plus, which is the first V/STOL craft to include the state-of-the-art APG-65 radar system. It was first flown in 1995. The Harrier II, of course, can operate in places where conventional aircraft cannot.

While previous versions of the Harrier had been designed to provide fast and effective support for Marine ground forces as well as interdiction missions, the addition of the radar meant that it could now perform a wide range of missions around the clock.

The radar, in conjunction with the aircraft's night-attack systems, increased the pilot's ability to perform air-to-surface and air-to-air missions in periods of darkness and bad weather. The Harrier II Plus radar also provided improved self-defense and pilot situational awareness.

The Harrier II is equipped with a Rolls-Royce Pegasus F402-RR-408 engine. It was developed through a trinational agreement between the United States, Spain, and Italy.

Harriers in Action

The Harrier first saw combat on May 1, 1982, during the Falklands War, operating off the HMS *Hermes*. The mission was the bombing and strafing of Port Stanley. Four days later the first Sea Harrier was shot down in combat, its pilot killed, by a surface-to-air missile. On May 9, a Sea Harrier sunk its first ship, an Argentine trawler, by bombing and strafing.

The Harrier was the first Marine Corps tactical aircraft to arrive in the theater during Operation Desert Storm, the liberation of Kuwait, in 1991. Harriers operated both from land bases and from ships in the Persian Gulf. During the 42 days of Desert Storm combat, 86 Harriers flew 3,380 sorties and 4,112 combat hours, and they delivered more than 6,000,000 pounds of ordnance.

In October 2002, six AV-8B Harrier jump jets aboard the 820-foot Tarawa-class amphibious assault ship USS *Belleau Wood* were used to support the war on terrorism in Yemen.

Today, the U.S. Navy's amphibious assault ships, used to deliver Marines close enough to the battle so that they can be flown to the battlefield, use AV-8B Harrier aircraft.

THE MODERN AIRCRAFT CARRIER

Now let's take a look at the aircraft that can be found on today's U.S. Navy aircraft carrier. We start with the F-14.

F-14 Tomcat

One squadron of F-14 Tomcats can be found on today's aircraft carrier.

In the late 1960s, General Dynamics had been contracted to design a new fleet defense jet for the navy. The company had no previous experience building carrier aircraft, and so it subcontracted the job out to Grumman, who had been making planes for the navy for decades. The job was to convert the F-111B, a previous-generation fighter, into a carrier craft that met all modern needs.

Grumman succeeded so well at this task that the jets are still being used more than 30 years later. The war in Vietnam was going on at the time and the navy was learning valuable lessons in what was needed in a modern fighter.

F-14 SPECIFICATIONS

Length: 62 feet, 8 inches
Wingspan: 64 feet, 1 inch
Height: 16 feet
Engines: Two F110-GE-400, capable of 27,400 pounds of thrust
Fuel capacity: 16,200 pounds
Maximum takeoff weight: 74,348 pounds
Armament: Any combination of Phoenix, AMRAAM, Sparrow, and Sidewinder missiles weighing up to 14,500 pounds; one 20mm M61 cannon

Grumman knew that it needed more than a good radar/missile platform. It needed a fighter with all the long-range/high-endurance attributes of a fleet defense missile carrier, a long-range radar/missile system, and dogfight/fighter escort capabilities.

Grumman looked at more than 6,000 configurations before deciding on the design, using the best of designs from previous Grumman aircraft. The F-111's variable geometry wings, TF30 engines, AWG-9 radar/fire control, and Phoenix missiles were combined with the F-4's tandem crew seating, and Sparrow and Sidewinder missiles.

Navy experience in Vietnam had taught the navy the need for an internal gun so, in the F-14 Tomcat, Grumman included the combat-proven M61 Vulcan 20mm six-barrel Gatling gun. Grumman also built in provisions for up to 14,500 pounds in air-to-ground or air-to-air weapons on the weapons stores stations. Several changes were made in the design over the years.

The F-14D, which is the version that is still being flown, made its debut in 1990.

Although there are no immediate plans for an F-14E—that is, no major upgrades are planned—the Tomcat is still scheduled to perform the navy's "outer air battle" mission well into the twenty-first century. The Tomcat continues to receive incremental improvements. New software upgrades are regularly being installed.

F/A-18 Hornet

Also on the modern-day aircraft carrier flight deck are three squadrons of F/A-18 Hornets. The most recent version of this jet is the F/A-18E/F, also known as the Hornet Strike Fighter.

The new version comes in both one-seat and two-seat versions. It was a significant improvement over the earlier Hornets. It can deliver greater fighting capabilities over a greater range, can carry more fuel, and is 25 percent larger. There is increased engine power, which allows for a quick response time.

F/A-18 Industry Team (McDonnell Douglas/ Northrop/General Electric/Hughes)

The F/A-18 has 11 wing and fuselage stations for weapons.

A new active matrix liquid-crystal touch screen placed in the upper center of the main instrument panel allows the pilot to call up altitude information, engine and fuel status, and weapons readiness virtually at eye level, with an unusually high contrast so that the display will not wash out in direct sunlight.

The new Hornet has 11 weapons stations, featuring AIM-9 Sidewinder air-to-air missiles on the wingtips; AGM-88 *HARM* (High-Speed Anti-radiation Missile) and the Harpoon Antiship Missile as well as the AGM-84H Standoff Land Attack Missile-Expanded Response (SLAM-ER) on the right wingtip inboard; the left wingtip inboard is armed with the AGM-65E Maverick, the AGM-154 Joint Standoff Weapon, and the BLU-109 Joint Direct Attack Munition (JDAM).

McDonnell Douglas Corp.

The F/A-18E4 Super Hornet was painted white and orange to provide high visibility for ground cameras during its three years of flight testing at Pax River.

When adapted as an electronic warfare aircraft, the Sidewinders are replaced by receiving pods, and a satellite communications (Satcom) receiver is added directly behind the cockpit.

The new design has altered the Hornet's airframe structure, lengthening the fuselage, tripling the size of the payload brought back to the ship.

F/A-18 SPECIFICATIONS

Length: 60 feet, 4 inches

Wingspan: 44 feet, 11 inches

Height: 16 feet

Maximum speed: Mach 1.8+

Combat ceiling: 50,000 feet

Combat radius: 660+ nautical miles

Armament internal: Lightweight M61A1 20mm cannon with 400 rounds of ammunition.

Armament external: 17,750 pounds maximum. Weapons include AIM-9 Sidewinder; AIM-7 Sparrow; AIM-120 AMRAAM; Harpoon; HARM; Shrike; SLAM-ER; Walleye and Maverick TV, laser and infrared-guided missiles; Joint Standoff Weapon (JSOW); Joint Direct Attack Munition (JDAM); and various current and future general-purpose bombs, mines, and rockets.

Weapons stations: 11 wing and fuselage stations.

The new Hornet F/A-18E/Fs are propelled by two General Electric F414 afterburning turbofan engines that provide 22,000 pounds of thrust, with a nine-to-one thrust-to-weight ratio. The fan gives 16 percent higher airflow; the combustor operates at lower metal temperatures; and the turbines are made of high-temperature resistant monocrystal blades.

This robust engine tolerates intense abuse and comes back for more. The Hornet had proven itself to be a reliable combat aircraft even before these upgrades. With them, they have a much improved speed, range, and efficiency.

History of the Hornet

In 1974, the U.S. Navy initiated the VFAX study to find a new, lightweight, multi-mission carrier-based fighter. Each carrier air group was composed of fighter aircraft, attack aircraft, reconnaissance aircraft, and patrol aircraft.

The requirement to carry out the various missions had often resulted in several different types of aircraft equipping the squadrons. Each different type of aircraft required spare parts, special tools, and specially trained pilots and mechanics. If the navy could find one aircraft that could carry out many different roles, it could save millions of dollars on spare parts and personnel. In addition, the carrier air group would become more efficient.

The study was just underway when funds were withdrawn from the program. The USAF had just gone through a study to develop its next fighter. In the course of the development, several major aircraft manufacturers had submitted designs that might well meet the navy's requirement without undergoing a lengthy and costly development study.

The navy looked at all the prototype aircraft and decided that the General Dynamics YF-16 and the Northrop YF-17 were the closest to its needs. However, both would need substantial revision to make them acceptable for work aboard an aircraft carrier. The firm that could best modify their design for work on the high seas would win the new contract.

Teaming Up

McDonnell Douglas, whose F-4 Phantom aircraft was replaced by the winner, approached Northrop with an offer to team up to develop not only a navy version of its design but one with many improved design features.

The new design was christened the Navy Air Combat Fighter. Melding McDonnell Douglas's naval aircraft experience with Northrop's design led to a superior aircraft. In January 1976, the design was accepted as the winner of the competition and the navy ordered prototypes built for testing.

Two distinct versions were ordered. The first was a two-seat version to be known as the F-18. The other was a single-seat attack version to be known as the A-18. The navy also ordered a trainer version that was designated as the TF-18.

The first of 11 prototype aircraft flew for the first time on November 18, 1978. The prototypes were impressive. The new aircraft, which was nicknamed the Hornet, was a cantilever, midwing monoplane with a twin tail. The aircraft had twin General Electric F404-GE-400 engines with afterburners. Each engine generated 16,000 pounds of thrust.

Packed into the airframe were the most advanced communications, flight controls, radar, and navigational equipment McDonnell Douglas and the navy could find.

Of course, the aircraft was adapted for carrier use. It was equipped with carrier launch and arresting gear. The wingtips could be folded up to increase storage space aboard ship and the landing gear was specially strengthened to allow for the shock of carrier landings. The prototypes were successful and after a full range of tests, the aircraft was accepted into the navy.

Replacing the Phantom

The success of the Hornet's new design convinced the Marine Corps that the Hornet would also be used to replace its aging McDonnell Douglas F-4 Phantom fighter and fighter-bomber jets. Since the Marine Corps routinely embarks its squadrons aboard aircraft carriers, the standardization made sense.

The first production version of the Hornet was delivered in May 1980 to VFA-125 stationed at Lemoore, California. This squadron was a joint Navy and Marine Corps squadron that would transition pilots to the new aircraft. By the time the first production version arrived, the nomenclature of the aircraft had changed to F/A-18. The difference between the two versions was a small amount of operational equipment on the aircraft and the ordnance load it carried.

The F/A-18 Hornet had a wingspan of 40 feet, 4 inches, with sidewinder missiles mounted on the outer wingtips. Without any ordnance creating drag, it had a top speed of 1,190 mph. It had a combat ceiling of 50,000 feet and in the fighter configuration had a range of 460 miles.

STING OF THE HORNET

The business end of the F/A-18 was quite impressive. It carried an M61 20mm six-barreled cannon with 570 rounds of ammunition. The gun was mounted in the nose. In addition to M61, the aircraft had nine external hard points—locations on an aircraft wing where weapons can be mounted.

The Hornet could carry 17,000 pounds of missiles, bombs, sensor pods, or extra fuel tanks. Among the weapons it could carry were the AIM-7 and AIM-9 air superiority missiles.

The new Hornet was quite successful in operational use. By 1984, three Marine Corps squadrons, VMFA 314, VMFA 323, and VMFA 531, had transitioned to the Hornet along with several navy squadrons. In that same year, a reconnaissance version was introduced.

Within a few years, the navy and McDonnell Douglas were at work to build an improved version. On September 3, 1986, the new F/A-18C was unveiled. It featured improved avionics for night flights, new General Electric F404-Ge-402 turbofan engines, and improved hard points that allowed the aircraft to carry the AIM-120 Phoenix Missile and the AGM-65 Maverick ground attack missile. The first F/A-18C was delivered to the Naval Warfare Center and was an immediate success.

The next improvement was to the two-seat night attack version. The aircraft had a Forward Looking Infrared Radar (FLIR) unit and improved attack computers for work at night. The new version was designated the F/A-18D and flew for the first time on November 1, 1988.

Within a few years the U.S. Navy and Marine Corps had fielded 37 tactical squadrons from air stations worldwide, and from 10 aircraft carriers. The U.S. Navy's Blue Angels Demonstration Team also chose the Hornet as its mount. However, as impressive as the aircraft was, it had to prove itself in combat. Its combat debut was not far off. During the Gulf War of 1991, the Hornet proved its immense value and versatility.

During Operation Desert Storm, the first war with Iraq in 1991, F/A-18s en route to bomb enemy targets were attacked by enemy fighters. Without jettisoning their bomb loads, they engaged and shot down the fighters and then went on to bomb their assigned targets. (Complete air dominance was the rule in Operation Iraqi Freedom as well.)

In the high-threat environment, the Hornets were certain to take damage from enemy antiaircraft guns and antiaircraft missiles. Several F/A-18s were damaged by enemy action. Despite the extent of the damage, all were able to make it back to their aircraft carriers or friendly airfields.

The vast majority were quickly repaired and most were flying combat missions the next day. Such was the ruggedness of the aircraft that during the course of the war they broke all records for mission availability and reliability.

Super Hornet

After the design of the F/A-18D, the engineers at McDonnell Douglas decided that the added weight of new ordnance would require a longer and stronger airframe. This requirement resulted in the proposal to build the F/A-18E and F. This version was officially designated the "Super Hornet."

The new airframe had 11 hard points and 17 cubic feet of growth space for electronic systems. The new versions could carry the improved APG-73 radar and had the room to accommodate future electronic improvements that might be needed.

The Super Hornet made its first flight at Patuxent River, Maryland, in September 1995. The F/A-18E/F was quite impressive. The design team not only enlarged the fuselage but also incorporated new technology into the aircraft. The Super Hornet incorporated low observable technology with improved radar and state-of-the-art defensive electronic countermeasures.

With these changes, the F/A-18E/F reduced its own vulnerability while increasing its lethality against air and ground targets. In practical terms the aircraft can carry 3,600 pounds or 33 percent more fuel. This allows the Super Hornet to fly up to 40 percent farther on a typical interdiction mission and to stay on station for 80 percent longer on a combat air patrol.

In January 1997, the Super Hornet conducted carrier qualifications aboard USS *John C. Stennis* (CVN 74). These tests involved both carrier launches and landings and deck handling operations for the pilots and flight deck crews.

All tests were successful, and with that the navy ordered the F/A-18E/F into production. The first operational cruise of the Super Hornet was onboard the USS *Abraham Lincoln* on July 24, 2002. The aircraft saw initial combat action on November 6, 2002. That action came when E models participated in a strike on hostile targets in the "no-fly" zone in Iraq. During the second war with Iraq during the spring of 2003, the F/A-18 E/F led the navy's attack on Iraqi defenses.

The Super Hornet can carry every tactical air-to-air and air-to-ground weapon in the navy's inventory. With the AMRAAM missile, enhanced radar, and advanced onboard sensor fusion capability, there is not a threat fighter in the world today—or projected to exist in the next 20 years—that the Super Hornet cannot decisively defeat and totally dominate in combat.

EA-6B Prowler

Also on the flight deck of a modern aircraft carrier you'll see four EA-6B Prowlers. Made by Grumman, the EA-6B Prowler is a twin-engine, mid-wing aircraft. Its airframe is modified from that of the A-6 Intruder airframe.

The EA-6B first saw action in the Vietnam War in July 1972. It is a fully integrated electronic warfare system combining long-range, all-weather capabilities with advanced electronic countermeasures.

More avionics equipment are located in a forward equipment bay and pod-shaped faring on the vertical fin. The cockpits are side by side for maximum efficiency, visibility, and comfort.

EA-6B PROWLER SPECIFICATIONS

Length: 59 feet, 10 inches

Wingspan: 53 feet

Height: 16 feet, 3 inches

Weight: Max gross, takeoff: 61,000 pounds (27,450 kg)

Primary function: Electronic countermeasures

Contractor: Grumman Aerospace Corporation

Propulsion: Two Pratt & Whitney J52-P408 engines (11,200 pounds thrust each)

Speed: Max speed with five jammer pod: 610 mph

Climb rate: 10,030 feet per minute

Range: More than 1,000 nautical miles (1,150 miles, 1,840 km)

Ceiling: 38,000 feet

Crew: Four (pilot and three electronic countermeasures officers)

Armament: Up to 4AGM-88A HARM missile

Date deployed: First flight, May 25, 1968

Operational: July 1971

The Prowlers received a major *ICAP* (Improved Capability) in 1976. This upgrade involved new displays, AN/ALQ-126 multiple-band defensive and radar deception gear, better jamming equipments, and a new "hard kill" capability with AGM-88A Harm missiles.

E-2C Hawkeye

For almost 40 years, the E-2C Hawkeye has been the navy's all-weather, carrier-based tactical warning and control system aircraft. The concept of an airborne early warning and command and control aircraft was born in the mid-1950s, due to the continuous improvements in early airborne radar. The first plane to perform this mission was the Hawkeye's daddy, the Grumman E-1 Tracer, which was based on the S-2 Tracker, an antisub aircraft.

The E-1 performed from 1954 until 1964, when it was replaced by the Hawkeye. The E-2 was the first carrier-based aircraft designed from the outset for the all-weather airborne early warning and command and control function.

E-2C SPECIFICATIONS

Primary function: Airborne early warning, command and control

Contractor: Grumman Aerospace Corp.

Unit cost: $51 million

Propulsion: Two Allison T-56-A427 turboprop engines; (5,000 shaft horsepower each)

Length: 57 feet, 6 inches

Wingspan: 80 feet, 7 inches

Height: 18 feet, 3 inches

Weight: Max. gross, takeoff: 53,000 pounds, 40,200 pounds basic

Speed: 300+ knots (345 mph)

Ceiling: 30,000 feet

Crew: Five

Armament: None

Operational: January 1964

In addition to this function, the Hawkeye has performed surface surveillance coordination, strike and interceptor control, search and rescue guidance, and communications relay. The navy calls the Hawkeye the "eyes of the fleet."

The Hawkeye made its combat debut in Vietnam, and also directed F-14 Tomcat fighters flying combat air patrol during the two-carrier battle group joint strike against terrorist-related Libyan targets in 1986.

During both wars against Iraq (1991 and 2003), the Hawkeye directed both land attack and combat air patrol missions over Iraq and provided control for the shoot-down of Iraqi fighter aircraft. The latest model of the aircraft, the E-2C, has been around since 1973.

The E-2 Hawkeye is not a weapon. It carries no arms. Instead it is part of the carrier's sensory system, part of the eyes and ears of the ship. Introduced in 1964, the Hawkeye's dominant feature is its radar dome mounted on top of the plane. The Hawkeye extends the detection range of a battle group by 298 miles for aircraft and 160 miles for missiles. It can also detect ships.

S-3 Viking

Also onboard today's U.S. Navy carrier are six S-3 A/B Vikings. The S-3A Viking entered fleet service in 1974. It replaced the S-2 Tracker. It is an all-weather, long-range, multi-mission aircraft. It operates primarily with carrier battle groups in antisubmarine warfare zones. It carries automated weapon systems, and is capable of extended missions with in-flight refueling.

PRESIDENT BUSH FLIES A VIKING

On May 1, 2003, 43 days after the beginning of Operation Iraqi Freedom, President George W. Bush announced to the nation that "major combat operations in Iraq have ended." He made this announcement to a national TV audience from the deck of the USS *Abraham Lincoln*. The ship, which was in the Pacific, was heading home for the first time in ten months.

The president landed on the carrier in the copilot seat of an S-3B Viking. President Bush was a fighter pilot during the 1970s in an F-102 Delta Dagger during his stint in the Texas Air National Guard.

He was asked if he had flown the Viking and admitted that the pilot had briefly turned over the controls to him. "Yes, I flew it," President Bush said. "Really exciting. I miss flying."

He then spent time shaking hands and having photos taken with many of the sailors and aviators aboard. He emerged from the Viking in a flight suit, his helmet tucked under his arm—but had changed into a suit and tie when he made his historic address to the nation.

The S-3 Viking, developed to counter the hard-to-hear Soviet nuclear submarines, carries a crew of four (pilot, copilot, tactical coordinator, and acoustic sensor operator). Debuting in 1972, it uses the AN/APS-116 search radar, OR-89 FLIR. The Viking carries 60 *sonobuoys (sonic detectors)* and is capable of carrying torpedoes, bombs, and depth charges.

The current version, the B version, has been around since 1981. The new version features improved acoustic processing, expanded ESM coverage, increased radar processing capability, new sonobuoys receiver system, and it is capable of housing the AGM-84 Harpoon ASM. The B version's main difference compared to the A can be distinguished by a *chaff* dispenser located on its aft fuselage. (Chaff consists of strips of metal foil or wire that is ejected from an aircraft into the air in order to confuse an enemy's radar.) Most A models have been converted to B standards.

The S-3B Viking is based on the S-3A, which was formerly configured for antisubmarine warfare (ASW). Today's Viking, however, is a top surveillance and precision-targeting platform with modern precision-guided missile capabilities.

S-3B VIKING SPECIFICATIONS

Primary function: Force protection, organic overhead/mission tanking

Contractor: Lockheed-California Company

Unit cost: $27 million

Propulsion: Two General Electric TF-34-GE-400B turbofan engines (9,275 pounds of thrust each)

Length: 53 feet, 4 inches

Wingspan: 68 feet, 8 inches

Height: 22 feet, 9 inches

Weight: Max design gross takeoff: 52,539 pounds

Speed: 450 knots (518 mph)

Ceiling: 40,000 feet

Range: 2,645 miles

Armament: Up to 3,958 pounds of AGM-84 Harpoon, AGM-65 Maverick and AGM-84 SLAM missiles, torpedoes, rockets, and bombs.

Crew: Two/four

Service Entry: 1975

The S-3B Viking is an all-weather, carrier-based jet aircraft. It provides protection against hostile ships while also functioning as the carrier battle groups' primary overhead/mission tanker. Extremely versatile, the aircraft is equipped for many missions, including day/night surveillance, electronic countermeasures, command/control/communications warfare, and search and rescue (SAR).

Among its features are several high-speed computer system processes which display information generated by their targeting-sensor systems. These systems include the Inverse/Synthetic Aperture Radar (ISAR/ SAR), and the infrared (IR) sensor and an Electronic Support (ESM) system.

The S-3B Viking employs an impressive array of airborne weaponry to engage and destroy targets. These include the AGM-84 Harpoon Antiship Missile, AGM-65 Maverick IR missile and a wide selection of conventional bombs and torpedoes. In the future, planned Viking aircraft will have a control capability for the AGM-84 Standoff Land Attack Missile Extended Range (SLAM-ER) missile.

All right, now—just when you've gotten your sea legs under you, it's time to return to land for a look at today's state-of-the-art land-based warplanes.

CHAPTER 12

STATE-OF-THE-ART WARPLANES

In this chapter, we look at the aircraft that are currently being used by the USAF. These warplanes include some veterans of combat, such as the F-16, as well as aircraft that are still under development, such as the F-22 Raptor.

THE F-16 FIGHTING FALCON

Although the F-16's official name is the Fighting Falcon, its nickname used by USAF pilots is Viper—because it strikes like a deadly snake. More than 4,000 F-16s have been built in a whopping 110 variations.

During the early 1970s, NATO held a competition for the best design of a new lightweight fighter plane. The winner was General Dynamics, which designed a fighter jet that weighed half of what the F-4 Phantom weighed.

Because of its low weight, the F-16, which entered service in the mid-1970s, can accelerate vertically (nose pointed straight up) and pull turns at 9 Gs—and it does this all with one engine. The flight controls are "fly-by-wire" and computerized. Fly-by-wire means there are no direct hydraulic or mechanical linkages between the pilot and the flight controls. Circuits send inputs from the pilot to the motors that move the various flight controls on the aircraft.

Prototypes

In 1974, two prototypes were built by General Dynamics. These were designated YF-16s. To keep maintenance simple, systems were placed behind easily removable access panels. Phil Oestricher, the top test pilot at General Dynamics at the time, was the first man to fly an F-16.

All the tests on the prototypes went well and General Dynamics was awarded a contract to build 15 of the aircraft. Eleven of these were single-seat F-16As. The other four would be two-seater F-16Bs. When these aircraft demonstrated outstanding performance, the USAF ordered 650 more.

USED AROUND THE GLOBE

The F-16 is the warplane used by the most different air forces. It has been flown by 20 other nations, not counting the United States, and is still flown by 16 foreign air forces. The reason: the F-16's combination of quality and affordability.

Among the nations that use the F-16 are Greece, Turkey, Israel, and Egypt. Israeli F-16s were used in 1981 by the Israeli air force to take out an Iraqi nuclear power plant before it could become operational.

The F-16 is powered by a single engine: the General Electric F110-GE-129 or Pratt & Whitney F100-PW-229. The fuel supply is equipped with an inert gas antifire system. An in-flight refueling probe is installed in the top of the fuselage.

Armament

Because the F-16 was originally conceived to be a dogfighter, it was intended to carry only a gun and Sidewinder air-to-air missiles. The potential for the F-16 to be used as an air-to-ground warplane was quickly realized and a wide variety of air-to-ground weapons were added to its arsenal.

It can still function as an air-to-air fighter. However, pilots can still shoot with the M-61A1 Vulcan 20mm cannon. The cannon's double-ended linkless feed system has a capacity of 500 rounds with a firing rate of 6,000 rounds per minute.

Nine pylons on the wings can hold a combination of weapons, external fuel tanks, and electronic countermeasures (ECM) pods. The pylons can even be used to deliver an atomic device.

F-16 SPECIFICATIONS

Purpose: Multi-role fighter
Wingspan (without missiles): 31 feet
Wingspan (with missiles): 32 feet, 10 inches
Length: 47 feet, 7¾ inches
Height: 16 feet, 5½ inches
Power plant: One Pratt & Whitney F100-PW-200 turbofan
Fuel capacity: 1,072 gallons in F-16A; 889 gallons in F-16B (plus provision for 300-gallon tank on fuselage centerline and two 370-gallon tanks under wings
Maximum speed: 1,350 mph at 40,000 feet (Mach 2.05); 915 mph at sea level (Mach 1.2)
Weight empty: 14,567 pounds
Maximum takeoff weight: 35,400 pounds
Armament: One General Electric M61A-1 Vulcan 20mm multibarrel gun port wing/fuselage fairing, with 515 rounds. Up to 12,000 pounds of external ordnance on nine stations, including wingtip AAMs.

Because the F-16 has the APG-66 Radar system and the AMRAAM (Advanced Medium Range Air-to-Air Missile), the pilot can shoot at targets beyond his visual range.

The F-16 is quite an upgrade over the F-4 that it replaced. It has twice the range, for example. There are switches on the throttle, side-stick controller, and radar control panel that allow the pilot to switch radar modes without taking his eyes off the target.

SCAMP

The F-16C and D models are the one- and two-seater upgrades of the original warplane. There are minor changes in the layout of the cockpit and all of the electronic and computer systems were improved.

The newest Viper is the F-16E, also known as SCAMP (Supersonic Cruise Aircraft Modification Program). This model has delta wings, can carry more fuel, and is able to take aloft a heavier payload. Also, takeoffs and landings require less room on the airstrip.

AWACS E-3: AIRBORNE WARNING AND CONTROL SYSTEM

The E-3 Airborne Warning and Control System (AWACS) represents the world's standard for airborne early warning (AEW) systems. Built by Boeing Aerospace & Electronics of Seattle, Washington, the E-3 fills the needs of airborne surveillance, along with a command, control, and communications (C3) platform.

The E-3 has superior surveillance capabilities. It is equipped with a "look down" radar. It can separate airborne targets from the ground and sea clutter returns that confuse other present-day radars. Its radar "eye" has a 360° view of the horizon. At operating altitudes it can "see" more than 200 miles. It can also detect and track both air and sea targets simultaneously.

The AWACS went into service in 1977. Since then it has earned the reputation as an international keeper of the peace in operations with the USAF and NATO.

In 1986, under an earlier foreign military sale by the United States, E-3 deliveries began to the Royal Saudi Air Force and were completed in 1987. Since then, the AWACS also has been purchased to fulfill AEW mission requirements of the United Kingdom and France.

In its tactical role, the E-3 provides quick-reaction surveillance and C3 necessary to manage both tactical and defensive fighter forces. The E-3 also can detect and track hostile aircraft operating at low altitudes over all terrain, and can identify and control friendly aircraft in the same airspace.

The AWACS's mobility permits rapid deployment in any intensity level of military action. In its strategic defense role, the E-3 provides the means to detect, identify, track, and intercept airborne threats. These capabilities can be applied in crisis management at trouble spots anywhere in the world.

A Militarized 707

The E-3 aircraft utilizes a militarized version of the Boeing 707-320B commercial jetliner airframe. It is distinguished by the addition of a large, rotating rotodrome containing its radar antenna and identification friend or foe (IFF) and data-link fighter-control/TADIL-C antennae.

Its avionics include surveillance radar, navigation, communications, data processing, identification, and display equipment. The heart of the information processing network is an advanced airborne version of the IBM command and control multiprocessing computer.

E-3 SPECIFICATIONS

Airframe span: 145 feet, 9 inches
Length: 152 feet, 11 inches
Radome height: 41 feet, 9 inches
Radome diameter: 30 feet
Radome thickness: 6 feet
Speed: 500-plus mph
Ceiling: 35,000 feet
Endurance: 11-plus hours
Armament: None
Range: 5,000 nautical miles
Crew: 21 (four flight crew, 17 AWACS specialists)

United States and NATO E-3s are powered by four TF-33 21,000-pound-thrust jet engines. E-3s delivered to Saudi Arabia are powered by four higher-performance CFM-56 engines. The new engines allow operation at higher altitudes, extending the horizon for radar surveillance.

History of the E-3

The first E-3 entered USAF service in March 1977, preceded by more than 10 years of competitive flyoffs, prototype design, and development. By 1981, 24 of the 34 AWACS on order had been delivered to the U.S. inventory and were designated "core" aircraft. The remaining U.S. aircraft, as well as 18 NATO E-3s, were delivered in electronic support measures (ESM) passive surveillance capability.

That improvement program also included these block enhancements: upgrading of the Joint Tactical Information Distribution System (JTIDS) to Tactical Digital Information Link-J (TADIL-J), improved computer capacity, and the ability to use the global positioning satellite system to pinpoint AWACS location anywhere in the world.

In March 1989, Boeing was authorized to begin production of Have Quick A-NETS, an improved communications system that provides secure, antijam radio contact with other AWACS, friendly aircraft, and ground stations to a degree not previously available. In the summer of 1989, a program was begun to improve AWACS's ability to detect smaller, stealthy targets.

The Peace Sentinel program, as the Saudi program was known, began in 1981 when President Ronald Reagan authorized the foreign military sale of five AWACS aircraft to the Saudi Arabian government. Also included in the government-to-government sale package were six E-3 derivative (KE-3) in-flight refueling tanker aircraft, along with spare parts, trainers, and support equipment.

In 1984, the Saudi government exercised an option to increase the tanker order to eight. The first Saudi E-3 was delivered in June 1986, with deliveries of the remaining E-3s and tankers completed by September 1987. In addition to building the aircraft, Boeing was selected by the USAF and Saudi Arabia to assist in operating and maintaining the E-3s and tankers in the kingdom. In the summer of 1989, Boeing issued subcontracts to three Saudi companies to assist in support work.

The AWACS fleet, providing an "eye in the sky," has been an important deterrent to aggression.

B-1B BOMBER: FRAUGHT WITH CONTROVERSY

The B-1 bomber program has been fraught with controversy almost from its inception. The aircraft, which was designed to replace the aging B-52 intercontinental bomber, proved too sophisticated and burdened with troubles to carry out the role. Many experts and military officials gave up on the aircraft. Despite the problems, though, the aircraft emerged in the Afghanistan "War on Terrorism" as a powerful strike bomber.

In November 1969, the United States Air Force issued a specification for a multi-role, long-range bomber, capable of flying intercontinental missions without refueling. Once near the target, the aircraft was expected to penetrate present and predicted sophisticated enemy defenses. The aircraft would carry both conventional and nuclear bombs.

After careful evaluation of the proposed designs, the air force selected the Rockwell design in June 1970. The engineers at Rockwell solved the problem of having the aircraft perform at high speed and low altitude by designing a unique variable geometry wing which could be swung out or in as the flight characteristics for a given mission dictated. The aircraft was complex and revolutionary, but if it worked it would provide the air force with an aircraft years ahead of any of its enemies.

To the Wind Tunnel!

A contract for five test aircraft was issued and Rockwell went to work on construction. The first full-scale mock-up was finished in November 1971.

The air force was impressed but asked for 297 changes to the mock-up. A total of 22,000 hours of wind-tunnel testing were conducted on the airframe even before the first full-scale prototype was begun. With all the testing complete and the proposed changes incorporated into the design, Rockwell began construction on the prototypes. The new aircraft was now, officially, designated the B-1A.

B-1A SPECIFICATIONS

The B-1A was 143 feet, 3½ inches long. It was 33 feet, 7¼ inches high. The aircraft had a wingspan of 136 feet, 8½ inches when fully extended and 78 feet, 2½ inches when fully swept back. The aircraft had an empty weight of 140,000 pounds and when fully loaded could take off at an incredible 360,000 pounds.

The first aircraft flew in December 1974. It was sleek, fast, and sophisticated. The prototype's swing-wing design allowed it to streak to Mach 1.25. With its wings extended, it could maintain stable flight at slower speeds for takeoffs and landings. Four General Electric 010-GE-102 turbofan engines powered the aircraft. The engines allowed the aircraft to take off with a maximum weight of 477,000 pounds.

The aircraft carried its offensive load in three separate bomb bays. It could carry a variety of different ordnance packages including bombs (maximum of 84 500-pound bombs) and missiles. The aircraft could fly 7,455 miles without refueling but had an in-flight refueling capacity that allowed it to reach any point on the earth.

A four-man crew consisted of a pilot, copilot, defensive systems operator, and offensive systems operator. Initially, the crew was seated in an escape capsule that came off the aircraft as a complete unit in the event of trouble. This feature was later replaced with standard ejection seats.

Nap of the Earth

The flight and bomb-carrying characteristics of the aircraft were impressive. However, the heart of the new bomber was its sophisticated navigation, radars, and electronic countermeasures suite. The aircraft could fly "nap of the earth" missions—that is, it could fly amazingly low over any terrain, up one side of a hill and down the other.

The 147-foot-long bomber could fly at 200 feet at speeds of 600 mph. It could jam enemy radars, confuse enemy radar tracking missiles, and penetrate any air defense on the planet.

Flying at high speed and low altitude left no room for error. When the advanced electronics failed during several flight tests, the crews were noticeably upset. The complex jamming arrays of the electronic countermeasures were so good that it did, on occasion, jam the electronics of the bomber itself.

Canceled and Resurrected

These and other problems led to extensive testing and modifications. Finally, in June 1977, President Jimmy Carter canceled the B-1 program in favor of the cruise missile program.

Proponents of the aircraft were undaunted. They realized that the cruise missile could not pack the threat or punch of the B-1 bomber. They knew that if they could resurrect the program and incorporate the modifications suggested during the test program into a new version of the B-1, they would have a winner.

CHAPTER 12: STATE-OF-THE-ART WARPLANES

On October 2, 1981, President Reagan announced that the air force was authorized to acquire 100 B-1Bs as part of the U.S. Strategic Modernization Program.

The B-1B or Lancer, as it was now called, incorporated a stronger airframe, better electronics, strengthened landing gear, improved engine design, and many other new features. Most importantly, the B-1B's electronic jamming equipment was improved. The infrared countermeasures, radar location, and warning systems were integrated to complement its low-radar cross-section and form a sound defensive package for the aircraft.

In addition, the new version of the bomber was equipped with a new electronics suite that consisted of the AN/APQ-164 multi-mode offensive radar also used for navigation and terrain following. The radar also allowed targets to be located and engaged under the worst weather conditions.

The first B-1B took to the air in October 1985. Much of the development and testing program had been accomplished on the B-1A, so the test flights proceeded quickly.

The Bone

The aircraft was accepted by the air force and the first production model was delivered in July 1985. Although it was officially known as the Lancer, the crews nicknamed it the B-one or "Bone."

The new aircraft was assigned to the nuclear deterrence role up to the Gulf War of 1991. Although it could have been used in attacking Iraqi targets in the Gulf, the air force decided to retain the aircraft in its primary role and it remained in the United States on alert to counter any nuclear attack.

Each of the big bombers could carry up to 24 B-61 and B-83 gravity nuclear weapons or the Lockheed AGM-69A Short Range Attack Missiles, or SRAMs. Quite a deterrent!

The fleet of B-1Bs was still expensive to operate. After they entered service, the B-1B fleet never achieved its objective of having a 75 percent mission capable rate. In 1992 and 1993, the B-1B mission capable rate averaged about 57 percent. According to the air force, a primary reason for the low mission capable rate was the level of funding provided to support the B-1B logistics support system.

Concerned about the low mission capable rate, the air force decided to leave several of the bombers as nuclear bombers while reconfiguring the others to carry conventional bombs. With proper funding and care, the availability of the B-1Bs rose to 84.3 percent. Although the availability rate varied, the B-1B was ready for combat.

Baptism of Fire

On the night of December 17, 1998, two B-1Bs attacked and destroyed an Iraqi Republican Guard Barracks at Al Kut, Iraq. The attack was part of Operation Desert Fox and was designed to punish Saddam Hussein for his failure to comply with United Nations directives. The attack was impressive and both bombers returned safely to friendly airfields.

Even as the air force planners were evaluating the B-1B's combat debut, another crisis in Kosovo was drawing U.S. attention. Ethnic hatred between Serbs, Albanians, and Kosovars erupted into a bloody civil war. The Serbian army decided to end the war by wiping out the Albanians and Kosovars. Despite United Nations demands to stop the massacres, they continued and the UN finally sent in a military force to stop the Serbs. Part of the military component was six B-1Bs from the 77th Bomb Squadron and two B-1Bs from the 37th Bomb Squadron, Ellsworth Air Force Base. The Lancers bombed the oil refinery at Novi Sad and the Ponkive Air Field in Yugoslavia. Both facilities were among the first to feel the fury of the B-1B. As the campaign continued, other targets that required the Lancers' range, heavy bomb load, and accuracy were added to the mission list. The eight bombers attacked and destroyed dozens of other targets during their campaign.

Bones over Afghanistan

The war in Afghanistan offered the B-1B a new opportunity to demonstrate its conventional war capabilities. Enemy troops dug in on hillsides and in caves required massive bomb loads to either bring them to their knees or bury them in their caves. The B-1B filled the bill. Fully loaded, the bomber can carry 84 Mk-82 nonprecision 500-pound gravity bombs.

The Lancer can also carry up to 30 cluster bomb units (CBUs)—89 per sortie for enhanced conventional capability against advancing armor. Each CBU carries 72 antitank mines and 22 antipersonnel mines. In the event heavier bombs are needed, the bomber can carry 24 2,000-pound Mark 84 bombs.

The B-1B can also carry the 24 GBU-31 Joint Direct Attack Munitions (JDAM), which consists of a guided one-ton bomb. This bomb has a circular error probable (CEP) of 39 feet. If the JDAM's GPS system fails, the bomb's internal guidance system will guide the weapon to within 90 feet of that target.

The aircraft is also equipped with the CBU-103 Wind Corrected Munitions Dispenser (WCMD), which allows cluster bombs to be dropped in windy conditions with a greater accuracy (CEP of 30 feet); the Joint Standoff Weapon (JSOW), which allows the crew to launch an accurate missile while still 74 miles away from the target; and the AGM-158 Joint Air to Surface Standoff Missile (JASSM), a cruise missile that can be launched while the aircraft is up to a maximum of 115 miles from the target.

VARIETIES OF JSOW

The JSOW comes in three variations:

- AGM-154A, which carries combined effects bomblets designed to attack area, personnel, and soft targets
- AGM-154B, which dispenses "smart bombs" designed to destroy tanks and other armored vehicles
- AGM-154C, which delivers a BLU-111, a 500-pound bomb designed to penetrate hard targets such as ships or concrete bunkers

Shortly after the start of Operation Enduring Freedom, the war against terrorism, the 28th Air Expeditionary Wing of the USAF was assigned B-1B bombers from the 7th, 28th, and 366th Bomb Wings—based, respectively, at Dyess AFB in Texas, Ellsworth AFB in South Dakota, and Mountain Home AFB in Idaho.

These aircraft were based on the British-controlled island of Diego Garcia in the Indian Ocean. Missions from Diego Garcia to Afghanistan lasted between 12 and 15 hours and covered distances of over 5,500 miles.

The initial attacks were made against Taliban antiaircraft radars, guns, and command centers. These attacks were made with precision-guided weapons. As the war progressed and the sophisticated enemy targets were obliterated, the B-1s were assigned to drop conventional munitions on enemy front-line positions.

Guided to their targets by Special Forces units using laser designators, the big bombers would swoop in at low altitude and demolish enemy positions with their 500-pound, 1,000-pound, and 2,000-pound bombs. The strikes were so successful that the B-1 soon began to replace the venerable B-52 as the workhorse of the bombing campaign.

B-1B SPECIFICATIONS

Primary function: Long-range, multi-role, heavy bomber

Manufacturer: Rockwell International, North American Aircraft (now the Boeing Company)

Power plant: Four General Electric F-101-GE-102 turbofan engines with afterburner

Thrust: 30,000-plus pounds with afterburner, per engine

Length: 146 feet

Wingspan: 137 feet extended forward, 79 feet swept aft

Height: 34 feet

Weight: Empty, approximately 190,000 pounds

Maximum takeoff weight: 477,000 pounds

Speed: 900-plus mph (Mach 1.2 at sea level)

Range: Intercontinental, unrefueled

Ceiling: More than 30,000 feet

Crew: Four (aircraft commander, pilot, offensive systems officer, and defensive systems officer)

Armament: Up to 84 Mark 82 conventional 500-pound bombs, or 30 CBU-87/89/97, or 24 JDAMS.

Date deployed: June 1985

Unit cost: $200-plus million per aircraft

The B-1B flew dozens of bombing missions over Afghanistan, as well as over Iraq during the Spring 2003 war against Iraq. Its powerful bomb load, wide range of weapons, and ability to fly "nap of the earth" missions made it a valuable part of the USAF arsenal.

F-117 STEALTH FIGHTER

With the end of the Cold War, the United States and its allies appeared to have air superiority for keeps. The major threat against U.S. airpower was no longer from other planes, but from ground antiaircraft fire.

Therefore, military planners placed less emphasis on speed in developing new aircraft and greater emphasis on stealth. Designers set about to create jets that, although they could not travel as fast as the speed of sound, could move in on a target at low altitudes (nap-of-the-earth technology); these jets were designed with a shape that made them all but invisible to radar and to those who might want to fire upon them from the ground. This was called "low-observable technology"—the fine art of being hard to see.

STEALTH = UFOS

During the years that the stealth fighter was test flown over "Area 51" in Nevada, sightings of it inevitably resulted in UFO reports.

"It darted this way and that," observers would say. "It's certainly beyond anything we on Earth could build."

Even after the F-117 went public, a flyover of New York City resulted in multiple calls to 911 with frightened observers reporting that flying saucers were "buzzing the Brooklyn Bridge."

Like U.S. spy planes, the F-117 stealth fighter, nicknamed the Nighthawk, was developed in complete secrecy. It is black in color and shaped like a flying wing.

The Nighthawk began in 1973 as design study Have Blue, to determine to what degree an aircraft could be made invisible to radar and IR detection systems. As a result of the study, two Experimental Stealth Tactical (XST) prototypes were built. They first flew in mid-1977. Production aircraft were ordered, and the first of these flew in June 1981.

The F-117A first saw action in December 1989 during Operation Just Cause in Panama. It was next used in combat during Operation Desert Storm in 1991. In both cases it proved that it could penetrate dense threat environments at night.

During Desert Storm it was the only coalition fighter to attack targets inside Baghdad's city limits.

F-117 NIGHTHAWK SPECIFICATIONS

Crew: One

First deployed: 1982

Primary function: Fighter/attack

Manufacturer: Lockheed Aeronautical Systems Co.

Power plant: Two General Electric F404 engines

Length: 65 feet, 11 inches

Height: 12 feet, 5 inches

Weight: 52,500 pounds

Wingspan: 43 feet, 4 inches

Speed: High subsonic

Range: Unlimited with air refueling

Armament: Internal weapons carriage with room for 12 smart bombs or missiles

Since then it has proven to be an effective first strike weapon in Yugoslavia and Afghanistan and in Iraq once again in 2003, during Operation Iraqi Freedom.

The Nighthawk is a one-seater powered by a pair of General Electric F404 turbofan engines. It can be refueled in the air and has fly-by-wire flight controls. Fifty-nine stealth fighters have been built. Fifty-five (52 F-117A and 3 YF-117) are still operational.

THE B-2

At the same time the United States was developing the F-117, plans were underway to develop a stealth bomber, the jet that would eventually become known as the B-2.

The work of making a fighter aircraft invisible to radar had been difficult. Making a bomber invisible was almost impossible. However, designers at Northrop were undaunted and, in the late 1970s, began the Advanced Technology Bomber program.

It was obvious that all America's top aircraft designers and companies would be needed to carry out this program and there was much interchange of information and technology among America's aircraft manufacturers.

Military Technical Journal

On November 22, 1988, the B-2 had its rollout ceremony at Air Force Plant 42 in Palmdale, California.

The result of all this effort appeared on November 22, 1988, when the B-2A bomber was unveiled.

The new bomber was powered by four General Electric F118–GE-100 turbofan engines, which generated 19,000 pounds of thrust each. The aircraft weighed 153,700 pounds empty and 375,000 pounds fully loaded. It could carry 50,000 pounds of conventional or nuclear bombs at a speed of 680 mph. It had a range of 6,000 miles without refueling and a service ceiling of 50,000 feet. However, what made the aircraft special was that it was all but invisible on radar.

The fuselage and wings were made of graphite and carbon fiber cloth and tape which was molded over a skeleton of titanium. The body contours, exhaust, flying surfaces, hatches, gear, and bomb doors were all specially engineered to reduce the radar image of the bomber as well as the infrared signature. Even the sophisticated radar was masked to keep enemy electronic intelligence experts from locating the bomber.

The first B-2 was delivered to the USAF on December 17, 1993. By that time the bomber had been tested for several hundred hours in all

conditions and had demonstrated that it had a lower radar signature than the F-117.

Since its arrival in service the B-2 has been involved in combat missions over Serbia, Afghanistan, and Iraq. In each case the aircraft performed flawlessly and achieved great accuracy with all its bombs. Still, new and improved versions of stealth bombers are already in the works. One such aircraft under design consideration is the FB-22, classified as a regional bomber, but with twice the bomb load of the B-2.

A-10 THUNDERBOLT: THE "WARTHOG"

Although its official name is Thunderbolt, everyone calls the A-10 the "Warthog." It ain't a pretty plane, but it does its job. Due to the big missiles and bombs it carries beneath its wings and the large double engines attached to its tail, it has a lumpy appearance.

The A-10 Thunderbolt II is a single-seat, twin turbofan aircraft specifically designed to provide effective antiarmor support for ground forces; to be deadly against tanks and other targets; to be able to carry large ordnance payloads, and have excellent range, and long-loiter capabilities near the battlefield; to survive intense antiaircraft fire, surface-to-air missiles, and attacks by other aircraft; and to maintain high sortie rates and operate from short fields, while permitting rapid servicing and easy repair of battle damage.

The Thunderbolt is operational with the Tactical Air Command at bases in the United States, Europe, and Korea. A-10s are also deployed with units of the Air National Guard and Air Force Reserves.

The plane has a wingspan of 57 feet, 6 inches, and an overall length of 53 feet, 4 inches. The craft stands 14 feet, 8 inches high. It weighs 22,141 pounds when empty and 42,500 pounds when fully loaded with fuel and ordnance.

The Thunderbolt II is known for its responsiveness, lethality, simplicity, survivability, reliability, and armament. The versatile and flexible A-10 has large-payload, long-loiter, wide-radius capabilities. The ability to operate under 1,000 feet ceilings with only 1-mile visibility makes the aircraft highly responsive to the needs of the ground combat commander.

Mounted internally along the aircraft's centerline is the GAU-8/A 30mm Gatling gun system. The GAU-8/A provides a cost-effective weapon to defeat a full array of ground targets encountered in close air support. The gun can fire between 2,100 and 4,200 rounds per minute.

The A-10's structure is conventional with approximately 95 percent of the airframe constructed from aluminum. Single curvature skins are used on all areas aft of the cockpit, permitting ease of maintenance. Redundant load paths used through the aircraft provide airframe reliability and damage tolerance. Numerous aircraft parts are interchangeable left and right, including the engine, landing gear, and vertical stabilizers.

JOINT STARS

The U.S. Air Force/Army E-8C Joint STARS (Surveillance Target and Attack Radar System), built by Northrop Grumman, provides precise tracking and targeting of ground targets and slow-moving airborne targets for battlefield management and peacekeeping operations. It looks like a huge commercial airliner.

The A-10 achieves its survivability through high maneuverability at low altitude combined with electric countermeasures, and chaff/flare dispensers.

The pilot and vital elements of the flight control system are protected by a titanium armor "bathtub"; self-sealing fuel cells are protected from fire and explosion by the installation of internal and external foam. The A-10's two separated primary flight control systems are further enhanced by a backup manual system permitting the pilot to fly the plane even if all hydraulics are lost.

The A-10 has consistently demonstrated its capability for sustained, responsive missions during sortie surge exercises. In a one-day surge effort conducted by the 81st Tactical Fighter Wing at RAF Bentwaters/ Woodbridge in the United Kingdom, a group of 89 missions-capable A-10s accumulated a total of 578.6 hours while flying 533 sorties in a 14-hour period.

The Story of "Pilot Dude"

The only air force pilot shot down over Iraq during Operation Iraqi Freedom in the spring of 2003 was flying an A-10 Thunderbolt. He was 37-year-old Maj. James (Chocks) Ewald. It happened on April 8 as he flew over Baghdad. According to the pilot, he wouldn't be alive today if he had been flying an F-16. He says his Warthog saved his life.

Ewald was flying his Warthog over Baghdad at less than 5,000 feet, heading toward the west, when his plane was hit by a surface-to-air missile that he never saw.

"It was like the hand of God moved the airplane," the pilot told the New York *Daily News* Washington Bureau during the summer of 2003. "There was a bang, then movement, and then a reddish glow." That was fire coming off the tail of his A-10. Ewald continued to fly the plane despite the damage.

He was uninjured by the missile hit. And it was a good thing, too, because he needed every ounce of strength to keep from losing control of the plane. He could see pieces of the plane falling off. Yet it flew.

"I didn't really know which parts they were but I figured I needed them," he later said.

He managed to get 40 miles south of Baghdad, where he felt there was a greater chance of landing or crashing in an area already under U.S. control. He got down to an altitude of 1,500 feet when he decided that the chances of making a safe landing were rapidly approaching nil. He ejected and parachuted safely to the ground, and the Warthog crashed in flames nearby.

Ewald got to his feet and was busy cutting off his parachute when he heard gunfire and could hear bullets whizzing by. At first he thought that he was under attack by Iraqis, but it turned out to be friendly fire. The flames in his crashed plane were igniting bullets. After the firing stopped, Ewald heard voices and hid in a drainage ditch. By the time the voices got close enough to be understood, Ewald heard, "Hey, pilot dude. Come on out, dude, we're Americans."

There had been an army engineering unit near the site of the crash and they had come to investigate. Within two days, "Pilot Dude" was in another Warthog flying sorties over Baghdad.

Upgrades to the A-10

The air force has plans to upgrade the A-10. These plans include …

- A precision engagement upgrade to give the pilot new cockpit displays, a digital stores management system, a Joint Tactical Radio System (JTRS) data link, and integration of the JDAM and WCMD.
- A targeting pod.
- By 2008, an upgraded automated chaff and flare system installation.

UNMANNED AERIAL VEHICLES (UAVS)

Until recently, all warplanes had pilots. But this is no longer the case. In the last two decades, unmanned warplanes have been developed, first as surveillance craft, and more recently as craft that can find and then destroy the enemy.

The Gulf War of 1991 convinced many military planners of the need for and viability of unmanned aerial vehicles (UAVs) for battlefield reconnaissance. During the war, the navy used UAVs to spot targets for the battleship. The Marine Corps used its UAVs to check for enemy activity in front of their forward positions. The air force and Special Forces used them to reconnaissance on heavily defended targets.

First Used in Vietnam

Drone aircraft had been used effectively during the Vietnam War. The Ryan Aeronautical Company developed the AQM-34N Firebee to perform these necessary but dangerous missions. The Firebee had a range of 2,400 miles, could fly up to 65,000 feet, and had a top speed of 420 miles per hour.

Despite its success, any information it gathered must be transmitted to a "chase" plane or retrieved from the Firebee when it was recovered. Although the information was important, it was often delayed while the information was processed or never recovered if the AQM-34N was shot down during the mission.

During the years between the end of the war in Vietnam and the Gulf War, the science of reconnaissance made quantum leaps, pictures went digital, cameras used fiber optics, navigation could be checked to within 3 feet of a given location, and data was transmitted to satellites and then to whatever source officials deemed appropriate.

Locating Scuds

One of the biggest problems of the 1991 Gulf War was locating Iraqi mobile Scud missile launchers. These six-ton missiles could carry a 2,205-pound conventional, nuclear, biological, or chemical warhead to a range of 174 miles and land within 3,280 feet of their assigned targets (although, as this is written, there is no indication that Iraq had a nuclear warhead).

The missiles were mounted on a Soviet-built mobile truck/launcher. Once the truck was at its assigned launching point, the crew could set up the missile, fire it, and be out of the launch area within 10 minutes. With thousands of square miles of empty desert, the launchers could be hidden almost anywhere. The only time they would become visible is when the missile was being set up and launched.

The ability of the Iraqis to maintain this capability gave them a strategic advantage. They could strike Israel, Turkey, Saudi Arabia, Kuwait, or any number of Middle-Eastern nations. After several Scud attacks, the Israeli government threatened to attack Iraq if the United States could not stop the missile attacks.

Reconnaissance efforts at every level were diverted to the task. Satellites were redirected to scan the empty desert to look for trucks with missiles onboard; and reconnaissance aircraft began flying missions deep into the desert to search for the trucks. Even Special Forces teams were dropped behind enemy lines, to search the desert for the elusive trucks. Eventually the effort paid off. Several Iraqi missile launchers were identified and destroyed by air strikes. However, not before several more Scuds hit Israel and Saudi Arabia.

It was obvious that in order to find an elusive target, some sort of electronic surveillance over a large area would be required. In a case such as the Scud missiles, a scenario that might be repeated in other wars, the surveillance would have to be from the air. The vehicle carrying out such a mission would have to remain in the air for a long period of time and be able to cover a wider area. It would also have to be able to detect moving vehicles and relay the information quickly to front-line commanders.

Global Hawk

The problem was assigned to the Defense Advanced Research Projects Agency (DARPA) in a joint program office with the departments of the USAF, Navy, and Army for the Defense Airborne Reconnaissance Office (DARO).

After the Gulf War, DARPA put out a specification for a new high-altitude, long-endurance UAV with a wide array of sophisticated abilities. Several civilian firms responded with proposals. The most impressive was the one submitted by the combined firms of Northrop Grumman Corporation, Teledyne Ryan Aeronautical, and Raytheon/E-Systems. They were given the task to develop the new UAV that was already named Global Hawk.

The prototype aircraft that emerged was a high-wing jet aircraft. It had a wingspan of 116.2 feet. The fuselage was 44.4 feet long. It had a bulbous nose that housed a 48-inch Ku-band wide-band satellite communications uplink. The long, narrow fuselage ended in a set of two high "V" tail planes. The prototype weighed 9,200 pounds empty and could get off the ground with a gross weight of 25,600 pounds.

Fully loaded for a mission, it could carry one ton of electronics surveillance equipment. The equipment was carried in two pods, one under each wing. Power came from the Allison AE3007H turbofan engine that gave the aircraft a top speed of 390 mph, a service ceiling of 65,000 feet, and a maximum endurance of 42 hours in the air.

Global Hawk can survey up to 40,000 square nautical miles per day per aircraft. It can detect moving vehicles going as slow as 4.5 mph. With the onboard cameras, Global Hawk can identify targets out to 30 miles, and with its radar it can find targets over 100 miles away.

Unlike other UAVs, which had a pilot who flew the aircraft by way of a camera mounted in the nose, the Global Hawk would be programmed to fly a set path, mapping and recording what it saw. The information would be instantly transmitted to a satellite and then relayed to surveillance experts stationed in a ground control station. The station consisted of two air-transportable, rugged shelters that would be used for mission planning, command and control, communications, and imagery quality control.

Programming the Key

Programming the UAV to accomplish all these various tasks is complicated. Most of the problems that plagued the early part of the program were caused by problems with the computer program. No one wanted a $10 million UAV loaded with complex, sophisticated, and classified sensors to crash or fall into enemy hands. Eventually the bugs were worked out and the aircraft made its first successful flight in March 1998. A successful test program followed.

In 2000, the Global Hawk won the Collier Trophy for the year's greatest aerial achievements in astronautics. It was the first unmanned vehicle to fly across the Pacific, to track an aircraft carrier battle group, and to track an individual ship. In all these tests the aircraft performed exceptionally well.

Initially the air force bought five Global Hawks. One was destroyed in an accident and two more were ordered as replacements. The initial buy called for a total of 30 Global Hawks to be procured. The plan is to build 51 aircraft through 2030.

In order to properly operate the new UAV, the air force chose Beale Air Force Base in California as its main base. The air force also designated 2,844 active-duty personnel and 310 civilians to maintain and fly the Global Hawk as well as collect and interpret the data.

The Global Hawk was developed too late to search for Scuds but it arrived just in time to hunt terrorists in Afghanistan. The terrain and the nature of the war were ideal for the UAV. Shortly after the war began the RQ-4 Global Hawk mapped the rugged terrain of Afghanistan, searched for terrorists on the ground, located their vehicles as they moved about the country, and alerted U.S. forces to the presence of enemy targets.

Effectiveness over Afghanistan

The UAV's long loiter time over a target area allowed American military experts to identify several routes used by the terrorists. Once identified, these routes were carefully watched by the Global Hawks and led to the interception and capture of several groups of enemy troops.

The success in Afghanistan has led to demands for more UAVs and allowed military planners to increase the number and types of missions assigned to the Global Hawk.

The Global Hawk has now been tested in combat. It is obvious that it will appear in future fights. The high-flying UAV will provide ground commanders with invaluable, real-time information on the battlefield and enemy deployments. The Global Hawks will give American combat commanders a real advantage over their enemies on future battlefields.

THE CIA PREDATOR: UAV WITH TEETH

The CIA-owned Predator drone is another robotic plane that is equipped for surveillance. But this UAV is also equipped to attack. It can locate a target and take it out—all without the risk of U.S. casualties.

PREDATOR SPECIFICATIONS

Length: 27 feet

Weight: 2,250 pounds

Speed: 84–140 miles per hour

Range: Can operate for as long as 16 hours while flying 454 miles from its controller

Ceiling: 25,000 feet

Armament: Two 100-pound Hellfire laser-guided tank-busting missiles

Personnel: While no humans fly inside the Predator, a crew of 55 is needed to operate one

The drone planes can patrol over a country such as Afghanistan for up to 24 hours without a rest and can fire sophisticated guidance missiles. Predators have been used with great effectiveness to support U.S. military forces in Kosovo, Iraq, and Afghanistan.

Future robotic flying surveillance—MAVs, micro air vehicles—will be much smaller. Therefore, they will be increasingly difficult to detect from the ground. After all, you get better pictures of the enemy when he doesn't know he is being photographed.

The Rand Corporation, MIT Lincoln Laboratory, and Defense Advanced Research Projects Agency have studied ways to shrink cameras, chemical sensors, communications gear, and weapons onto mini-drones. They would be able to do things that the Predator can't because of their size and increased agility. For example, the new mini-bots would be able to fly into buildings. The aerial robots could track hazardous clouds, for example, all the time.

PREDATOR ARMAMENT

The Predator is equipped with AGM-114 Hellfire missiles. The Hellfire can be equipped with three types of warheads: single explosive, double explosive (for new armored vehicles with reactive armor), and a "delayed-blast fragmentation" warhead.

The Predator drones were specially equipped with the Hellfire missiles for the war in Afghanistan. The missiles are mounted underneath the drone plane's wings. The Hellfire missiles weigh 100 pounds apiece and are laser-guided.

MCDONNELL DOUGLAS C-17 GLOBEMASTER II

Today's state-of-the-art USAF cargo plane is the McDonnell Douglas C-17 Globemaster II, which became operational in 1995. It flew most of its first 10,000 flying hours during routine operational missions of the 17th Airlift Squadron out of Charleston Air Force Base in South Carolina, and from the Royal Air Force's base in Mildenhall, England.

C-17 AIRFRAME SPECIFICATIONS

Wingspan: 169 feet, 9 inches
Length: 174 feet
Height: 55 feet, 1 inch
Fuselage diameter: 22 feet, 6 inches
Power plant: Four Pratt & Whitney PW2040 (military designation F117-PW-100); 40,440 pounds thrust each

Over the years, the flexibility of the workhorse has been impressively demonstrated. It was used out of Howard Air Force Base in Panama during U.S. operations there. It flew out of several USAF bases in Europe during operations in Bosnia and Kosovo, and participated in the war against Iraq in 2003.

When it was introduced, the C-17 immediately set 22 world records, including a short takeoff and landing mark. Crew members love the cargo jet. They applaud its flexibility and agility. The C-17 gives the USAF the capability to fly big loads into airfields that, up until the 1990s, were accessible only to small airplanes.

F/A-22 RAPTOR

Although the F-15 performed brilliantly over Kosovo and in the two Gulf wars, it has become increasingly vulnerable to surface-to-air missiles. Military planners have long known that you have to look ahead, and you can't assume that the next war will be anything like the last war. It isn't enough to have air superiority, you have to keep it. A nation must plan ahead so that air superiority can be assured in the future.

F-22 SPECIFICATIONS

Wingspan: 44 feet, 6 inches
Wing Area: 840 square feet
Length: 62 feet, 1 inch
Height: 16 feet, 8 inches
Power plant: Pratt & Whitney F-119
Weight empty: 31,670 pounds
Maximum takeoff weight: 60,000 pounds
Maximum speed: 921 mph
Ceiling: 50,000 feet
Crew: One
First flight: September 7, 1997

Lockheed's F-22 is the first fighter jet to combine state-of-the-art fighter capabilities with stealth technology. It can fly at Mach 1.5 without using its afterburners, and yet can be all but invisible to enemy radar and SAMs. It has what is called "first-look, first-shot, first-kill" capability. It is not only hard to see, but it has the ability to "see" enemy aircraft from farther away than any warplane ever.

The Raptor has undergone four years of testing, the most of any warplane in history. Each Raptor will cost approximately $84 million.

The F-22 is armed with six AIM-120C Advanced Medium-Range Air-to-Air Missiles (AMRAAM) located in the ventral bays. The F-22's side weapons bays (one on each side) hold one Aim 9 Sidewinder missile. In addition to the F-22's internal weapons bays, it is capable of carrying stores externally. Four underwing stations are able to support up to 5,000 pounds.

There is room in the lower weapons bays to accommodate one 1,000-pound GBU-30/32 Joint Direct Attack Munition (JDAM) per side. A simple GPS (global positioning system) inertial system guides the weapon to its target.

The aircraft has an M61A2 internal cannon mounted just above the right wing root. To keep the craft stealthy, an inward opening door covers the muzzle until the weapon is fired.

Each Raptor has two F119 engines, which develop more than twice the thrust of current engines under supersonic conditions and more thrust without afterburner than conventional engines with afterburner.

The F-22 is scheduled to enter operational service in 2004.

So there you have it, warplanes from the wooden biplanes of World War I to the state-of-the-art supersonic and stealth warplanes of today. From the moment airplanes were invented, the country that has controlled the sky has controlled the war, and there is nothing to indicate that this will change anytime soon.

WARPLANE MUSEUMS

American Airpower Museum
Farmingdale, Long Island, New York
Located in hangars alongside New Highway,
south of Conklin Avenue.
Website: Americanairpowermuseum.com
Open Thursday–Sunday, 10:30 A.M.–4:00 P.M.

American Airpower Heritage Museum
Midland International Airport
PO Box 62000
Midland, Texas 79711-2000
Phone: 915-563-1000
Website: www.airpowermuseum.org
Monday–Saturday, 9:00 A.M.–5:00 P.M.;
Sunday 12:00 P.M.–5:00 P.M.

Arizona Wing Hangar
PO Box 2969
Mesa, Arizona 85214
Phone: 480-924-1940 or 480-981-1945
Website: www.ArizonaWingCA.org
Open daily 10:00 A.M.–4:00 P.M.

Castle Air Museum
Castle Air Force Base
5050 Santa Fe Drive
Atwater, California 95301
Phone: 209-723-2178
Website: www.elite.net/castle-air/
Open daily in the summer 9:00 A.M.–5:00 P.M.;
otherwise 10:00 A.M.–4:00 P.M.

Cosford Royal Air Force Museum
Shifnal
Shropshire, England TF11 8UP
Phone: 019 0237 6200
Website: www.rafmuseum.org.uk/cosford
Open daily 10:00 A.M.–6:00 P.M.

Hendon Royal Air Force Air Museum
Grahame Park Way
London, England NW9 5LL
Phone: 020 8205 2266
Website: www.rafmuseum.org.uk/hendon
Includes the Royal Air Force Museum, the Battle of Britain Museum, and the Bomber Command Museum. All three museums open daily 8:00 A.M.–6:00 P.M.

Intrepid Sea, Air and Space Museum

West 46th Street and 12th Avenue
New York, New York 10036
Phone: 212-245-0072
Website: www.intrepidmuseum.org

Open weekdays 10:00 A.M.–5:00 P.M.;
weekends 10:00 A.M.–6:00 P.M.

Smithsonian National Air Space Museum

Independence Avenue at 4th Street, SW
Washington, D.C. 20560
Phone: 202-357-2700
Website: www.nasm.edu

Open daily 10:00 A.M.–5:30 P.M.

Planes of Fame Museum

7000 Merrill Avenue
Chino, California 91710
Phone: 909-597-3722
Website: www.planesoffame.org

Open daily 9:00 A.M.–5:00 P.M.

U.S. Air Force Museum

Wright Patterson Air Force Base
PO Box 1903
Dayton, Ohio 45433-7102
Phone: 937-255-3286
Website: www.wpafb.af.mil/museum

Open daily 9:00 A.M.–5:00 P.M.

AIR SHOWS

Abbotsford International Air Show
Abbotsford, British Columbia, Canada
Abbotsford Airport
Held annually in August.
www.abbotsfordairshow.com

California International Air Show
Salinas, California
Salinas Municipal Airport
Held annually in October.
www.salinasairshow.com

Canadian International Air Show
Toronto, Canada
Takes place over Lake Ontario;
viewed from the Canadian
National Exhibition.
Held annually in August.
www.cias.org

Cleveland National Air Show
Cleveland, Ohio
Burke Lakefront Airport
Held annually in August.
www.clevelandairshow.com

Dayton Air Show
Dayton, Ohio
Dayton International Airport
Held annually in July.
www.usats.org

Indianapolis Air Show
Indianapolis, Indiana
Mount Comfort Airport
Held annually in September.
www.indyairshow.com

New York Air Show
Riverhead, New York
Grumman/Calverton Airfield
Held annually in September.
www.newyorkairshow.org

Prairie Air Show
Peoria, Illinois
Greater Peoria Regional Airport
Held annually in July.
www.prairieair.com

Southport Air Show
Manchester, England
Southport Seafront
Held annually in September.
www.southportairshow.com

Stuart Air Show
Stuart, Florida
Witham Field
Held annually in November.
www.stuartairshow.com

APPENDIX C

BIBLIOGRAPHY

Books

Angelucci, Enzo. *Illustrated Encyclopedia of Military Aircraft*. Edison, New Jersey: Chartwell Books, 2001.

———. *The Rand McNally Encyclopedia of Military Aircraft*. New York: Galley Books, 1990.

Baldwin, Sherman. *Ironclaw: A Navy Carrier Pilot's Gulf War Experience*. New York: William Morrow and Company, 1996.

Beaver, Paul. *Carrier Air Operations Since 1945*. Harrisburg, Pa.: Arms and Armour Press, 1983.

Bowman, Martin W. *The B-24 Liberator, 1939-1945*. New York: Rand McNally & Company, 1989.

Boyne, Walter J., USAF (Ret.), and Barrett Tillman. *Alpha Bravo Delta Guide to the U.S. Air Force*. Indianapolis: Alpha Books, 2003.

Bridgman, Leonard, ed. *Jane's Fighting Aircraft of World War II*. New York: Crescent Books, 1994.

Chant, Christopher. *The History of Aviation*. London: Tiger Books International, 1998.

Condon, John Pomeroy. *Corsairs and Flattops: Marine Carrier Air Warfare, 1944-1945*. Annapolis, Md.: Naval Institute Press, 1997.

Consolidated Aircraft Company. *Consolidated B-24 Liberator General Aircraft Book*. Fort Worth: Tex., 1943.

Couhat, Jean Labayle, and Bernard Prezelin. *Combat Fleets of the World, 1988-89: Their Ships, Aircraft and Armament*. Annapolis, Md.: Naval Institute Press, 1988.

Crane, Conrad C. *American Airpower Strategy in Korea: 1950-1953*. Lawrence, Kans.: University of Kansas, 2000.

Craven, Wesley Frank, and James Lea Cate, ed. *The Army Air Forces in World War II, Volume One, Plans and Early Operations, January 1939 to August 1942*. Washington, D.C.: Office of Air Force History, 1983.

Davis, Larry. *B-24 Liberator in Action*. Carrollton, Tex.: Squadron/Signal Publications, Inc., 1987.

———. *U-2 Spy Plane in Action*. Carrolton, Tex.: Squadron/Signal Publications, Inc., 1988.

Emme, Eugene M. *The Impact of Air Power*. New York: D. Van Nostrand Company, Inc., 1959.

Fahey, James C. *Ships and Aircraft of the U.S. Fleet*. Annapolis, Md.: Naval Institute Press, 1986.

Flintham, Victor. *Air Wars and Aircraft: A Detailed Record of Air Combat, 1945 to the Present*. New York: Facts on File, 1990.

Fredette, Raymond H. *The Sky on Fire*. Washington, D.C.: Smithsonian Institution Press, 1991.

Futrell, Robert. *The United States Air Force in Korea, 1950-1953*. Washington, D.C.: United States Air Force, Office of Air Force History, 1983.

Goldberg, Alfred, ed. *A History of the United States Air Force, 1907-1957*. Princeton, N.J.: D. Van Nostrand Company, Inc., 1957.

Grant, Zalin. *Over the Beach: The Air War in Vietnam*. New York: W. W. Norton Co., 1986.

Griess, Thomas E., ed. *The Second World War: Asia and the Pacific*. Wayne, N.J.: Avery Publishing Group, Inc., 1984. Prepared by the Department of History, United States Military Academy, West Point, New York.

Halliday, Jon. *Korea, the Unknown War*. New York: Pantheon Books, 1988.

Hezlet, Sir Arthur Richard R. *Aircraft and Sea Power*. New York: Stein and Day, 1970.

Jackson, Robert. *Fighter Pilots of World War II*. New York: St. Martin's Press, 1976.

———. *Fighter!: The Story of Air Combat, 1936-1945*. New York: St. Martin's Press, 1979.

Johnson, Vice Marshal J. E. *Full Circle*, New York: Bantam Books, 1984.

Lawson, Captain Ted W. *Thirty Seconds Over Tokyo*. New York: Random House, 1943.

Lindley, John M. *Carrier Victory: The Air War in the Pacific*. New York: Elsevier-Dutton, 1978.

MacDonald, Steve. *Historic Warplanes*. Secaucus, N.J.: Chartwell Books, 1995.

Mobley, C. A., and Michael Benson. *The Complete Idiot's Guide to Aircraft Carriers.* New York: Alpha Books, 2003.

Mondey, David. *The Concise Guide to American Aircraft of World War II.* Secaucus, N.J.: Chartwell Books, Inc., 1994.

———. *The International Encyclopedia of Aviation.* New York: Crown Publishers, Inc., 1977.

Morrison, Samuel Eliot. *History of United States Naval Operations in World War II, Volume II, The Rising Sun in the Pacific, 1931-April 1942.* Boston: Little, Brown and Company, 1988.

Morrison, Wilbur H. *Pilots, Man Your Seats!: The History of Naval Aviation.* Central Point, Ore.: Hellgate Press, 1999.

Musciano, Walter A. *Warbirds of the Sea.* Atglen, Pa.: Schiffer Publishing Ltd., 1994.

Pisano, Dominick A., Thomas J. Dietz, Joanne M. Gernstein, and Karl S. Schneide. *Legend, Memory and the Great War in the Air.* Seattle: University of Washington Press, 1992.

Polmar, Norman, and Timothy M. Laur, ed. *Strategic Air Command: People, Aircraft and Missiles.* Baltimore, Md.: The Nautical & Aviation Company of America, 1990.

Powers, Francis Gary, with Curt Gentry. *Operation Overflight: The U-2 Spy Pilot Tells His Story for the First Time.* New York: Holt, Rinehart and Winston, 1970.

Rich, Ben R., and Leo Janos. *Skunk Works: A Personal Memoir of My Years at Lockheed.* New York: Little, Brown and Company, 1994.

Stokesbury, James L. *A Short History of Air Power.* New York: William Morrow and Company, Inc., 1986.